The Aid Lab

Critical Frontiers of Theory, Research, and Policy in International Development Studies

Series Editors: Andrew Fischer, Uma Kothari, and Giles Mohan

Critical Frontiers of Theory, Research, and Policy in International Development Studies is the official book series of the Development Studies Association of the UK and Ireland (DSA).

The series profiles research monographs that will shape the theory, practice, and teaching of international development for a new generation of scholars, students, and practitioners. The objective is to set high quality standards within the field of development studies to nurture and advance the field, as is the central mandate of the DSA. Critical scholarship is especially encouraged, within the spirit of development studies as an interdisciplinary and applied field, dealing centrally with local, national and global processes of structural transformation, and associated political, social, and cultural change, as well as critical reflections on achieving social justice. In particular, the series seeks to highlight analyses of historical development experiences as an important methodological and epistemological strength of the field of development studies.

The Aid Lab

Understanding Bangladesh's Unexpected Success

Naomi Hossain

OXFORD
UNIVERSITY PRESS

OXFORD
UNIVERSITY PRESS

Great Clarendon Street, Oxford, OX2 6DP,
United Kingdom

Oxford University Press is a department of the University of Oxford. It furthers the University's objective of excellence in research, scholarship, and education by publishing worldwide. Oxford is a registered trade mark of Oxford University Press in the UK and in certain other countries

First Edition published in 2017

Published in the United States of America by Oxford University Press
198 Madison Avenue, New York, NY 10016, United States of America

British Library Cataloguing in Publication Data
Data available

Library of Congress Control Number: 2016945506

ISBN 978–0–19–878550–7

This book is dedicated to Alfaz and Kathleen Hossain, who gave me the chance to learn about the matters discussed here, and the heritage to want to do so

Acknowledgements

This book took a couple of years to write, but it draws on more than twenty years of research and consultancy work in Bangladesh. Since 1994, I have personally interviewed and 'focus grouped' at least a few hundred Bangladeshis in villages, towns, and metropolitan areas across Bogra, Chandpur, Chapainawabganj, Chittagong, Dhaka, Dinajpur, Gaibandha, Jamalpur, Khulna, Kurigram, Lalmonirhat, Nilphamari, Rangamati, Sirajganj, Tangail, and my own 'home district' of Rangpur. I am very grateful to those people for the time and insights they have offered into the development project of Bangladesh. This book would not have been so thoroughly grounded in the contentious realities of development if I had not had the opportunity to meet these people and hear their views. I should also acknowledge that those activities were primarily funded by the UK Department for International Development (DFID), and it is to its credit that it has usually insisted on testimony gathered from people who live with poverty and powerlessness as part of the evidence base for understanding development.

I have been very fortunate in my choice of bosses in those years of my research which have contributed most to this account, and should in particular single out AMR Chowdhury, Imran Matin, and Mick Moore for having encouraged and enabled me to research the issues that interested me most, even when I had no idea why I wanted to ask such questions. The IDS very kindly let me have a long year off to write this book, and I am grateful to my team leader, Anuradha Joshi, and the Institute's Director, Melissa Leach, for making this possible, and to Patta Scott-Villiers for inheriting a most unwieldy project so that I could write. I should note that the IDS is not responsible for any errors of fact or judgement in this book.

Although I had no specific funding to write this book, it was spurred in particular by a project called *Food Riots and Food Rights: The Moral and Political Economy of Accountability for Hunger* (2012–14) which was funded by the Department for International Development-Economic and Social Research Council (DFID-ESRC) programme on poverty (grant number ES/J018317/1), on which I was the Principal Investigator. The finding that it was 'because of the famine' that Bangladesh had relatively successfully weathered the global food crisis of 2007–12 fatefully turned my attention to this little-studied but plainly pivotal event in the nation's brief but turbulent history. I must in particular acknowledge my colleague and friend Professor Ferdous Jahan of Dhaka University for our collaboration on this and related issues over the decade of our partnership. She will recognize the outcome of several of our debates in the analysis here.

Several people provided invaluable comments on early drafts. In particular, Rosalind Eyben, Marie Jo Cortijo, Penelope Mawson, Samer Al-Samarrai, and two anonymous referees gave invaluable detailed feedback, in some cases on more than one draft. I have not incorporated all of their suggestions, but those I did have improved the text immeasurably. I am also thankful to Andrew Fischer and his series co-editors for taking the book on as part of the Development Studies Association series, and to Adam Swallow at Oxford University Press for his patience as I sorted out my ideas.

Many colleagues and friends provided useful critical sounding boards for the ideas as they emerged, in particular Saku Akmeemana, Afsan Chowdhury, Mirza Hassan, Habibul Hoque Khandker, Sohela Nazneen, Patta Scott-Villiers, Sarwar Lateef, and again, Ferdous Jahan. My thinking about the fate of the 'patriarchal bargain' in Bangladesh was closely shaped by some very interesting (at least, they were for me) conversations with Naila Kabeer over the years. Several people generously answered questions or gave help on specific areas of analysis, including Nabil Ahmed, Tariq Omar Ali, Firdous Azim, Gary Bass, Ben Crow, Stephen Devereux, Marcus Franda, Alan Greig, Meghna Guhathakurta, Jaideep Gupte, Samia Huq, Neamat Imam, Tom Lavers, Dolf te Lintelo, John Pilger, Aruna Rao, Lucy Scott, Dina Siddiqi, and Matthias Vom Hau. I am extremely grateful to Tahrat Naushaba Shahid for the exceptional quality of her research support towards the end of this process, and there are one or two late additions that have greatly improved the flow and avoided error that owe to her diligence and expert knowledge. I must also thank Sadik Hasan Shuvo for his excellent assistance in scouring the (somewhat depleted) newspaper and library resources on the 1974 famine. Md. Ashikur Rahman very ably and kindly translated Sheikh Mujib's speech at the UN in 1974. Staff at the US Library of Congress helped me find theses and documents that I might not otherwise have been able to access.

For their moral support I thank in particular Rosaleen Cunningham, Eve Goff, Paul Hossain, Rebecca Hossain, Rob Jenkins, Nadia Khan, and Isabel Rodriquez, and my colleagues in the Power and Popular Politics cluster at the IDS. As always, Alfaz Hossain provided me with a comfortable space in which to work, and his household looked after me exceptionally well in those long final writing days. My family has been supportive throughout and I am forever grateful to Samer Al-Samarrai, who consented to—and co-financed—my long year off as we moved across continents, and to Sophia Al-Samarrai, whose childhood has no doubt been blighted by dinner-table conversations about the horrors and injustice of famines in Ireland and Bengal.

Contents

List of figures

List of tables

Acronyms

AL	Awami League
ASA	Association for Social Advancement
BAIRA	Bangladeshi Association of International Recruiting Agencies
BAKSAL	Bangladesh Krishak Sramik Awami League
BBC	British Broadcasting Corporation
BBS	Bangladesh Bureau of Statistics
BDT	Bangladesh *taka*/currency
BGMEA	Bangladesh Garments Manufacturers and Exporters Association
BIGD	BRAC Institute of Governance and Development (formerly BRAC Development Institute and Centre for/Institute of Governance Studies)
BNP	Bangladesh Nationalist Party
BRAC	Previously, Bangladesh Rural Advancement Committee
BRDB	Bangladesh Rural Development Board
CDF	Credit and Development Forum
CIA	Central Intelligence Agency
CPD	Centre for Policy Dialogue
CSP	Civil Service of Pakistan
DOTS	Directly Observed Treatment Short course (tuberculosis therapy)
EPI	Expanded Program on Immunization
EPZ	Export Processing Zone
FAD	Food Availability Decline
FYP	Five Year Plan
GBP	British pound/currency
GDP	Gross Domestic Product
GED	General Economics Division (Planning Commission)
GFMD	Global Forum on Migration and Development
GSP	Generalised System of Preference
ICDDR,B	International Center for Diarrhoeal Diseases Research, Bangladesh

ILO	International Labour Organization
InM	Institute for Inclusive Financial Development (formerly Institute of Microfinance)
JSD	Jatiya Samajtantrik Dal
MDGs	Millennium Development Goals
MFA	Multi Fibre Arrangement
MFI	Microfinance Institution
MoF	Ministry of Finance
MVA	manual vacuum aspiration
NAP (B)	National Awami Party (Bhashani)
NGO	Non-governmental organization
ORT	Oral Rehydration Therapy (diarrhoea treatment)
PFDS	Public Food Distribution System
PL480	United States Public Law 480; the law governing US food aid policy
RCT	Randomized control trials
RMG	readymade garments
RMMRU	Refugees and Migratory Movements Research Unit, at the University of Dhaka
SDGs	Sustainable Development Goals
SME	Small and medium enterprise
UBINIG	Policy Research for Development Alternative (English translation)
UNDP	United Nations Development Programme
UNROD	United Nations Relief Operation in Dacca; the UN-administered post-war reconstruction effort by the international community
USAID	United States Agency for International Development
USD	United States dollar/currency
VGD	Vulnerable Group Development
VGF	Vulnerable Group Feeding
WFP	World Food Program

Part 1
The Paradox

1

Bangladesh's Surprising Success

1.1 The Idea of Bangladesh

Bangladesh leaves but a light imprint on the international imagination. 'Bangladesh—Sheikh Mujib', said the middle-aged republican in Northern Ireland, when I explained my ethnic origins. 'Bangladesh—Muhammad Yunus', said the young imam in South Sumatra, Indonesia, to the same. Yes, in both cases. Also floods and climate change, Rana Plaza and that disposable shirt you have on, labour migrants, and an increasingly impressive cricket team. This may be changing, but few people without a Bangladesh connection will know more about the world's eighth largest country.[1]

Relatively unimportant for politico-religious extremism, uninteresting from a geopolitical point of view, and not famous as a tourist destination either, Bangladesh punches well below its weight in terms of recognition value. And yet the country has played a major unacknowledged role in the world order as we know it. This role is ideological: the story of Bangladesh's development is told as a parable of the success bred by an early and sustained commitment to economic liberalism. A poor, populous country chooses the path of global capitalist development, resisting many of the temptations of *dirigisme* opted for by so many power-happy post-colonial elites. A particularly dominant retelling of this is a fairy tale of female empowerment that has helped amplify and reinforce powerful messages about the essential rightness of global capitalist development. That Bangladesh—that notorious basket case, with its hungry millions, that byword of bywords—has dragged so much of its population out of poverty is surely proof the development experiment works. If Bangladesh can do it, anywhere can.

Many countries, in particular but not only in Asia, have enjoyed sustained economic growth rates, transforming their economies from populous resourceless

[1] By population. At an officially estimated 160 million, Bangladesh ranks after Nigeria but above Russia. http://www.bbs.gov.bd/Home.aspx (accessed 25 July 2016).

backwaters into export-oriented powerhouses, in the decades since the Second World War. Those who have visited Malaysia or Mauritius may scoff at the idea of Bangladesh's 'success'. But success there undeniably has been. As with other poor countries that relatively early on established the market-friendly economic reforms that laid them open to the boons of global economic integration, Bangladesh has seen sustained economic growth and significant structural transformation from a substantially agrarian base to an economy dominated by exports, chiefly of readymade garments and labour services. Through strategy, circumstance, and perhaps a little luck, these transformations from agrarian to export-oriented and industrial societies have been more pro-poor and less unequalizing than in some other countries that developed quickly. This pro-poorness is partly explained by a second feature of Bangladesh's surprising achievement, which is its pronounced gains in the domain of human development: Bangladesh does far better on key health, education, and gender equality indicators than its income and stage of economic development would suggest. People live longer, healthier lives; have fewer children, more of whom survive to adulthood; and school more of their sons, and in particular their daughters, than in other countries at comparable levels of economic development or with similar social structures. There has been some interesting discussion of how this has come about, but to date none of why.[2]

The idea of Bangladesh's development success remains contentious in some circles, not least because deprivation, ill-being, and oppression remain significant problems: almost fifty million Bangladeshis still live below the ungenerous national poverty line (BBS 2011). Yet the successes—lower infant and maternal mortality, childhood disease, and hunger; gains in mass education, women's rights, and managing disasters—are real enough, and they made the country stand out in the international race for the Millennium Development Goals (Bhattacharya et al. 2013). They are all the more remarkable because the country started from such a low base and with such limited resources of its own. The 'basket case' label (famously but wrongly attributed to Henry Kissinger) may have been unkind, but it was not an inaccurate assessment of the new nation's prospects in the aftermath of its bloody war of liberation from Pakistan in 1971.

Development success is also, in the Bangladesh case, paradoxical: its chronically unsettled politics and corrupt, captured state foretell fragility and division, not shared progress. Some scholars explain this success by showing that 'bad' governance can be fully compatible with economic growth if contending elites can at least hold off on disagreeing about the basis for growth and the distribution of its rewards (Khan 2013; Hassan 2013). Others argue that there

[2] For instance, Asadullah, Savoia, and Mahmud (2014); Chowdhury et al. (2013).

remains a puzzle, because that growth was pro-poor and accompanied by effective public and private investments in human development (Asadullah et al. 2014; Mahmud et al. 2008). It has never been obvious why an elite known best for corruption and violent winner-takes-all politics should have committed its country to a progressive, inclusive development pathway. Key questions for scholars and practitioners of development in the past decade have been: how did Bangladesh achieve human development with such weak governance? If Bangladesh did, can other countries, too?

This book argues that Bangladesh's successes, as well as its signal governance failures, must be understood in the light of its political economy conditions. Both are best understood as the outcome of an interlocking set of agreements or contracts between key actors. This book departs from other analyses by extending the analysis downward and upward: it is not only the national elite whose interests and ideas and institutions matter, but also their relationships with the masses over whom they rule, and with the international community, on whom they depend for recognition and aid resources. *The Aid Lab* also departs from other analyses by historicizing the political economy of Bangladesh's development, showing how these agreements emerged or were crafted in the aftermath of the critical event in its history. Perhaps the most important insight of the book is that this critical event was not, as might reasonably be assumed, the traumatic liberation struggle that founded the country. Instead, the origins of Bangladesh's innovative pro-poor public action can be traced to the devastating famine it suffered in 1974, only three years after independence: as many as 1.5 million people—2 per cent of the total population, overwhelmingly the rural landless proletariat—died in this catastrophe, having already been starved, displaced, terrorized, and otherwise harmed during the liberation war of 1971.[3] Shortly after, the once-heroic nationalist leader Sheikh Mujib was brutally assassinated alongside his family, and fifteen years of military rule followed. The fallout from the famine reset the terms of the development project in Bangladesh, making gross failure too costly and too painful for the ruling elite and their allies in the aid complex to countenance.

In the shadow of the 1974 famine, the agreement on development came to include, first, a ruling class consensus that their own survival depended on human development and basic social protection. This ensured that protection against natural disasters and food shocks was institutionalized as a state priority, helped protect key policies to transform the population through health and education against political competition and corruption, brought

[3] I cite the mortality figure considered most authoritative in the scholarship of the famine (Alamgir 1980). Other estimates of famine mortality are available and are used (including by Nobel Prize-winner Amartya Sen), but with less or no discussion of methodologies and provenance.

poor rural women to the forefront of development, and ensured the elite policed themselves to deliver these essential public goods.

Second, a social contract between rulers and ruled committed the former to providing at least a basic minimum protection. This recognized the unusual degree of exposure faced by the rural landless masses to the elements, the volatilities of global markets, and the general vicissitudes of life. Basic protection meant not only support in times of crisis but also particular efforts to reach poor rural women, to raise their capacities to protect themselves. In exchange for basic protection, the masses granted legitimacy and authority—the foundations of rule. For reasons of political history and social structure, the ruling class in Bangladesh derives its legitimacy not from traditional status, religious leadership, cultural superiority, or even adherence to democratic process. A regime that fails to deliver basic protection against crises of food, flood, cyclones (and so on) lacks legitimacy, rapidly loses authority, and is vulnerable to plotting and overthrow by contending elites. At the same time, development could not proceed without the basic protections being in place in this acutely ecologically fragile and globally exposed setting. These were the lessons of the famine.

The third part of the agreement was to pursue broadly pro-market, pro-poor economic and human development strategies in return for recognition and resources from the international community. Because failure was not an option, pride in national self-determination—in a home-grown development ideology that resisted global economic integration—became an unaffordable luxury. The contending elites in the driving seat of development policy agreed their political (and actual) survival depended on making development work: ideology, political process, even culture could be jettisoned in the pursuit of growth and human progress. Whatever seemed to work could be policy. The challenges were large, numerous, and often reversible, but a clear-eyed view of what needed doing and how held across regimes of all political stripes. This included accepting aid conditions and creating space for the non-governmental action for which Bangladesh is now so fêted.

In accepting its role as the international experiment in aid, Bangladesh fulfilled its side of the development bargain with the international community. This book's title, *The Aid Lab*, serves as a reminder that for the international community, Bangladesh functions and has primary purpose as a colossal human experiment in development models. In providing resources, technical knowhow, and discipline, the international community has met its part of the development contract with this least developed country, and is largely satisfied with the result. It is not only in the big question of its choice of development model that Bangladesh serves as a laboratory for aid, but also in its actual experiments with delivering services to people in great need. Bangladesh has some of the most admired and emulated approaches to public health and fertility control; providing basic education, social protection, and credit; and tackling hunger. Because it serves as the world's aid lab, and no doubt because its human subjects are so numerous, Bangladesh's many innovations and experiments have been much pored over and dissected. We know a great deal about what happened here, but understand little about why.

1.2 Bangladesh as Cinderella

The idea of Bangladesh as a development success is a twenty-first-century trope, a deliberate and striking contrast to its 1970s role as the poster-child for Malthusia. Chief of the cheerleaders for international aid, Jeffrey Sachs, spotlighted Bangladesh's development success as early as 2005:

> Bangladesh was born in a war for independence against Pakistan in 1971. That year, it experienced massive famine and disarray, leading an official in Henry Kissinger's department to famously label it 'an international basket case'. Bangladesh today is far from a basket case [He provides illustrative statistics of human development progress]... Bangladesh shows us that even in circumstances that seem the most hopeless there are ways forward if the right strategies are applied, and if the right combination of investments is made. (Sachs 2005, 10)[4]

Rock star Bono wrote the foreword to Sachs' book, which was published by Penguin and has been cited several thousand times, so let us assume his view is influential. Contrasting Bangladesh with also very poor Malawi, both of which Sachs had recently visited, the author describes a dawn vision in Dhaka of long lines of garments workers en route to the factories. He suddenly realizes they are all young women. Rich country protestors campaign for better working conditions, but they would do better to protest the trade protectionism at home that prevents more such garments jobs from being created:

> These young women already have a foothold in the modern economy that is a critical, measurable step up from the villages of Malawi (and more relevant for the women, a step up from the villages of Bangladesh where most of them were born). The sweatshops are the first rung on the ladder out of extreme poverty. They give lie (sic) to the Kissinger state department's forecast that Bangladesh is condemned to extreme poverty. (Sachs 2005, 11)

He is not unaware of the hardships these young women suffer: a newspaper article contained 'poignant, fascinating, and eye-opening' stories of long hours, harassment, lack of rights in the factories. But

[4] There was not actually a famine in either 1971 or 1972—at least not in Bangladesh (some say it was exported, with the refugees, to India). See Chapter 5 for a full account. But it is certainly true to say that the post-war period was one of mass hunger and chaos.

> what was most striking and unexpected about the stories was the repeated affirmation that this work was the greatest opportunity that these women could ever have imagined, and that their employment had changed their lives for the better.
>
> Nearly all of the women interviewed had grown up in the countryside, extraordinarily poor, illiterate and unschooled, and vulnerable to chronic hunger and hardship in a domineering, patriarchal society. Had they (and their forebearers (sic) of the 1970s and 1980s) stayed in the villages, they would have been forced into a marriage arranged by their fathers, and by seventeen or eighteen, forced to conceive a child. Their trek to the cities to take jobs has given these young women a chance for personal liberation of unprecedented dimension and opportunity.
>
> (Sachs 2005, 12)

Sachs also visited a group of rural women members of a credit group run by the non-governmental organization BRAC (formerly the Bangladesh Rural Advancement Committee). With their tiny food-trading businesses and beautiful saris, these women 'presented a picture every bit as dramatic as that of the burgeoning apparel sector' (Sachs 2005, 14). None of these women wanted more than two children, a remarkable change from the fecund situation in the 1970s, when six or seven were normal. He concludes:

> Bangladesh has managed to place its foot on the first rung of the ladder of development, and has achieved economic growth and improvements of health and education partly through its own heroic efforts, partly through the ingenuity of NGOs [non-governmental organizations] like BRAC and Grameen Bank, and partly through investments that have been made, often at significant scale, by various donor governments that rightly viewed Bangladesh not as a hopeless basket case but as a country worthy of attention, care, and development assistance.
>
> (Sachs 2005, 14)

Bangladesh is powerful as an aid-justifying idea partly because its unpromising start made any success so entirely unlikely. But the idea of Bangladesh is so powerful in the twenty-first century partly because its successes satisfy both the soft-hearted liberal and the gung-ho neoliberal. Those on the political left remain largely unconvinced, but as they play such a minor and specialized role in contemporary debates about economic development, they do not spoil my point. Despite its continuing troubles—and there remain many and new ones to come thanks to climate change—Bangladesh provides the photo op that convinces sceptical taxpayers in the West that development works and the aid flows should continue. Bangladesh is the smiling, more often than not sweetly female, face of global capitalist development. Better yet—she often wears a headscarf as she goes about enjoying her new economic and political freedoms, signalling that moderate Islam can couple with global capitalism. What's not to like?

It is well to be wary of self-aggrandizing stories of success, in the aid industry or any other. Yet like all myths, this one gets much power from core truths.

Early entry into global markets was vital in a densely populated place with no resources other than its rural masses. Innovative social entrepreneurs devised clever ways of reaching those people at scale and sustainably, even figuring out how to bring millions of secluded, unschooled, traditional village women into markets from which they were traditionally excluded. Aid donors did a lot. They provided finance and technical assistance; they documented, analysed and evaluated, learning about what was working; and they granted Bangladesh's development project the international community's seal of approval. The way the average Bangladeshi lives now is vastly different—and, in respect of basic securities and freedoms, particularly for women and girls, measurably better—than forty years ago.

So Sachs' narrative contains many truths. But like most development blueprints it is a caricature, exaggerating and minimizing for effect (Roe 1991). What stands out most here is the emancipatory potential for women of the flourishing non-profit sector and the unstoppable transformative forces of export industry. Sachs invests the promise of low-paid jobs for the girls in the global economy with a particular moral power, an example of what Nancy Fraser calls the 'new romance of female advancement and gender justice' (Fraser 2012, 10). There is all the charge of the attraction of opposites in this romance: custom, parochialism, and the chains of patriarchy meet the white-knuckle pace of change in the globalized fast-fashion industry. And the moral power of anything that promotes female advancement packs an even greater punch at a time when gender equality has become a tenet of, a motive for, and a motif of the war on Islamist extremism.

But after the excitement of having 'stepped up' into factories and credit markets subsides, the downsides of being the cheapest industrial workforce in Asia and in collective micro-debt to the tune of USD 4.2 billion give pause.[5] Is this what empowerment looks like? It no longer feels like enough, if it ever was. But perhaps that is what empowerment does—raises expectations so just the chance to earn some cash, what once felt like such a step up from the village, stops being enough; you start to want rights, to secure those earnings, to organize if not, and to do so in safety. The largest and most visible effort by women to empower themselves, the garments workers' struggle for basic workers' rights, has happened with neither moral nor actual support from the aid industry. Its clear implications are that workers cannot live on the wages that the global economy is willing to offer them. But political and collective forms of empowerment may not be consistent with the fairy tale.

[5] Moazzem and Raz (2014) estimated that in 2011, Bangladeshi garments workers had the lowest wages in Asia; even Cambodian workers had higher wages. Micro-credit figures are from www.mixmarket.org (accessed 3 February 2015).

There are other silences in this idea of Bangladesh's success. You would be forgiven for forgetting that Bangladesh's gains were 'partly through its own heroic efforts'. Sachs' respectful reference to the role of a sovereign state in directing its own development is drowned out by the role of NGOs and donors, whom it is clear have full freedom to operate in this space. It is a fair sketch in a way. In drawing a positive image of Bangladesh, it makes intuitive sense to minimize the role of a state which it is difficult to characterize other than as chronically corrupt, driven by a violently divisive politics and a venal, pathologically mutually antagonistic leadership.[6]

1.3 The Political Economy of Development Success

Scholars and aid donors increasingly recognize that a country's development pathways are determined less by the technical correctness of its policies than by its political economy conditions, and specifically the nature of its main political settlements or agreements among elites.[7] For Bangladesh, it has been convincingly argued that sustained, broad-based development was the fruit of an elite agreement to enable economic growth through openness to global markets, accepting that even political opponents would need to be able to benefit. Khan (2013) shows how the institutions and incentives to make growth possible emerged after its initial 'failed populist authoritarianism' generated political crisis and anarchy following an all-out grab for national resources by politically connected elites in the early 1970s. The idea of a political settlement on growth through business-friendly policies is backed by the simple fact that more than half of Bangladesh's Members of Parliament had business or industry as their primary occupation throughout most of the 2000s (Jahan and Amundsen 2012; Jahan 2015).

Hassan (2013) argues that the elite agreement to let growth happen was one of three lower-level bargains on which the overall political settlement rested. The second was an unstable but occasionally functional agreement on the rules of the political game that emerged out of the fifteen years of military rule (1975–90). This was to adhere to multiparty elections and democratic competition to share political power, in order to gain the internal and external legitimacy of an elected regime. The elite took this so seriously, even while recognizing their own inability to police themselves and their faction followers,

[6] There may be many hundreds of donor and newspaper reports saying as much, but for an authoritative perspective on Bangladesh's governance see the *State of Governance* series by the Institute of Governance and Development at BRAC University (formerly the Institute of Governance Studies, and before that, the Centre for Governance Studies; http://bigd.bracu.ac.bd/index.php/s-reports/147-sog-reports, accessed 25 July 2016).

[7] See Di John and Putzel (2009); Khan (2010); Laws (2012).

that for more than a decade after 1996, a non-party caretaker institution was constitutionally mandated to oversee political transitions. The third bargain was a 'social provisioning contract', in which the state committed to at least basic service provisions for the masses. This 'triple-lock' political settlement, Hassan argues, is the key to Bangladesh's relatively inclusive development success (Hassan 2013).

While these accounts of the political settlement are correct in essence, both grant somewhat too much autonomy to the elite. Both neglect the relational and negotiated nature of the political settlement and the role of both external actors and the Bangladeshi masses in their explanations. To the extent that the broad-based growth pathway adopted by Bangladesh after its brief and disastrous flirtation with state 'socialism' was pro-poor, they do not convincingly explain why the elite needed this to be the case. This book shows how the political fallout from the 1974 famine, hard on the heels of the 1970s cyclone (the neglect of which turned popular opinion against West Pakistan rule), reasserted the social contract between rulers and ruled. It put in place a contract of basic protection against the ecological disasters and global economic volatilities to which the rural proletariat had been exposed for at least a century (Bose 1986). That contract in turn depended on an agreement with the international community to provide the aid resources and knowhow needed to transform the population in order to prevent subsistence crises along the lines of 1974 (or 1970, 1943, etc.).

In signing up to aided development Bangladesh was required to open itself not only to global markets, but also to a range of experimental policy and programmes in the name of poverty alleviation. Both Khan and Hassan implicitly assume that choices of the pathways of development were clear-cut and given, and that ideas played no important role in how interests were conceived and institutions evolved. But there are reasons to believe that the motivations for going down this path included not just growth, but an inclusive, labour-intensive variant of the model. This was the obvious choice from a limited menu, but acutely low levels of human development meant it was not necessarily easily achieved. Ideas about development matter in their own right, and Bangladesh has hot-housed and showcased many. This is both because its options were initially so limited that new ideas urgently needed to be tested in this difficult environment and because in opening itself to aid and development, Bangladesh found itself exposed to a rapid and rich traffic in liberal development thought and practice. Both the relationships within which the elite found themselves and their ideas about the appropriate models of development mattered to how the political economy functioned.[8]

[8] Following Hickey's critique of political settlement theories in relation to development outcomes (Hickey 2013).

1.3.1 *The Domination/Development Contract*

There are many problems with the idea of a social contract, not least that in liberal political philosophy it assumes autonomous actors freely choosing to be rulers in a nation-state setting. The use here departs from liberal social contract theory in two ways. First, by extending it to transnational relationships and institutions of aid. It is not usual to see international parties as part of the social contract establishing the state, but nor is it unheard of. Rawls' 'law of peoples' sets out the principles of a supra-national social contract in which aid, human rights, and famine relief are instances of the kinds of exchange the contract may entail (Rawls 1993). The content of the mutual obligations and expectations in this instance has to do with aid programmes to reduce poverty, accelerate growth, and speed global economic integration.[9] Hickey's caution about where the social contract stops being a useful concept for development is instructive, pointing to the need for more transformative and politically empowering forms of public action than donors can manage (Hickey 2011).

Second, the social contract is acknowledged to be a relation of domination: power always permeates the contract, establishing the unequal terms on which parties are contracted and the unequal costs of breaking it (Pateman and Mills 2007). The acute dependence on aid with which Bangladesh was born sharply reduced the range of possible pathways of development to those which were minimally acceptable to its donors (Sobhan 1982). As for the masses, it is all but impossible to conceive of their participation in this contract as voluntary, free, or autonomous. Following Pateman (1980), we can ask—can consent be said to have taken place in any meaningful sense of the term? Has granting 'consent' made it possible for the developed to hold their developers to account? Or is consent beyond the scope of a population facing Malthusian annihilation?

To avoid making the social contract metaphor work harder than it can, note that consent may amount to little more than agreeing not to resist (Lipset 1959). But that does not make it meaningless: not resisting is not the same as actively rejecting. The legitimacy of a regime depends not on continual active support, just on it not being withdrawn. And unlike in the established democracies of the West, it is possible to observe moments in a post-colonial country's history when the contract is actively renegotiated or reset. The idea of consent may mean more in developing countries precisely because the nation (who is in it, what it stands for) is a relatively recent construction,

[9] Those interested in such distinctions will recognize this as the difference between Hobbesian contractarian approaches, which are seen as substantive, or specifying the normative content of the contract, and Kantian contractualism, in which the contract is the thing, and the norms to which it binds people are not specified.

as is the polity that will distribute its power and the state that will administer it. In the writing of new constitutions, mass migration, major insurgencies, and significant declines in political trust (Norris 1999), it is surely possible to read something very like acts of mass assent or dissent.

And in understanding the times when the contract was broken, as this book does in its discussion of the famine of 1974, we start to see why consent matters. The silence about this time is too heavy to explain without delving into its psychology. But it leaves an impression of a nation that learned the hard way why protection against crisis had to be hardwired into its system, protected against political regimes, open to others to help. To fail again as in 1974 would in future be known to spell the end not only for a ruling fraction, but for the class more generally. So the social contract is a useful device, because the mechanics of the contract can be discerned empirically, if not with ease. There is enough evidence to make sense of the mechanisms through which contracts have been broken or honoured in the early part of Bangladesh's development, and to make sense of the costs and consequences of broken contracts for elite groups at different levels. Take, for instance, the effects of the broken patriarchal bargain for poor and landless women household heads, forced into manual labour on public works schemes, against all their society's rules and norms. When contracts break, and parts of society are no longer protected or supported, there is a clear role for the state.

1.4 The Aid Lab and Its Ethics

Visitors to Matlab in Chandpur, southern Bangladesh—the 'world's longest running health project' (source: Wikipedia)—are said to be surprised when they learn the name is a real place-name, and not a contraction of MATernal and Child Health LABoratory. They are surprised because Matlab has been at the heart of advancements in our understanding of, precisely, maternal and child health, and is internationally renowned as a large human laboratory. Appropriately enough, Matlab actually means 'plan' or 'idea' in Bangla; it therefore refers not to the science of the foreigners but to a clever scheme in the vernacular.

It is as the international experiment in aid, the aid lab, that Bangladesh has fulfilled its side of the development contract with the international community. The idea of the aid lab helps keep in focus some of the defining features of Bangladesh's development journey, but it is a troubling label. It prioritizes an outsider's view of Bangladesh, from the not-always-pleasant gaze of the development industry. It suggests a treatment of human beings as scientific subjects—as means and not as ends. And it seems to negate the point made above—that politics and the state have mattered in these achievements, suggesting instead the insulation of the clever scientist, toiling away at her experiments under 'lab conditions' without hindrance from the real world.

As we have already seen, Bangladesh's status as the Aid Lab reflects its lack of alternative geostrategic significance and the terms of its incorporation in a developmental social contract. This deliberately problematic metaphor makes us keep in mind that the country's geostrategic and ideological role in the world is as the 'test case' for global capitalist development (Faaland and Parkinson 1976). A flat, small space with an accessible and homogenous population, the country has many qualities suited to social experimentation. Many experiments with poverty reduction have been tested on its soil. Bangladesh's status as aid lab has several implications for its place in the world, and is a reminder that comparatively small, less developed, aid-dependent countries are shaped by their place in a larger whole in a way that a Brazil, China, or India never could be. For Bangladesh, global connections and global perceptions matter a great deal. This is true whether you stitch jeans for America, build stadiums in Qatar, buy banks or telecoms, or send your kids to the Ivy League or the LSE.[10]

When aid officials and diplomats come to Bangladesh they seek not minerals or land or geopolitical advantage, but to demonstrate that the social, economic, and political model they promote works. The country's greatest product is ideational, an idea of Bangladesh. The key point here is that external intervention in this misbegotten Malthusia has been motivated by something close to altruism. It is the gift of the scientist who wants to learn the truth, the visionary that desires to share her vision—not of the colonialist grabbing your wealth. If aid is about making the world safe for capitalism to enter, it is not clear that anyone has been particularly desperate to get into Bangladesh. Because it lacks any obvious material benefit to the donor, the contract endows its donors with a particular kind of power: the gift that is not returned, leaving the recipient in permanent debt.[11]

As an aid lab, the inner workings of Bangladesh's policies and projects are exposed—global public property for researchers and aid missionaries and media. The bell jar hothouses some ideas; others, less easily marketable in a policy and intellectual space crowded with free market doctrine, have withered. But the experimentation has produced many justly celebrated successes that Bangladesh has gifted back to the world. Among the pioneering development

[10] Hickey warns us off of 'methodological nationalism' in thinking about the politics of development, reminding us that global influences may be particularly important for developing country elites (Hickey 2013). Global influences and networks matter in particular to the elites of small, open countries like Bangladesh.

[11] As we know from the economic anthropology of gift exchange (Mauss 2002; Parry 1986). On the specific and considerable problem of altruism and reciprocity in aid exchanges, see Stirrat and Henkel (1997).

NGOs that eventually grew so large, the most successful had actual laboratories: research centres that tested emerging ideas about what worked. A famous example is BRAC's Research and Evaluation Division, which works in close partnership with the International Center for Diarrhoeal Diseases Research Bangladesh (ICDDR,B), one of the world's largest applied public health research institutions. Together they pioneered major innovations in oral rehydration therapies, maternal and child healthcare delivery, and tuberculosis treatments that have saved unknown millions of lives.[12]

The experiments in the aid lab have been real as well as metaphorical, and the ethical standards of the science have often been low. In its large numbers, densely situated and affordable to reach, the Bangladeshi population has often been an inviting prospect for testing risky initiatives, and the pressure to take interventions 'to scale' has resulted in disasters where a more cautious respect for human life and rights would have put a stop to matters. A UNICEF/World Bank project celebrated for delivering 'safe' water to 80 per cent of the population by promoting shallow tubewells in the 1970s turned into 'the largest mass poisoning of a population in history', having failed to test the groundwater for arsenic (Smith, Lingas, and Rahman 2000, 1093). An estimated seventy-seven million Bangladeshis have had heightened risk factors for cancers and other diseases as a direct result (Argos et al. 2010). To date, there has been no accountability for the ongoing disaster, and a 2003 lawsuit against the British Geological Society for not testing for arsenic in the preparation of the project failed.[13]

Another notorious instance was the testing of the fertility control implant Norplant during the 1980s. In the 1995 BBC Horizon series documentary 'The Human Laboratory', the activist director of UBINIG, Farida Akhter, described how the implants were being marketed to uneducated slum women to control their fertility without informing them that the drugs were unapproved and experimental. Potential side effects were not explained to the women, nor, once they were experienced, recorded in the data. Women reported having been coerced and threatened to keep the implants in. The United States Agency for International Development, USAID, defended the ethical standards of these drug trials it had sponsored in the slums of Dhaka and in conflict-ridden, deeply poor Haiti, denying all wrongdoing. The dark side of the aid lab comes into focus. Women's health rights activist Nasreen Huq said:

> When you conduct a trial in this sort of setting, you are simply taking advantage of them being poor. You've access, cheap access, to subjects, and you can write it up as a successful trial. You're not in any way advancing science, you're taking

[12] The author's first job was on a joint BRAC-ICDDR,B project on women's empowerment, in the very centre of the Aid Lab.

[13] See Hossain (2006); Buncombe (2010).

> advantage of a situation in which women are poor and they don't want to have more children, and by providing this method, or conducting this trial, you are not in any way letting them out of their desperate situation. I mean, I have been trained in science and I'm sorry, this is not science. (BBC 1995)

For Farida Akhter, Bangladeshi women were preferred because they were cheaper and more easily controlled than guinea pigs. Betsy Hartmann, another researcher familiar with the aid discourse in Bangladesh, argued that 'the population bomb' was seen as the biggest threat in Washington: 'now we're fearing these Third World peoples. Does this mean that you promote Norplant like a weapon in the war against population growth?' (BBC 1995).

The militant Malthusianism that drove American attitudes in the 1970s and 1980s has faded, at least in respect of the bodies of Bangladeshi women. But there is a residual utilitarianism in development-think in this context that makes interventions like the Norplant 'weapon' and poisonous groundwater sources likely. Utilitarianism is a pragmatic response to the fear of large numbers, the logical implication of the knowledge of quite how many people are crowded onto a sinking, eroding piece of land. F. H. Abed, the founder of BRAC—an organization famous worldwide for its ability 'to scale'—has as his mantra 'small is beautiful, but big is necessary', a gentle mockery of the alternative economics popularized by E. F. Schumacher at precisely the same time he was founding BRAC. Abed believes in the need for small-scale innovation, but only if it can be blown up to reach millions: there can be no laurels for tiny perfection in a place where tens of millions have desperate need now. The failure to treat each human as an end in her own right is justified thus: when fifty million have been pulled out of poverty, what does it matter if two or three or ninety have had their rights and dignity trampled on to achieve this end?

People who know Bangladesh know why this makes sense as a rough-and-ready moral philosophy of development. But it is a crude utilitarianism that justifies the trampling of human rights and permits fascistic tendencies, the suppression of dissent and competition included. Under emergency conditions of 'triage', such errors are understandable. One of the conclusions of this book is that a utilitarian calculus that neglects human rights no longer suits a country at the stage to which Bangladesh has advanced. It is time—long overdue, some would argue—to negotiate a new social contract for development.

1.5 About This Book

1.5.1 *Motivations, Approach, Politics, and Positionality*

I wrote this book as part of a continuing conversation with colleagues and friends—experts in development and on Bangladesh as well as others—about what has changed in Bangladesh and why. I wrote it partly with the aim of puncturing the unwarranted air of self-congratulation in the aid industry discussion of the Bangladesh 'paradox'. It is unwarranted first because the methods used on Bangladesh and Bangladeshis were often illiberal and unethical. A laboratory mentality continues to justify practices in Bangladesh (and elsewhere) on the basis of the ends. Certainly the population may benefit when these experiments go well. But does that justify means that would not be used on a more powerful country, a less impoverished people? What happens when the treatment of nations and their people like subjects without regard to their rights becomes institutionalized as public (aid) policy—worse still, marketed as a recipe for development success? Part of my concern here is to remind practitioners and scholars of the need for vigilance against the suggestion that a 'state of exception' prevails which permits abrogation of national sovereignty and human rights on the grounds of some greater good. The 'triage' to which the Bangladeshi people were in effect subjected around the time of the 1974 famine should never be repeated, even if the effects of the shock had positive final fruits. The costs, in human life and misery and political violence and disruption, were immense.

A second reason why the aid industry (in which I include NGOs) should not credit itself for Bangladesh's success is that this depended more fully on the politics being right than has been acknowledged to date. Other countries without geopolitical significance have also had large amounts of aid poured into them, without similar human development success. Many have been smaller and less challenged by ecology than Bangladesh. Others have found less grudging patrons among the aid donors. Many countries have had NGOs, big, small, international, innovative, and otherwise. The reasons Bangladesh succeeded ultimately owed to the powerful political imperative to do so, because the process of national liberation and its aftermath built a social contract to protect the population against subsistence crisis, and it was on this foundation that human development could proceed. It was this contract—a contract of domination, it is true—that permitted aid and its organizations to work alongside and with the state. It is understandable that the technocrats and bureaucrats that manage aid should sideline the significance of messy political struggle in explaining development outcomes. But I worry their hubris will catch them up if they expect to replicate the Bangladesh success in other, less politically receptive, settings.

Many readers of this book will, I expect, have a personal or professional link to Bangladesh, and be familiar with these debates. Some will have firsthand or scholarly knowledge of these events. They may disagree with my approach or my interpretation; they may think I have left out crucial facts that bias me one way or another. However this book is received, I anticipate debate. One possibility I have considered is that some may view my work as partisan, as giving succour to an 'anti-liberation' agenda which seeks to blacken the name of the 'Father of the Nation' Bangabandhu, Sheikh Mujibur Rahman, the nationalist hero who led Bangladesh's liberation struggle—and whose party, the Awami League, was in power at the time of the famine. Bangladeshi scholarship can be highly politicized along partisan lines, particularly with respect to contentious matters in the early part of our short history as an independent nation. Any mention of the 1974 famine may be seen as potentially taking a position against the Awami League, the party in power at the time. It is true that as a study of politics this is necessarily a political book. But I refuse a partisan position. Nationalist and domestic party politics matter, but they are hardly central to the argument. Nor—and it may be prudent to make this plain from the outset—does my argument lay blame for the pivotal famine squarely at the door of the government of the time: I believe, and show, that the tragedy was all but inevitable under post-war conditions, and that aid donors played a distinctly murky part in establishing those conditions, and in the famine itself.[14] In fact, I conclude that the distinguishing feature of Bangladesh's one and only famine is that the political leadership did not try to conceal it: by contrast, they publicized the crisis in a vain effort to get help. Mujib was personally devastated by these events, as were others among the political and policy elite. This is why the famine played the role of immediately orienting Bangladesh on a human development pathway—a role comparable events arguably failed to play in the Ethiopia of the time, for instance. And so this is less an analysis of parties and political leaders than one of global aid relations, class, and the politics of ecology. None of Bangladesh's human development successes would have happened without national liberation; that it took a further phase of violence and struggle for the social contract on which that success rested to emerge does not make that any less true.

Some readers may suspect my personal motivations for writing a book likely to reopen old sores, so let me put them out there. I bring to this story the biases, experience, insight, and shibboleths of twenty years of working on and living in Bangladesh, all as part of the aid industry. I have been a consultant, an NGO (BRAC) staffer, and a researcher, in and outside of Bangladesh. I draw on a great deal of my primary and secondary research, as well as my experiences and observations, in the argument constructed here. At some times I write as an analyst and a scholar, but at others I write about things I have seen or heard or done. My role in the industry means I have had a ringside

[14] A role which has never been given the close scrutiny it deserves. A group of scholars is currently developing research plans to study the role of the US Government and other aspects of the famine in detail, to ensure the lessons are not lost to posterity.

view of the changes, but also that I am bound to some parts of the story of Bangladesh's development success more than others. I do feel that I have an unusual perspective on these matters, having worked closely and extensively with people from all walks of life in those twenty years—farmers; ministers; industrialists; members of Parliament; beggars; traders; journalists; factory workers; rickshaw-pullers; aid bureaucrats; NGO staff; teachers; nurses; policemen; doctors; landless labourers; market stallholders; activists; military leaders; writers; religious leaders; district, upazila, and union officials; chairs and members; and so on. I have personally spoken with several hundreds of people in Bangladesh about the issues I cover here. And I have spent time thinking about what they told me, and analysing what it all meant. I draw on those twenty years of research and publication in this book.

I deliberately chose not to conduct additional research for this book, because I had accumulated more opinion and material than I could ever write about. I also knew that there was already a vast body of literature, most of it by Bangladeshi scholars, most of it ignored in development research and writing, on which to draw. As the bibliography indicates, I have drawn freely on all sorts of published material about Bangladesh without feeling confined by discipline or domain. I have not used Bangla-language secondary sources (apart from a small number of newspaper articles) largely because (as my Bengali is self-taught) key English-language sources on which I have drawn have parsed them better than I ever could. I have, however, used United States Government State Department and similar official declassified sources. This has led to an apparent anti-American bias in the book, which I am unable to correct. By this I mean not that I would remove any of the critical reflections on the role of the US government, but that I wish I could also have included similar critical reflections on the role of the UK, Canada, and other aid donors, including those from the Gulf states, in directing Bangladesh's domestic policy. But there are few states as transparent as the United States, and indeed as powerful as it was during the 1970s. All the material I cite is freely available online. This is quite remarkable given that I have not even cited some of the most inflammatory commentaries by US government officials regarding the new nation of Bangladesh.

Some people feel that non-Bangladeshis, and people of Bangladeshi extraction living elsewhere, have less right or place to comment on the place than those who stay. There is something in that; there is an innate authority to authenticity that I cannot claim. But proximity does not always make for the most objective analysis, and distance has its benefits. In fact, I first conceived of this book when I was living in Indonesia. Researching the risks Indonesians faced in their lives, I was amazed by the number and severity of disasters people there pack into a lifetime: volcanoes, earthquakes, droughts, tsunamis, pestilence, colonialism, war, famine, economic crisis . . . It was clear that local societies, informal governance, public policy, as well as economic, cultural, and religious behaviour, were all closely structured to respond to the risks people faced. After several years of travelling around Java it struck me that the only other place I could think of where the people faced so many external shocks was the country I knew best. My distance-proximity has helped in other ways. I am part-Bangladeshi, enjoying the advantages of an insider and few problems of over-identification with the society I study. I often misunderstand things because my Bangla is rough, but people are always happy to correct me. I expect they will continue to do so after they have read *The Aid Lab.*

On the title: most people dislike it. I do myself. But the story I am telling here is not a pretty one. I have called it *The Aid Lab* despite very good alternative suggestions because of the difficult fact at the core of the narrative: that Bangladesh's development history—indeed, its very existence—hinged upon its precarious and clientelistic relation to (chiefly) western aid donors. With this title, I want us to keep in mind that whatever the power of its national politics in bringing about positive change at home, Bangladesh is located, on historically adverse terms, in a global political economy with vast power and influence over its pathways to human progress. Bangladesh has been disciplined accordingly. If anything, this makes its achievements all the more remarkable. It is with great satisfaction that I show in the final chapter how Bangladesh now markets itself as a sophisticated model of development, poised not only to resolve the thorniest future challenges of human existence but also to instruct others on how to do so.

1.5.2 *Structure*

The book is organized into four parts. After the initial introductory chapters (Part 1), the chapters proceed in a roughly chronological order.

PART 1: THE PARADOX

The introductory section sets out the motivations for the book, the key debates and themes with which it engages, and some of the debates about Bangladesh's achievements to date (Chapter 1, 'Bangladesh's Surprising Success'). Following this, background is provided, setting out some facts and figures of Bangladesh's success and showing why Bangladesh is seen as a success story (Chapter 2, 'From Malthusia to the Bangladesh Paradox'). It then unpicks the 'triple-lock' political settlement in Bangladesh with a close look at the substance of the development contract, through an examination of the Bangladeshi elite, its relations with the mass of citizens and externally with the international community and aid donors, and the perceptions, interests, and relationships among these groups (Chapter 3, 'The Elites, the Masses, and Their Donors').

PART 2: THE BASKET CASE

The second part takes us back to the period immediately following independence. It looks at how the context for development policy was set by the devastation of the war, the preceding decades of rural impoverishment and subsistence crises, the condition of the civil administration, and the aid-dependent international relations with which the strategically insignificant Bangla Desh was burdened. Drawing on the work of feminist scholars, it focuses in particular on the broken patriarchal bargain, the result of wartime rapes, widowhood, and abandonment, as the start of the state's early recognition of 'the woman problem', and its relatively strong emphasis on women's development (Chapter 4, 'The Breaking of the Patriarchal Bargain and the Emergence of the "Woman Issue" ').

A chapter on the famine of 1974 puts this tragedy at the centre of the analysis (Chapter 5, '1974'). This critical juncture showed that the growing rural proletariat was relentlessly buffeted by market and environmental shocks, and that women were acutely vulnerable. The famine is treated as the single most important cause in a re-negotiation of the social contract that laid the foundations for the successful project of national development.

PART 3: THE TEST CASE FOR DEVELOPMENT

In the third part we start to see the national development project emerge. The after-effects of the famine and its lessons for development more generally are taken up in a chapter that discusses the politics of reforms in food security, and experiments with social protection and poverty reduction (Chapter 6, 'Never Again: The Long Shadow of Famine'). Next we turn to an exploration of institutional innovations such as NGOs and vertical campaigns to reach the rural masses with health, fertility control, and education. These pioneering development efforts were about changing the bodies and minds of the mass of Bangladeshis, and they came with strong commitment from the Bangladeshi elite, for whom the people had to be equipped to engage with development (Chapter 7, 'Making Bangladeshis').

PART 4: THE BENGAL TIGER

This brings us full circle to the idea of Bangladeshi development success. In the fourth and concluding section, we look at the changes in Bangladeshi society that are unsettling the old bargains and demanding a more challenging set of rights to be protected. We see a highly globalized population, with skills wanted in the wider world economy (Chapter 8, 'Aerotropolitans and Cinderellas: Bangladeshis in the Global Economy'). But these are generally low-level skills, learned in a public service regime that can deliver only basic services, creating a low-skill equilibrium trap. When they go abroad to work, as when they work at home, they are unprotected. Those not fortunate enough to have steady public or private sector jobs are the flexible workforce of global capitalism, chronically precarious as a result of that position. These groups are increasingly restive, prone to unruly politics and excluded from the mainstream policy agenda. In the conclusion (Chapter 9, 'Post-Malthusian Futures: Towards A New Social Contract') it is argued that to incorporate this group, the elite will need to agree to a re-settlement that makes more stringent demands than the basic protections of the past. This will include protecting workers from a world workplace that strips them of their citizenship and workers' rights, even while it struggles with the implications of climate change and global economic turbulence.

2

From Malthusia to the Bangladesh Paradox

2.1 Legacies of Colonial and Neo-colonial Rule

The war of liberation in which Bangladesh won its independence from Pakistan was the second in a two-part struggle against colonial exploitation and neo-colonial underdevelopment. The province of Bengal had historically been the wealthy centre of the East India Company, later of British Imperial rule. In their long rule over Bengal, the British presided over the agricultural settlement of large portions of the East Bengal delta, maximizing revenue without investment in agriculture or the population by concentrating control over land in the hands of non-cultivating *zamindars*. By the late nineteenth century East Bengal was characterized by increasing population pressures and declining landholding on the one hand, and growing integration into the global capitalist economy on the other. Smallholder farmers across much of East Bengal were more precariously positioned than the medium-sized *jotedars* (placeholders for revenue-collecting *zamindars*), largely because of their different histories of land settlement and access to credit. These 'demographic and market pressures intersected most obviously at a microcosmic level on the tiny jute-growing plot of the east Bengal peasant' (Bose 1986, 36). Unable to subsist on the proceeds of rice cultivation on ever tinier plots, peasants shifted into potentially more lucrative jute production, exposing them to the volatilities of global commodity markets and the oppressive dependence on local credit relations. By 1920, there was little unsettled land left on which to expand production, and production yields remained about the same for a quarter of a century. The famine of 1943–4 (whose wider effects pre- and post-dated this period; see Mukherjee 2015) did much to accelerate the process of impoverishment and loss of land in the east of Bengal. By 1960, a conservative estimate was that one-fifth of the rural population of what was by then the east wing of Pakistan had no land of their own (Van Schendel 2009; Abdullah et al. 1976). By the mid-1980s, in the country that was by then Bangladesh, around half the rural population was landless (Turner and Ali

1996; Lewis 2011), signalling that the intervening quarter-century had seen a dramatic increase in landlessness.

Independence from Britain and partition from India in 1947 changed little in these underlying patterns of underdevelopment. Industrial development, in particular processing of jute products, had been concentrated in West Bengal; the eastern part of Bengal remained in the weak position of commodity producer once it was turned into East Pakistan. The disruption to industry and business after independence illustrates the extent to which industry had been neglected in East Pakistan:

> Overnight a vacuum was created in large areas of modern industry, banking, insurance, foreign and domestic trade, inland water transport and shipping. At the same time the developed trading and supply relationships which had been built up by this expatriate bourgeoisie to serve the Bangladesh economy were severed. In 1969/70, 35% of Bangladesh's imports and 32% of its exports had been direct to West Pakistan. Again overnight Bangladesh had to find new sources of supply for raw cotton, yarn, cloth, oil seeds, long staple rice, tobacco and variety of manufactures. In the export sector, markets for tea, paper and newsprint, and matches were severely affected whilst markets for jute goods, hides and skins and leather were partially affected. This meant that not only was it necessary to find new sources of supply and markets but new classes, institutions and skills had to be developed to fill the vacuum created by the departing Pakistanis. (Sobhan 1982, 2)

This gap in turn reflected the nature of the landed, business, and industrial elites, who had been predominantly drawn from among non-Bengalis or Bengali Hindus. The new nation faced the uphill challenge of economic development with only an 'intermediate class' of lawyers, academics, and other professionals to play the role of a class of entrepreneurs and industrialists (Kochanek 1994; Sobhan and Ahmad 1980; Bertocci 1982). Indeed, a major motivation for Bengali independence was that the eastern wing of Pakistan had been neglected by development policy and aid expenditure in the two decades since partition. This was partly deliberate, a neo-colonial strategy, and partly de facto, the result of a failure to correct for the unequalizing effects of a drive towards private sector-driven industrial development in which rural livelihoods and human development were of minor relevance (Sobhan 1969). It also reflected the view of the ruling elite that maintaining the political settlement across the bifurcated country meant military power, which meant a viable economy (Khan 2013); investment in growth (rather than subsistence) sectors such as the manufacturing industry meant that the poor, agrarian citizens of East Pakistan were disproportionately neglected compared to their counterparts to the west.

Neo-colonial rule inevitably rested on inequitable distributions of political power that finally proved untenable. Khan (2013) shows how the exclusion of

East Pakistani elites from the benefits of growth destabilized the political settlement in the 1950s. When Ayub Khan seized power in 1958, a combination of authoritarian violence and effective subsidies to industrial investors maintained the settlement through the 1960s, leading to a growing concentration of economic and political power among a small group. Growing inequality between the industrial elite—the 'twenty-two families' said by Pakistani Chief Economist Mahbub ul Haq to control Pakistan's industrial and financial assets in 1965—and the rural masses was sanctioned as part of this development drive. Over the 1960s, and despite praise for Pakistan's apparent economic growth success, class and regional inequalities grew ever more glaring and ever more intolerable for the intermediate classes over in East Bengal:

> With the benefit of hindsight, the praetorian LAO (limited access order, or political settlement) failed to allocate sufficient rents to potential organizers of violence and allocated too many rents to client capitalists, a group that included almost none from the eastern wing. An emerging alliance between excluded business interests and excluded political interest in East Pakistan proved to be devastating for the stability of the regime. (Khan 2013, 36)

Most foreign aid was military aid, and this stayed in the west where the military/political leadership were. Foreign exchange earned from the jute exports of Bengali peasants was transformed into industrial investment in the west. As early as 1956, East Pakistani economists highlighted the unevenness of investment and development outcomes, arguing that a 'two economy' approach disadvantaged the East. Between 1959–60 and 1969–70, per capita gross domestic product (GDP) rose by 17 per cent in East Pakistan, but by 42 per cent in the west; per capita income was one-third higher in the west than in the east in 1959–60, and two-thirds higher by 1969–70 (Islam 1972; Van Schendel 2009). By 1970 there was widespread acceptance that West Pakistan had treated its eastern half as a colony: industrial investment was heavily concentrated in the east; foreign exchange earned in the east from jute exports funded development in the west; coveted positions in the state were dominated by West Pakistanis (Khan 1995; Maniruzzaman 1988; Ghosh 1990) and the fruits of development confined to the elites of the west (Khan 1995; Khan 2011); within the army, Bengali officers were frequently passed over for men from the west, and the top brass were rarely from the east. By the time of independence in 1971, the east had built up no modern heavy industry or financial services of its own, and the separation left a large gap in domestic and foreign trade and transport services, among others.[1]

[1] See Nurul Islam's memoir (Islam 2003) and Rehman Sobhan's blistering analysis of the causes and effects of Bangladesh's aid dependence (Sobhan 1982).

Resistance to this uneven distribution inevitably emerged. A key moment was the 1950s' language movement. This student-led struggle succeeded in blocking the imposition of Urdu in public life, a move which would have marginalized Bengali, the language spoken in the east. Responding to widespread popular struggles of the late 1960s in Pakistan (themselves influenced by youth struggles elsewhere during the late 1960s (Raghavan 2013)), democratic elections were called for in late 1970. But with only weeks to go before the polls, one of the worst disasters ever to befall the region, and indeed one of the deadliest cyclones in world history, struck the coast of East Bengal, centring on Bhola. Given the significance of its timing in the independence struggle, and, I argue, the development history, the treatment of Bhola in political history is surprisingly cursory.[2] For this reason, I discuss it in detail.

2.2 The Bhola Cyclone of 1970

No political history of Bangladeshi nationalism fails to link the Bhola cyclone to the Awami League election landslide that unleashed the struggle for independence weeks later, but elite-centred accounts routinely ignore the significance of the environment in political history (Ahmed 2013; Iqbal 2010). Bhola was a critical juncture (USAID 2007, 42), a 'perfect storm' that crowned a series of natural disasters which made ever plainer the neglect by the Pakistani state and the need for an alternative political dispensation to serve the interests of its precarious peasantry. It was a national disaster, whose 'socio-psychological impact fell on the entire incipient Bengali nation' (Khondker 1995, 176).

The Bhola cyclone, one of the deadliest tropical storms in world history, struck the Bay of Bengal on 12 November 1970. It was forecast to be of moderate intensity, and radio warnings only started late in the afternoon (not that anyone trusted these messages). Travelling at 150 mph at high tide, it generated a 20-foot tidal wave that swept at least a quarter of a million people and possibly twice as many, with their animals, crops, and houses, into the Bay of Bengal.[3] One man watched helplessly as his five children were swept away by a howling frenzy of water, wind, and flying debris. Almost half the population were washed away in one area. People spoke of the wave as similar to a bombing raid—presciently, it turned out, with the Pakistani army raids only four months into the future (Schanberg 1970).

[2] Apart from Nabil Ahmed's provocative essay 'Entangled Earth' (Ahmed 2013) and Habibul Haque Khondker's work on the politics of disaster (Khondker 1992).

[3] On the cyclone itself, see Frank and Husain (1971); on its epidemiology Sommer and Mosley (1972).

Disastrous though it was, the Bhola cyclone was no freak occurrence. The coast around the Bay of Bengal is highly exposed to tropical storms and tidal surges (Frank and Husain 1971, 438); almost half of deaths from tropical cyclones since the nineteenth century have been around the Bay of Bengal (in Paul 2009). Historical records suggest severe cyclones occurred on average twice or less frequently per decade from the 1790s to the 1900s, at which time the average rose to around three per decade. The 1960s were a decade of unusually intense cyclonic activity, with ten major events, or one each year (Frank and Husain 1971 citing Husain 1966).

Around two million people lived in the most damaged areas; a million acres of crop were destroyed and a further million damaged (World Bank 1970); 400,000 houses and 3,500 schools were damaged, and 65 per cent of total fishing capacity destroyed (Frank and Husain 1971). Four months later one million people still depended on relief (Sommer and Mosley 1972). The government of Pakistan knew that coastal East Bengal was often buffeted by cyclones and tidal bores, and it took some preventive and ameliorative action (Reilly 2009). But disasters of this kind were accepted as part of the landscape. It was days before news of the catastrophe reached even Dhaka (then Dacca), let alone the capital Islamabad so much further away. *New York Times* journalist Sydney Schanberg described the Pakistani government's view of their failure to tackle the cyclone:

> Because natural disasters are so common and so difficult to control in East Pakistan, and because resources are so limited, the central Government pleading helplessness, has tended to ignore the disasters and invest its resources elsewhere.
>
> (Schanberg 1970)

There was little to impede the cyclone on its way to its victims. Many of these islands were too new to even have the protection afforded by mature trees, and the Sundarbans forest that once covered that part of the coastline had been cleared over the preceding century, partly thanks to colonial policies.[4] The government of Pakistan had established a programme to develop cyclone protection, warning, and shelter systems; deliver relief; and reduce vulnerability by re-zoning land settlement after the North Indian Ocean cyclone season of 1960, but it was designed without regard to the people it should protect and had little impact (Islam 1971).

Since 1970, there has been investment in preventive infrastructure such as embankments, technically superior and credible early warning systems, and networks of somewhat more user-friendly cyclone shelters and evacuation routes, as well as in safe water and food supply and other relief systems

[4] On environmental history in the colonial period, see Iqbal (2010) and on patterns of settlement in the Bengal delta see Bose (1986).

(Alam and Dominey-Howes 2015). Crucially, there has been an emphasis on building the administrative and human capacities to prepare and respond speedily and effectively when disasters strike. The more severe cyclone Gorky in 1991 killed a still tragically vast 143,000 people, but cyclone preparedness had improved in the intervening twenty-one years, and many lives were probably saved. In 2007, Cyclone Sidr was as severe in magnitude as the Bhola storm, but the death rate was one-hundredth of that in 1970.[5]

The Bhola cyclone dramatized the arguments for independence better than any campaign or manifesto. The cyclonic sixties had already put disaster management on the political agenda of the nationalists. Among its commitments, Sheikh Mujib's Awami League manifesto prominently featured commitment to flood relief, while the National Awami Party (Bhashani wing, or NAP (B)) campaigned on a platform of protection against natural disasters. The veteran NAP leader, 'friend of the farmers' Maulana Bhashani, had declared in September that

> if concrete steps were not taken to correct interregional inequities and to protect Bengal against the destructive vagaries of nature, East Pakistan would be forced to separate from the western wing and develop friendly relations with whomever it wanted. (Sisson and Rose 1990, 30)

Indeed, the first direct democratic elections in Pakistan's history had originally been scheduled for July, only to be postponed to 7 December because of excess flooding in the east. Thus the cyclone struck Bhola only three weeks before the much-anticipated election, perfectly timed to politicize the Pakistani regime's lackadaisical relief effort. Whether deliberately callous or not, the Pakistani government's cyclone relief effort was certainly slow and careless of appearances. Getting off to a sluggish start, there was an effort to imply that Bengali political leaders were crying wolf and overstating the devastation by claiming a million victims. The international community shouldered the burden of supplying and distributing relief from the outset, and were 'more responsive than the central government of Pakistan' (Khondker 1995, 180). Although slow to act and reliant on external aid, the Pakistani authorities retained control, keeping political considerations paramount: Indian offers to lend aircraft to help with relief were declined. Two recent books on the birth of Bangladesh linger on the details of Yahya's callousness: Raghavan (2013) depicts the architect of Pakistan's return to democracy surveying the cyclone damage from the air, en route back from a successful trip to China (which he did not cut short), nursing a hangover with a few beers and pronouncing that

[5] On cyclone preparedness see Haque (1997); Chowdhury et al. (1993); Paul (2009; 2012); Paul et al. (2010); Paul and Dutt (2010); Alam and Collins (2010); Haque and Blair (1992); Karim and Mimura (2008).

it did not look so bad after all; Bass (2013) has him touring with a gold-topped cane. After a week in which no assessment of damage or declaration of national disaster was made, and under growing public pressure from domestic and international media and private displeasure from the friendliest of Western powers (that is, from Richard Nixon and Kissinger), Yahya apologized and made assurances that all necessary steps would be taken.

The political significance of the cyclone response was its timing. This display of unconcern took place only three weeks before an election scheduled to return Pakistan to democracy after its almost unbroken history of military rule. This was a major mass electoral event, and the ruling elite had fielded candidates (Baxter 1971). The political imbecility and grotesquely bad timing of the cyclone response all but defies explanation. Were the Pakistani authorities truly unable to guess that a few hundred thousand East Pakistanis washed out to sea might cause ructions? That their survivors might have a grievance against a state that failed to get its boots muddy? Apparently this was beyond their imagination. A powerful editorial in *Forum*, a left-leaning magazine from East Pakistan, summarized the political lessons:

> A people's government would have had its chief executive with his cabinet sitting in Bhola... personally directing relief operations... The demand for popular government is thus no casual whim of ambitious politicians. It is an imperative for the survival of 70 million people. We have no illusions that elections are the end to our problems. They will merely record before our people and before the world the basic urge of the people of East Pakistan to rule themselves. It is a demand which on (sic) longer needs elaboration or justification. It now only has to be registered loud and clear. If this demand once made is ignored by our ruling classes, the next stage in the struggle for democracy will unveil itself. There is still time for statemanship [sic] which preserves this nation in peace and amity. But this can only be demonstrated if the people of East Pakistan speak with a clear voice. Our dead have voted with their lives: Let the living speak with their votes. (reproduced in Ghosh 1990, 190)

One political champion of the Bhola cyclone victims was the fascinating figure of Maulana Bhashani, 'friend of the peasants', Sufi *pir* or saint, Islamic preacher and theorist, and leftist firebrand leader of the National Awami Party (NAP (B)), an offshoot of the early Awami League. Bhashani was then 85, with seventy years of organizing peasants and the disenfranchised under his belt, credited with having led the recent movement that forced General Ayub Khan to resign. Bhashani's messages of Islamic equality and non-communalism in the struggle against oppression and the risks of peasant life spoke to what many people who subsisted precariously together in this delta feared and needed.[6]

[6] Several young scholars are researching the 'Red Maulana' at present, but to date Abid Bahar and Peter Custers are the most prominent studies of his political thinking and organization (Custers 2011; Custers 2010; Bahar 2003).

The Red Maulana was the first political leader to arrive on the scene. Hearing the news on the radio (or in the newspaper, depending on legend) by his sickbed, he famously sprang up and made the gruelling journey to the cyclone areas. Abid Bahar paints a moving picture of Bhashani touring the area with great assiduousness and sadness. At Friday prayers in Noakhali, he preached that people should prepare for *jihad* or a struggle against injustice. He later told the press that the people had told him: '*Ora keu ashe ni*'—'none of them came'. He returned to stage a huge event in Dhaka where he notoriously declared 'Assalam Alleikum' to Pakistan—an ironic greeting, which he followed up with the call 'Independent East Pakistan Zindabad!', calling for independence. Finally, he and NAP (B) withdrew from the elections, apparently from a combination of respect for the victims and an unwillingness to legitimize the elections.[7]

In November 1970, the Awami League's Sheikh Mujibur Rahman was riding a wave of popularity after his recent release from jail; he followed Bhashani three days later with an angry speech about the failings of Pakistan. When asked if this now meant independence, he promised: 'not yet.' Mujib made the crucial point that the cyclone failure was a failure of the Pakistani state, not just of the Yahya regime (Ludden 2011): in this political dispensation the state was structurally and functionally incapable of protecting the people on its far southeastern fringes. After Bhashani's exit, the Awami League inherited the mandate to protect the masses of the peasants against such crises.

As wave follows storm, three weeks after this display of unfeeling, the first properly democratic elections produced a landslide for Sheikh Mujib's Awami League: they won 160 of the 162 National Assembly seats allotted to East Pakistan, with around 72 per cent of the vote, and 288 out of the 300 East Pakistan provincial assembly seats, in 'possibly the greatest victory of any party in a free and contested election anywhere' (Baxter 1971, 212). The cyclone put a shine on what was always going to be a victory, making it sharper and more pregnant with possibility, ensuring the Awami League's 'six-point' demand for regional autonomy under a federal system was not only a serious contender but the only real game in town. But regional autonomy was not to happen, and by March 1971 the Pakistani army had attacked its erstwhile compatriots in a vicious and bloody struggle that lasted nine months and killed hundreds of thousands, and possibly many more.

[7] Other views suggested political strategy played a part, for Bhashani (who may have feared NAP (B) would not win many seats) (Feldman 1978; Baxter 1971) and for the Awami League, who deemed it tactical for the election to go ahead while their campaign messages captured the outraged mood of the moment (Ghosh 1990).

2.3 The Liberation War and After

Had regional and world political powers been less willing to sacrifice the population of East Pakistan to Cold War exigencies or convenient notions of state sovereignty, its economic weakness on achieving independence would have been less pronounced. The immediate concerns of the post-conflict scenario included devastated infrastructure, looming famine, returning refugees, and freely roaming armed militia, while its seventy-five million residents subsisted mainly on the proceeds of rice cultivation and jute, in turn dependent on global market conditions. Less visibly but no less vitally for the tasks of reconstruction, nation-building, and development ahead, the conflict had decimated its social structure and intelligentsia, with the Pakistani army having specifically targeted its cultural and intellectual leadership in the 'Operation Searchlight' campaign conventionally viewed as an attempt at genocide (Akmam 2002).[8]

The mortality figures from combat and associated deaths from disease and hunger are unknown, but credible estimates reach as high as half a million, making the conflict one of the bloodiest in recent history. The official figure of deaths from the war is three million and although the methodology and documentation for that figure have not been established, debate about this figure is to be prohibited under the proposed War Crimes Denial Act. Taking together the displacement of tens of millions as a result of the conflict, and the 'exported famine' of 1971–2 in a population already weakened by endemic poverty and hunger, cyclone, and floods, a total conflict-related excess mortality in the magnitude of a million or more by 1972 is fully within the realms of the possible.[9] The UN relief operation estimated the material damage of the war at $1.2 billion (about $7 billion in 2015 prices), in a country whose gross national product (GNP) was estimated at USD 4.5 billion and whose recurrent expenditure was only USD 1.1 billion in 1970 (World Bank 1972). Losses of around $300 million (USD 1.7 billion in 2015 prices) were estimated for reductions in agricultural outputs alone. But by the end of 1973 much of the basic reconstruction work was complete, as a result of a coordinated and reasonably

[8] A more recent analysis is critical not only of the specifics of the charge of genocide in the Bangladesh case, but of the validity of the concept at all (Gerlach 2010).

[9] The mortality statistics from the conflict are a point of debate (see Bergman (2011) for a summary) and of contemporary political contention, with the Awami League resisting any attempt to question the orthodoxy that three million people were killed by the Pakistani army. In 2014, the International Criminal Tribunal convicted a journalist of contempt of court for debating the mortality figures (specifically for querying the 'fact' of three million deaths: *The Guardian* 2014). Refugee figures are less controversial: of an estimated population of seventy-five million, almost ten million people were documented by the Indian government as having crossed the border to India during the war, with a high proportion believed to be Hindu. Between March and December 1971, an average of 36,000 people crossed into India every day (Myers 1973).

successful relief effort under the UN Relief Operation, Dacca (UNROD) (Faaland and Parkinson 1976).

The human impacts of the war were less easily made good. During the war, in addition to the ten million who fled to India, almost seventeen million people were internally displaced. More than two million people were homeless in June 1972, and 1.5 million homes had been destroyed. The already limited rural health services had been destroyed by the war (Greenough and Cash 1973). In November 1971 alone, 2,000 people were admitted to the Cholera Hospital in Dhaka, the largest number ever admitted in a single month (note that November is in the dry season, not the usual season for cholera). A smallpox epidemic broke out in one of the Calcutta refugee camps, and the disease (all but eradicated prior to the war) then travelled back with returning refugees (Sommer, Arnt, and Foster 1973). The effects of the war on nutrition were particularly dramatic; famine predicted in 1971 and 1972 was averted (or exported) only after a vast relief effort (Curlin et al. 1976; Bose 1972; Chen and Rohde 1971).

The impacts of the war on marital and family structure and on women's citizenship marked a permanent break in the old patriarchal bargain that shaped gender relations. A possible 200,000 to 400,000 rapes resulted in an estimated 26,000 pregnancies. Sexual violence was part of the war strategy, and women, gender, and social relations were traumatized. In addition, social and cultural norms mean women are likely to have been disproportionately affected by the hardships of hunger, displacement, and widowhood. Gender relations never fully recovered after the war and the social disorder that followed (Kabeer 1988).[10]

Partition and war also weakened the civil administration. West Pakistanis had dominated the ranks of the respected Civil Service of Pakistan administrative corps, and many senior Bengali officials remained stranded in the west after the war. But on their return, officials rapidly became demoralized with the party politicization of civil administration, as well as with the corruption of networked party people. New laws institutionalized the politicization of all levels of the civil administration, removing the meritocratic recruitment procedure and strengthening political control over governance (Islam 2003; Maniruzzaman 1975a, b; Jahan 1973). All of this underlined the fact that Sheikh Mujib's gifts were in political mobilization, not public administration (Mascarenhas 1986).

Politically, the liberation struggle mobilized numerous groups of young leftists, many of them with experience of guerrilla warfare and firsthand experience

[10] See work by Bina D'Costa, Nayanika Mookherjee, and Yasmin Saikia. The work of these authors will be discussed in further detail in Chapter 4, 'The Breaking of the Patriarchal Bargain and the Emergence of the "Woman Issue"'.

of rural life; others were drawn from the student wings of political parties with organizational experience. At the same time, security and law-and-order conditions were weak, as armed groups roamed the countryside, looting and terrorizing. All of this presented a threat to the authority and capacity of the new regime, even while popular expectations of the new government were high. The undisciplined and inexperienced Awami League party rapidly deteriorated into a corrupt, venal, and inept government.[11]

2.4 The Basket Case

Few nations have been born with such unpromising prospects. Bangladesh found no friends among the powerful nations during its bloody liberation struggle, and support was slow to emerge even once nationhood was achieved (with India's reluctant intervention). It now seems difficult to imagine that a territorially split state straddling 1,000 miles of its main military enemy was ever thought viable, but there was nothing inevitable about the break-up of united Pakistan (see, in particular, Raghavan 2013). After the failed Prague Spring of 1968 and the Biafran independence movement of 1970, it seemed unlikely that an independent nation-state would emerge from the conflict. All the major global powers viewed the military crackdown on East Pakistan as a matter for national sovereignty, despite credible accounts of genocide early on (Bass 2013).

There were powerful reasons for this deaf–blindness. The independence struggle was politically inconvenient for the US, for whom the Pakistani military leadership were brokering relations with China. It was undesired by India and the Soviet Union, which neither viewed secessionist movements kindly at home nor encouraged popular independence struggles on the doorstep of their own unruly movements. And Bangladesh was already seen as economically unviable—a densely populated part of the world prone to natural disaster and famine, with high levels of poverty and low levels of economic development, and no natural resources. From the outset, aid and economic prospects coloured foreign policy.

The extent of the 'tilt' in White House foreign policy (led in the Nixon administration by National Security Advisor, later Secretary of State, Henry Kissinger) to the Pakistan side has been closely documented in Gary Bass's account of the US's role in the genocide in East Pakistan: 'the Bengalis became collateral damage for realigning the global balance of power' (Bass 2013, xv). The affiliation with West Pakistan was personal as well as political, and White

[11] Ahmed (1983) offers a detailed catalogue of the dimensions and causes of this deterioration and the response to them at the time.

House foreign policy ignored witness accounts of genocide from its own diplomats and abetted Pakistan despite an official ban on military support to either side. At the height of the military crackdown, the then-US representative to Dhaka 'blasted the United States for silence in the face of atrocities, for not denouncing the quashing of democracy, for showing "moral bankruptcy" in the face of what they bluntly called genocide' (Bass 2013, xiii). The 'Blood telegram' was named for the Consul, Archer Blood, but it could equally have referred to what the US had on its hands.

It was at the height of the war that the infamous 'basket case' epithet was used. It is worth putting that moment in context, because the label has had such lasting power over the country's international image and national identity. While not an inaccurate assessment of the country's short-term prospects, the 'basket case' label was as much about political, ideological, and indeed military 'tilt' as an assessment of the economic prospects of a country at war.

The label was used during a high-level crisis meeting of the Washington Special Actions Group (WSAG) early on in the war.[12] The meeting covered military briefings, aid, and strategies for bringing about a ceasefire and withdrawal of (Indian, not Pakistani) forces. Kissinger wondered whether the US could prevail on Jordan to send Pakistan arms under conditions where the US was legally constrained from doing so, and showed concern about a likely backlash against Urdu-speaking minorities, but no response is recorded when similar fears were raised about the fate of the Bengali population in West Pakistan.

It was towards the end of the meeting that Kissinger raised the possibility of famine, apparently apropos of nothing that has gone before:

DR. KISSINGER: (to Mr. Williams [Deputy Administrator, USAID, Chairman of Interdepartmental Working Group on East Pakistan Disaster Relief]) Will there be a massive famine in East Pakistan?

MR. WILLIAMS: They have a huge crop just coming in.

DR. KISSINGER: How about next spring?

MR. WILLIAMS: Yes, there will be famine by next spring unless they can pull themselves together by the end of March.

DR. KISSINGER: And we will be asked to bail out the Bangla Desh [sic] from famine next spring?

MR. WILLIAMS: Yes.

[12] The meeting comprised the President's National Security Advisor (Kissinger) and senior officials from the National Security Council, including U. Alexis Johnson, Under Secretary of State for Political Affairs; Alexander Haig, Deputy Assistant to the President for National Security Affairs; and Maurice Williams, Deputy Administrator, Agency for International Development (USAID) and Chairman, Interdepartmental Working Group on East Pakistan Disaster Relief.

DR. KISSINGER: Then we had better start thinking about what our policy will be.
MR. WILLIAMS: By March the Bangla Desh will need all kinds of help.
MR. JOHNSON: They'll be an international basket case.
DR. KISSINGER: But not necessarily our basket case.
MR. SISCO [Assistant Secretary of State for Near Eastern and South Asian Affairs]: Wait until you hear the humanitarian bleats in this country. (US Department of State 1971)

Now that we know the US withheld food aid to Bangladesh in 1974 on grounds that trade with Cuba made it ineligible for food aid under the US Public Law 480 (PL480), this exchange cannot help but ring alarm bells. With the benefit of this hindsight, Kissinger's questions suggest an unseemly alacrity to think about 'what our policy will be' regarding a possible famine in a country whose birth he had hoped and worked to abort. Seen in this light, the comment 'not necessarily our basket case' reads like an idea to shape humanitarian policies on the basis of political considerations.

The term 'basket case' originated in the First World War to refer to a soldier who had lost all four limbs and was deemed helpless, and the use of the term to describe East Pakistan confirmed—if there had been any doubt—that the US had 'tilted' to West Pakistan (Anderson 1972). The term took on a very specific character in relation to Bangladesh when *The New York Times* published an editorial in October 1972 about the vast aid being poured into the relief effort, only for as much as two million tons of food aid to be stolen by 'hungry hyenas' for re-sale in Indian markets (*The New York Times* 1972). The 'basket case' label came to mean not only hopelessness in terms of the need for aid, but also a case from which the aid leaked (Bari 2008). Thus in its earliest days, the problem of underdevelopment with weak governance came to be seen as a defining concern for aid.

2.5 Nasty, Brutish, and Short

Callous and politically motivated though the 'basket case' label certainly was, it was not, in 1971, inaccurate about Bangladesh's prospects. An early CIA report noted that independence meant that the 'rather unique phenomenon' of Bangladesh could finally be seen. No longer hidden among or averaged out by membership of a nation dominated by less precarious and more prosperous communities in Pakistan or India, it was suddenly obvious that 'so much of (sic) poverty (was) shared by so many squeezed into so little a land area' (CIA 1972, 6, citing National Plan 1972–3). In independent Bangladesh, the CIA discounted the long-term prospects of the political energies of liberation, predicting instead that the inevitable disappointment in its material fruits would lead to wider regional destabilization:

> [T]he formidable and probably insoluble nature of these problems will make East Bengal—be it East Pakistan or Bangla Desh—an object of concern to its people, its neighbors, and the world in general for the foreseeable future. With 70 to 80 million people packed into an area the size of Florida, unable to grow enough food to feed itself, almost devoid of natural resources, facing a decline in the sale of jute (its principal export), periodically subjected to floods and cyclones, East Bengal will be plagued by economic privation and political crisis. (CIA 1971, 13)

Apart from its remarkable political energies, the odds were not in Bangladesh's favour, posing a challenge to the project of aided development:

> Even under the best of circumstances, Bangladesh constitutes a critical and complex development problem. The population is poor (per capita income of $50-$70, a figure which has not risen over the past 20 years), overcrowded (population density is nearly 1400 per square mile), short-lived (life expectancy at birth is well under 50 years), in many cases unemployed (perhaps 25-30 percent), and largely illiterate (under 20 percent literacy rate). (World Bank 1972, i)

These Hobbesian framings were political acts, not merely a catalogue of dismal facts: their diagnosis was on the basis of contemporary economics, pushing political relations firmly out of view. As Rehman Sobhan points out, the problems were not merely of financing gaps:

> [t]he disruptive effect of this decisive [political] break with the past has been seriously underestimated by analysts who seem to see the problem as one of direct substitution of resources, sources of supply and social forces. (1982, 3)

Many of Bangladesh's contemporary economic fragilities could be directly traced to the political subjugation of its people prior to independence. Bangladesh was exceptionally weak economically in part because it had suffered nine months of Pakistani bombardment and an all-but-scorched-earth policy that killed, maimed, or displaced as much as one-third of the population. Behind that catastrophe lurked decades of neo-colonial rule that had stalled and sometimes even reversed economic and human development. Pakistani rule had in its turn been enacted upon a population and landscape that was at the coalface of British imperialism, bearing the brunt of policies of extraction and enforced commodity production for the global economy for generations. Whether Pakistani or British, the state consistently failed to protect the population against the frequent ecological and subsistence crises. In several instances, including the 1943–4 famine, the state had been instrumental in causing the disaster and vulnerability to its effects. If a shopping list of economic problems said nothing about the politics that had historically thwarted and undermined the fragile economy of the Bengal Delta, it could equally say little about what development might be unleashed in a sovereign state, and about how the population might respond to a different distribution of resources and chances.

2.6 The 'Test Case for Development'

Nature was always cast as an enemy of Bangladesh's development in the authoritative external framing, in contrast to the Bengali cultural ideal of *Sonar Bangla* or golden Bengal, rich with fertile natural beauty. The aesthetics of landscape may feature in nationalist ideology but they have limited significance in development discourse. Instead, nature was seen as unpredictable and violent towards the humans that sought to extract a living from the land. The agricultural livelihoods and nourishment of the majority depended—and continue to depend—on the annual flooding that keeps the soil rich and the main rice crop watered, so in a key respect, the precarity of the population with respect to nature is also the reason for its settlement in these parts, and why it thrived to the extent it did.[13]

Despite the frequency with which natural disasters have caused social, economic, and political crises, the intimate relation between ecology and social and state formation in East Bengal has often been ignored or treated as an add-on to historical and social-scientific analyses (Iqbal 2010). Within development, an influential assessment of Bangladesh typified Malthusian views of the relationship between people and nature:

> It must be the fond hope of most educated people that man can control events and his own future. There is little to give credence to that view in the situation of Bangladesh. There can be little prospect of a spontaneous movement to reduce the increase in population and it is impossible to see how a much larger population can be given any prospect of attaining the type of living standards to which the Western world has become accustomed. Nature, not man, is in charge of the situation in Bangladesh. (Faaland and Parkinson 1976, 1)

These statements from the former Resident Representative (chief) and Senior Economist at the World Bank Mission in Dhaka in the early 1970s set out the idea that Bangladesh's lack of resources and ample development challenges made it the 'Test Case for Development'. With nature 'in charge of the situation', the 'prospect of attaining a spontaneous movement' to stem population growth was, these World Bankers argued, dead in the water. In this authoritative early expression of 'the development problem' there is a morbid

[13] On ecological history, see Iqbal (2010). Bose (1986) maps the settlement of the region across its agro-ecological zones. See also Van Schendel (2009) for an overview.

note to the view of the relationship between man and nature: absent a 'spontaneous movement' to address human over-reproduction, and the certainty that more Bangladeshis will never attain Western living standards, what might happen?

From the point of view of international development, ecology is unkind both in its lack of natural resources and in its hostility to human progress:

> All of this would not matter if Bangladesh were rich in natural resources and underpopulated, if it were effectively governed and if its social order and economic system were geared to growth, but none of these things obtain. The terrain, in relation to the number of people that inhabit it, is inhospitable and often hostile. It is dominated by mighty rivers which in depositing silt both form and flood the territory over which they flow; in the monsoon the rainfall is intense and unpredictable; the one certainty is that much of the land will be covered with water, and loss of life and interruption to production from flooding may be considerable. Even more dangerous are the cyclones which unpredictably can inundate vast areas of land and cause great damage and loss of life. (Faaland and Parkinson 1976, 3)

Forty years on, this statement is of interest because of what has not changed in Bangladesh's favour. The population has almost doubled; the country's reputation for corruption leaves it bouncing along the bottom of governance indices; and nature has become more hostile, with a rising number of climate change-related events.[14] Nor have natural resources been found on any important scale. This lack is significant, because it helps to explain why the project of national development came to depend so entirely on investing in its potential human wealth. Some of Bangladesh's leadership appeared to have hoped they were sitting on undiscovered unearned riches of oil and gas, although prospecting dates back a century in the region (Van Schendel 2009) and to date, no viable oil fields have been found. Nevertheless, in its early years, and particularly at the moment of its most acute economic crisis in 1974, the possibility of oil and gas appeared to be held out to foreign powers as a reason to stay engaged in a desperate Bangladesh (see Anderson 1976).

The terms of the aid quid pro quo can be read in an exchange between Prime Minister Sheikh Mujibur Rahman and President Gerald Ford in late 1974. In this conversation, Mujib has come seeking urgently needed food aid, with famine conditions peaking at home:

> Mujibur: [Following a statement about the floods and the global commodity crisis] If we could control the floods, we could be self-sufficient in five years. We produce rice, jute, wheat, and tobacco. We have big gas deposits—10-20 trillion cubic feet. We were almost self-sufficient in fertilizer but our plants were damaged. With our

[14] See Dastagir (2015). Bangladesh was ranked fifth among the countries experiencing the effects of climate change in the period 1993–2011, with 242 events in that time (Kreft and Eckstein 2013).

own gas and fertilizer plants we could begin to export fertilizer, except for inflation. (US Department of State 1974)

As busy world leaders, both men cut to the chase—the country's geostrategic significance. For Mujib, the point is the urgent need for food aid, and, knowing that US interests centre on the crisis price of oil, he moves swiftly on to the possibility that Bangladesh may have reserves of the precious resource. Ford sizes up Bangladesh as a potential participant in a 'despairing chorus line' of low-income countries praying for OPEC to lower oil prices at the height of the first oil crisis of the 1970s (Rothschild 1976, 296). He makes no effort to hide the limited strategic value of Bangladesh. After brief enquiries into membership of the international financial institutions and population size, the meeting ends with Ford assuring imminent food aid. In fact, the aid was delayed further, until after Bangladesh made its final shipment of jute sacks to Cuba, for which reason the US had delayed its food aid in the first place.

Bangladesh continues to explore the possibility of the natural resources it is hoped will assure its national prosperity (Prasad 2014). In the meantime, the propositions of fiscal sociology[15] suggest that the absence of natural resource wealth or a prosperous population to tax could well be reasons why Bangladesh's development policies turned towards earning 'strategic rents' as a 'test case for development', an international laboratory for the testing of aid models and theories. Opening itself to the ideas of foreign aid earned it that aid, but also led it to develop the economy and population in ways that could be taxable (see Moore 2004). In the medium term, the continued flow of foreign aid depended on the pursuit of economic and human development policies in line with the dominant development paradigm. This, as we will see presently, included pro-economic growth policies of openness to global markets, and investments in the health, fertility control, education, and food security of the poor masses.

2.7 National Liberation as Social Revolution

While the West viewed Bangladesh as at worst a basket case and at best a test case, many involved in the liberation struggle took quite the opposite view, seeing it as the start of a social revolution. The nationalist movement relied on youth cadres of the left who had mobilized the rural masses on revolutionary platforms. For reasons of nation-building, political compromise, and ideological

[15] '*Fiscal sociology* [is] a macro-historical paradigm that captured, embodied, and laid bare the dominant drivers of societal, economic, and political change' (Moore 2004, 293) by uncovering how states' dependence on their sources of revenue shapes their formation, including the effectiveness and reach of their bureaucratic organization and the nature and quality of the state–society relationship.

principle, the new government of the new country established 'socialism' among its four key principles (also 'secularism', 'nationalism', and 'democracy'). The Constitution adopted in December 1972 declared the provision of food, clothing, shelter, education, health care, jobs, and social security through planned growth to be the basic responsibility of the state (Maniruzzaman 1988; see also Sobhan and Ahmad 1981). 'A socialist economic system' was to be established with a view to ensuring a just, egalitarian society, with 'the people' controlling the means of production (Khan 1996, 206). Notably, given the significance of the Bhola cyclone in the 1970 election, the Cyclone Preparedness Programme started at this time, presaging Bangladesh's later disaster-management proficiency.

No notable 'socialist' agenda was achieved in the chaos of the post-war years, other than the nationalization of economic assets. Efforts at land reform failed to tackle asset inequalities (Jannuzi and Peach 1980), and Mujib's 'macroeconomic populism' proved unsustainable (Hossain 1996a; 1996b). Disillusionment with corruption and nepotism set in early. Economic crisis struck, and the new state deployed its paramilitaries to address law and order. And then, as Chapter 5 discusses, the famine of 1974 unfolded. By early 1975, a constitutional amendment had replaced Parliament with a presidential system and soon after a single-party state, under the Bangladesh Krishak Sramik Awami League (BAKSAL), intended to incorporate workers, students, farmers, freedom fighters. Donor pressure peaked, and before the end of Sheikh Mujib's regime the policies of nationalization and state-planned development had already been reversed: private investment ceilings were raised, public sector investment curbed, and the *taka* devalued in 1974–5 when the government agreed to limited reforms in return for aid (Sobhan 1982). This was not a total capitulation to donors, as many in the administration were leaning in this direction already. But the ideological tenor of the coups in 1975 indicated that there was still support, including within the political elite and within groups with control of the means of violence, for a radical economic agenda.

The rupture in development policy came with the emergence of the new political settlement when General Zia Rahman came to power in 1975, restoring control of the state in effect to the same class of people—military and civil bureaucrats—who ran Pakistan. This group was in power for the next fifteen years. Zia came to power on the back of a series of military coups during which Sheikh Mujib, his family, and other Awami League leaders were killed in particularly brutal acts of violence. The coup which eventually placed Zia at the helm of state was led by leftist military groups, radicalized by the experience of the Independence struggle, and linked to the Marxist Jatiya Samajtantrik Dal (JSD) party. Zia was believed to be sympathetic (Lifschultz and Bird 1979), but as a pragmatist rather than an ideologue (see Jahan 1980; Franda 1982) he recognized the destabilizing potential of the situation, and the need to establish order. He purged the army of radicals and cracked down on the JSD, further fragmenting the left (Lifschultz and Bird 1979; Maniruzzaman 1980).

Zia's shift to the right surprised no one who was alert to the context. There were problems with India violating water agreements by diverting water away from Bangladesh during the dry season, and internal security was threatened by leftist and underground groups (with Indian assistance). The army remained divided and Zia himself was the target of twenty or more coup attempts in the months before his death. And the economy was still in crisis (Maniruzzaman 1988). The international community had been pushing hard for more market-friendly policies, and saw little benefit to aiding a country that showed signs neither of developing its economy nor of controlling its population (as we will see in Chapter 7). The international community apparently welcomed Zia after the 'democratic risks' entailed by Mujib (Sen 1986, 306)—Mujib was never popular with the US and Kissinger took a strong personal dislike to him (Chapter 8). Zia accordingly reoriented economic policy in the desired direction through the Revised Industrial Policy of 1975, as the World Bank had pushed for divestiture of state-owned enterprises and promotion of private industry. Many top-ranking former Civil Service of Pakistan (CSP) officials removed under Mujib were reinstated by Zia, so that liberalization was also promoted from within government (Franda 1982; Islam 1986–7; Maniruzzaman 1988). State ideology was rewritten, with the Constitution amended in 1977 to reinterpret 'socialism' as 'economic and social justice' and replacing 'secularism' with 'absolute trust and faith in the Almighty Allah' (Maniruzzaman 1988, 215; Ahamed 1978; Jahan 1980; Kochanek 1994), in a bid to appeal to both the Middle East and the more conservative religious sentiment in the country.

This sharp shift to the right was politically possible because this was a new authoritarian regime taking office after profound economic and political crisis (Franda 1982). The re-installed upper bureaucracy were predisposed to this redirection, but the position of other interest groups on the need for reform is less clear. Although observers have claimed that Zia's policies were the outcome of a 'bureaucratic-industrialist nexus' (see, for example, Islam 1984 and 1986–7; Zafarullah 1987; Quadir 2000), there is little evidence that Zia even tacitly struck bargains with the tiny demoralized industrial elite, who proved unsupportive of initial reforms (Humphrey 1990). The decimated left and other opposition groups were in no position to oppose this shift. But although reform may have been politically possible because the authoritarian government was insulated against potential opponents, it seems to have been motivated most by the need to legitimize the regime with the Bangladeshi people, by providing stability and avoiding a repetition of the economic crisis of the mid-1970s, and with the international community. Zia's reforms were cautious and limited, but they signalled a break with the past ideology that attracted aid (Humphrey 1990; Kochanek 1994). Notably, food security took top billing.

This book argues that the famine played a significant part in this policy rupture. It did so in a general sense, in that the declining legitimacy of the government and perceived threat of insurrection and instability directly caused by the famine were among the factors contributing to the long political crisis of 1975.[16] Under the political settlement that finally emerged, there was both a move towards liberalizing economic policy in general, and new organizations and institutions to protect against crises of subsistence specifically. The famine had demonstrated that protection against the hunger and health crises associated with commodity shocks, wars, and natural disasters was an important lower-level institution on which the overall balance of political power rested. The need for aid in general and food aid in particular pushed the new government into the laps of the aid donor nations, predominantly North American and European, after the initial attempt at independence from Cold War alignments showed the lengths or depths to which the superpowers were willing to go even in a geostrategically unimportant country.

Zia was assassinated in 1981, and was replaced by General Ershad in 1982. The move towards the market gathered pace under Ershad's National Industrial Policy. Denationalization, privatization, and the promotion of foreign investment were key elements of this policy, which initially were only really popular with the World Bank (Kochanek 1994). Apart from devaluing the taka, Zia had done little to liberalize the financial sector, but Ershad attempted to do so with his Financial Sector Reform Programme, which was later stepped up considerably under Khaleda Zia's first government (1992–6; Quadir 2000). The weakly authoritarian Ershad regime was sensitive to public pressure, particularly from organized labour and professional elites (Humphrey 1990; Maniruzzaman 1992), but enjoyed considerable support from the small new business elite with whose emergence the regime is closely associated (Dasgupta 1996). By the end of the Ershad era, in 1990, the market orientation of economic policy was firmly established. Trade unions gradually accepted the inevitable (see World Bank 1994, 49–53), and other groups adapted to the new situation in the absence of alternatives (on the position of farmers, see Abdullah and Shahabuddin 1997). By 1988, 'people [had] come to believe that drastic reversal of the privatization program [was] neither possible nor desirable' (Humphrey 1990, 90).

Economic reform has been slow and uneven (see World Bank 1994a; 1994b; Quibria (ed.) 1997), but it has consistently pushed a growth agenda, and one which is labour-based and therefore broadly pro-poor in orientation. This

[16] As, it seems, was a desire to re-establish Islam as a governing principle. See Shehabuddin (2008).

process has continued through more than two decades of multiparty democracy, and despite chronically violent political transitions. The government of the Bangladesh National Party (BNP) under Begum Khaleda Zia (1991–6) accelerated the policy regime it inherited from Ershad's civilianized military regime (1982–90). The Awami League briefly lived up to its reputation as the more left-leaning of the major parties, embracing the market only after it lost the 1991 elections on a platform of renationalization. That the most left-leaning of the major parties had finally signed up to liberal economic reform may also reflect the fact that India's Congress Party, on which the Awami League patterned its policies, had discarded its more statist left policies. But on assuming power in de facto coalition with Ershad's Jatiya Party in 1996, the Awami League government of Sheikh Hasina (1996–2001) also fell in line, and resolved not only to pursue but to speed up market-based reforms (Economist Intelligence Unit 1996; Baxter 1998). It is not clear that there is much to distinguish the major political parties when it comes to economic development policy, and only slightly more on social policy. Viewed over the past half-century, the country has enjoyed a rising and stable economic growth rate in the past thirty years, compared to its striking volatility before 1980 (see Figure 2.1).

A significant feature of the political settlement in Bangladesh has been the caretaker government institution. This system, in place from 1996 until 2013, provided for a non-party appointed caretaker regime to oversee political transitions, agreed as the new rules of the electoral game after a deadlock confrontation in 1996 resulting from the incumbent BNP attempt at rigging the general election. This worked well for all of two general elections. By 2006, it was clear that the ruling BNP were again trying to rig the election, this time by manipulating the leadership of the caretaker government; this deadlock was resolved not with a new agreement between the parties, but through a military-backed extension of caretaker rule to two years. This period was notable mainly for its largely failed anti-corruption drive and political party reform effort, and in particular for the comparatively peaceful resumption of multiparty rule within two years. Donors financed a sophisticated electronic voter list that generated an accurate electoral roll for the 2008 election. The BNP had been particularly weakened by the wholesale assault on the political classes, and that election was won overwhelmingly by the Awami League, on a manifesto that included tackling the food price spike that had plagued the unfortunate caretaker regime. During the Awami League's term starting in 2009, their large parliamentary mandate enabled them to remove the provision for a caretaker government and to establish a long-overdue process of justice for the war crimes of 1971. The war crimes tribunal posed a major threat to the Jamaat-i-Islami, the well-organized centre-right Islamic party, with their strong links to Pakistan and the anti-liberation counter-struggle; several of their top leadership have now been convicted and hanged for war crimes. This in turn has helped stir up

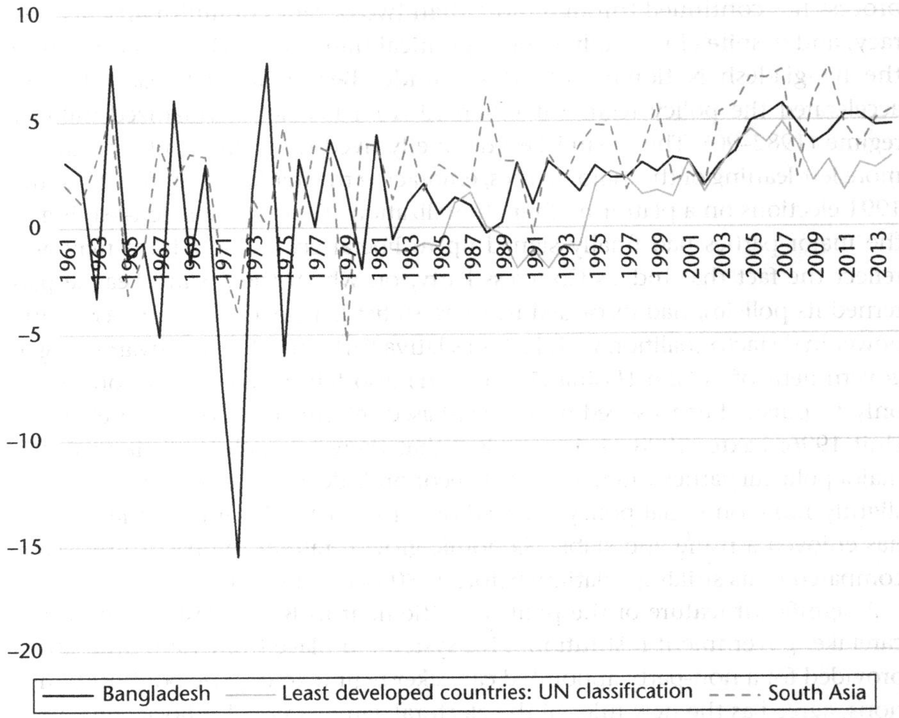

Figure 2.1. GDP growth rates, Bangladesh and comparator regions, 1960–2015
Source: World Development Indicators. Accessed 17 April 2016. http://databank.worldbank.org/data/reports.aspx?source=world-development-indicators.

fundamentalist sentiment and sharpened the divide between (substantially educated middle-class) secularists and Salafist tendencies and Islamist groups. Since 2014, a series of high-profile murders of 'atheist bloggers', some of them foreign nationals, has encouraged the government to clamp down on freedom of speech, targeting in particular social media. In a significant break with the quarter-century history of democracy, the Awami League won an unprecedented second term, in an effectively uncontested (yet formally legal) election. As of late 2015, the political settlement was increasingly shaping into a system with a single dominant party, after twenty-five years in which politics had been a competition between well-matched opponents.[17]

While the rules of the political game appear to grow more dysfunctional, it is the democratic period that has presided over the most rapid progress on

[17] For core definitions, concepts, and phasing and characterization of different political settlements, this draws on Khan (1995; 2011; 2013). I rely on BRAC University's *State of Governance* reports for details of events since 2006.

Table 2.1. Selected human development indicators, 1961–2011

Human development indicators	1961	1971	1981	1991	2001	2011
GNI per capita, PPP (current international $)				890	1420	2780
Adult literacy rate, population 15+ years, both sexes (%)			29	35	47	
Mortality rate, under-5 (per 1,000)	258	223	194	133	84	47
Pregnant women receiving prenatal care (%)					40	55
Life expectancy at birth, male (years)	48	48	56	61	66	69
Fertility rate, total (births per woman)	7	7	6	4	3	2

Source: World Development Indicators, accessed 23 December 2015.

human development. Table 2.1 offers some insights into selected areas. Human development performance has become an important domain in which governments can demonstrate their guardianship of the national development project, as well as the commitment and capacity of the state to delivering services that primarily benefit the poor segments of society. This includes relatively impressive rates both of economic growth and, perhaps more to the point, of poverty reduction and human development. Since the early 2000s, the pattern of economic growth has become more pro-poor, and, compared to others in the region, the pace of poverty reduction both faster and with a slower rise in inequality (World Bank 2013).

2.8 A Development Success: The 'Positive Deviant'

From this unlikely start, Bangladesh emerged as a development success within a few short decades. The pace and extent of its achievements are unexpected because of the low base and fast progress that mean it even outstrips comparators on some indicators (see in particular World Bank 2003; Ahluwalia and Mahmud 2004; Asadullah et al. 2014). And those achievements appear to have come about despite weaknesses in its governance that by conventional wisdom should have impeded economic growth and public service delivery, limiting gains in human development (World Bank 2006; IGS 2006; Lewis 2011). The record of Bangladesh's achievements was set out for inspection by the World Bank in a text box recording the 'phenomenon' in no less a document than its own Annual Report:

> Bangladesh is 1 of only 18 developing countries with an annual growth rate that has never fallen below 2 percent. Since the 1990s, economic growth has been steady at 4 to 5 percent annually, with relatively low inflation and stable domestic debt,

> interest, and exchange rates. Its gross domestic product growth rate has accelerated by 1 percentage point every decade, despite floods and other weather-related catastrophes. This growth, coupled with an impressive decline in population growth rates, has led to a doubling of annual per capita growth from 1.6 percent in the 1980s to 3.3 percent from 1990 to 2004. The country has achieved universal primary education and has an equal number of girls and boys in secondary school, and it is on track to reach the Millennium Development Goal in child mortality.
>
> These growth and development gains have taken place despite widely held perceptions of weak governance, a phenomenon referred to as the Bangladesh conundrum. If not addressed, poor governance will be a growth constraint, particularly in critical areas such as power and transport. (World Bank 2006, 40)

This description of Bangladesh's development success focuses on macroeconomic fundamentals. It does not specify how growth put children in school or stopped infants from dying, but in the omission by implication indicates that modest but steady economic growth is the source.

Labour-based growth may have been the only real possibility for a resource-poor country, but it was also one which contending elites came to be capable of sharing the benefits of (on which latter point, see Khan 2010; Hassan 2013). And it can be argued that the badness of Bangladesh's governance has been overstated, at least to the extent that it limits growth: endemic corruption is characteristic of early stages of economic development (Khan 2002). But Bangladesh's (human) development successes do not owe chiefly to its economic growth, whether or not it was consistent with weak governance. Poverty reduction and human development have not owed exclusively to growth (see, for instance, Sen and Hulme 2004). Bangladesh has done better on human development than its (actually quite modest) economic growth would predict: given its low average income levels, its human development and social indicators are relatively strong (Mahmud et al. 2008; Asadullah et al. 2014). Bangladesh is famous for its service delivering development non-state organizations, but its 'positive deviance' does not owe exclusively to these large and innovative programmes. Instead, the gains in public health, education, food security, and other domains owe to a potent mix of public, donor, and private for-profit as well as non-profit providers in the achievement of public goals (Chowdhury et al. 2013).

As early as 2010, the World Bank concluded that the paradox was resolved and that the answer to Bangladesh's surprising successes in economic development lay in the actions of a strategic (or lucky) state, which ensured governance was functional in six key areas. Successive governments, it was argued,

- developed 'sound' macroeconomic policies that created space for the private sector to flourish;
- improved disaster-management capacity, 'reducing considerably their macroeconomic impact';

- took 'wise public expenditure choices within a limited fiscal envelope', for example, on rural infrastructure, public health, and education;
- created space for and partnerships with NGOs and the private sector on public service delivery;
- supported family planning, girls' schooling, and women's employment, '[u]nleashing the development potential of half its population';
- encouraged and enabled labour migration and remittances. (World Bank 2010, 7).

These are indeed some key areas of policy success (see also Sen et al. 2007), and many of these achievements depended on both macroeconomic and social policies and programmes. This in turn implies a degree of political will and state capacity not usually associated with Bangladesh. Why were these, and not others, the protected domains of 'good enough governance' (as Merilee Grindle has put it)? Under a political settlement characterized by authoritarian and later competitive clientelism, why did 'successive governments' behave in this way? This book addresses these questions.

2.9 The MDG Consensus

Most recently, Bangladesh's image in the aid world has been associated with its successes on the Millennium Development Goals (MDGs). These have proven the perfect vehicle for Bangladesh's development ambitions, allowing political leaders to showcase achievements to a world audience that knew it only as the basket case, and on whose financing its development project still depended to a significant (but fast declining) degree. By 2015, Bangladesh had partly met goals on poverty and hunger, and on universal primary education; it had met the goals on gender equality (probably) and on both maternal and child mortality; it had also made progress on the other goals on environmental sustainability and combating HIV/AIDS, malaria, and other diseases, but was behind on some nutrition, and on water and sanitation, targets (GED 2015a). Among the Least Developed Countries, only Rwanda ranks higher in terms of its MDG performance, and Cambodia ranks alongside Bangladesh (Bhattacharya et al. 2013). Bangladesh has done well enough to be spoken of as a 'role model' (Imran 2015). The international recognition this has earned is important to the political leadership. The Minister for Planning saw fit to occupy much of his preface to the last MDG progress report with listing six recent prizes and other recognition for the Prime Minister's leadership of the MDG challenge (GED 2015a, preface).

Less widely remarked upon is the political consensus on which these achievements rest. Much is made, particularly by donors with short memories, of differences in the public policies of the ruling coalitions or parties. But these differences pale into insignificance compared to the vast swathes of common ground on the MDGs, an invisible consensus. All three ruling groups (the Awami League, the Bangladesh Nationalist Party or BNP, and the military-backed caretaker regime of 2006–7) issued reports over the last decade of the MDGs which all made similar points about the achievements; the need to address lagging areas; connections between economic growth, poverty reduction, and human development; the need to fill financing gaps (with more aid); and the government's strong and continuing commitment to the MDGs. The first MDG report was issued jointly with the UN, but from then on it has been issued by the government.

There are shades of difference in the ways in which these commitments are justified, and these take on the colour of ideological distinctiveness. In 2005, a time when economic debate in Bangladesh was centring on the country's position vis-à-vis world trade, then-Finance Minister Saifur Rahman ended his preface to the progress report with a stern reference to unequal trade rules:

> For countries like Bangladesh to meet the MDG commitments made at the 2000 Millennium Summit, industrialised countries must honour their commitments to finance development in developing countries. Trade barriers must be lifted and both the rich and the poor must be allowed to benefit from globalization so that we can all move towards a more equal world. (GED/UNDP 2005, preface)

The pro-globalization and free trade inflection is consistent with the then-ruling party BNP's historical alignment with trade and industrial interests, and its stewardship of the early shift to pro-market policies. By contrast, in her speech to the High Level Plenary Meeting on the MDGs, Prime Minister Sheikh Hasina explained the state commitment as follows:

> During my last tenure as Prime Minister, our government took steps to mainstream MDGs in our national development plans. The aim was to ensure national ownership of the MDGs, and to demonstrate our commitment to achieve them, within the stipulated timeframe of 2015. The planning and budgeting process since 2001, thus: sought to achieve the MDGs as part of our national development. During our present tenure, we have set a Five Year Plan to achieve the MDG targets, as a step towards making our country a middle income and a 'Digital Bangladesh' by 2021, the Golden Jubilee Year of our independence. This is on way to achieve finally 'Sonar Bangla' or 'Golden Bangladesh' as dreamt by my father and Father of the Nation, Bangabandhu Sheikh Mujibur Rahman. (Wazed 2010, 1–2)

This personalization of the political will to develop is characteristic of Awami League political discourse, as is the use of socialistic-sounding 'Five Year Plans' and reference to the cultural ideals of the nationalist struggle. The lessons of history echo in the Prime Minister's reflections on the factors retarding progress:

> [T]he world food and energy crises of the past year, the ensuing global economic recession, world trade decline, dismal investments and the impact of climate change have retarded our pace for achieving the MDGs. Yet Bangladesh has been able to achieve satisfactory progress, with the support of the UN system, and bilateral and multilateral partners. (Wazed 2010, 1–2)

The old problems of commodity shocks, vulnerability to world trade fluctuations, and 'natural' disasters recur, as does the issue of reliance on external aid. But this is no longer Sobhan's 'crisis of external dependence'; the agenda is now broadly agreed between donors and the political elite. In the main, and indeed in the detail, the differences between the rules of the political parties with regard to how they approach development are almost undetectable. And that consensus arose out of a painfully learned understanding of how Bangladesh is positioned vis-à-vis global commodity and trade markets, ecological disasters, and aid financing.

3

The Elites, the Masses, and Their Donors

3.1 Relations of Domination

It helps to think of the political economy of development in Bangladesh as resting on the maintenance of a specific form of social contract: that political authority and legitimacy are earned and reproduced, minimally, by protecting the masses against crises of subsistence and barest survival, and lost or weakened with the failure, or appearance of weak will, to do so. The anthropologist Jahangir summarizes the political *quid pro quo* crisply: '[i]n the rural areas of Bangladesh the perception of a good government depends on: whether a government is able/unable to feed its people in times of crisis' (Jahangir 1995, 93). Governments may do many other things, and they may fail to do many other important things, but at the moment of crisis, subsistence and survival are to be safeguarded at all cost. The Bhola cyclone politicized the need for such protection for a people and a place so thoroughly exposed to global economic volatility and highly destructive environmental events. The subsistence crisis contract was arguably part of the rationale for sovereignty, but the political settlement (or balance of power between elites) needed to meet its terms was not achieved in the immediate aftermath of independence; instead, it emerged out of a painful process of learning. The loss of political legitimacy at a time of (and as a result of) acute subsistence crisis confirmed that the ruling elite—any ruling elite, regardless of who they were and where from—needed the commitment and the capacity to provide that protection if it was to assure the legitimacy and authority it needed to rule.

It is true that the idea of a social contract has been applied to so wide a range of empirical, theoretical, and normative concerns as to be capable of meaning almost anything to almost anyone (Boucher and Kelly 1994). But it is a helpful device, both in the 'thick' sense of helping to describe the empirical facts and in the thinner, as a narrative device for theorizing the story of Bangladesh's development (Pateman and Mills 2007). Certainly the struggle for sovereign rule in Bangladesh (as in other post-colonial states) resembles the emergence of a social contract in Rousseau's sense as the 'institution of civil or political society in a social compact... designed to secure pre-existing moral rights and duties' (Boucher and Kelly 1994, 4). In the case of the state that emerged to govern the Bengal Delta, there was a Lockean sense of protecting society against the 'inconveniences of nature' (Boucher and Kelly 1994, 6). This primeval language fits with the idea that the wild destructiveness of the Bhola cyclone triggered the independence struggle by mandating sovereignty for the people so affected.

Social contract thinking also makes sense of the relationships underpinning development as a 'relationship between the ruler and the ruled that is... contractual, explicitly or implicitly, and which specifies or implies the respective rights and duties of the contractees' (Boucher and Kelly 1994, 10). As we will see, both elites and masses see their relationship in terms of rights and duties, and of a somewhat vague notion of its enforceability through the threat of non-support. 'Constitutional contractarianism' of the kind at work here draws attention to the costs of broken contracts, namely the loss of political legitimacy for rulers and of protected rights for the ruled. In relation to the politics of development at least, a social contract has come to be thought of as 'a good thing', implying

> more legitimate, peaceful and consensual forms of political authority [and] stronger commitment to social justice that can help relocate public policy within the realm of rights rather than patronage. (Hickey 2011, 427)

In other words, in development thinking, the social contract has appeared as a liberal ideal, loosely inspired by Rawlsian conceptions of justice (Hickey 2011; Pateman and Mills 2007). But the idea of a social contract need not suggest freely consenting people participating in a development project of their choosing (in the case here). The survivors of Bhola or the Pakistani army crackdown of 1971 may have been enthusiastic nationalists, but they could not consent to being ruled in the sense of free choice on a footing of equal power. Their 'consent' must be treated as constrained by their personal physical, economic, and political vulnerability, as the assent of people with the most limited of alternatives. Nevertheless, they had much to gain from an agreement to be protected against crises of survival and subsistence in return for either their enthusiastic democratic support or their passive acceptance of elite rule. And so an agreement could be reached between grossly unequal parties who stood to gain, or not to lose, from the agreement. We can read this through signs within popular political culture that even the relatively powerless can make it costly to break the agreement, if only through the passive acts of non-compliance that make it difficult to govern—the classic 'weapons of the weak' (Scott 1987).

That the weak have some weapons in a political society so thoroughly dependent on popular legitimacy is not the only reason to retain the idea of the social contract. Mills' idea of the 'domination contract' is helpful in explaining how the elite and the masses come to be in a relationship that works, despite its inequities, to deliver adequate legitimacy for rule for one side and enough protection to survive and to advance for the other (Pateman and Mills 2007). The domination contract also characterizes the relationship between the ruling elite and the aid donors on whom they came to depend in the early post-war years. Again, the notion of consent is one of form for a ruling class facing the destruction of its developmental ambitions at the first hurdle, within a couple of years of assuming office. Agreement to take what turned out to be the first steps towards liberalizing economic reform was forged, or forced, upon a governing elite that had lost its legitimacy early on, and was soon to learn the violent costs of that loss. But what to the political elite of a developing nation was an (unfamiliar) experience of domination may to aid donors have been the rightful authority to influence policy in a client country in the interests of its population. In a discussion of the application of social contract theory to the political economy of development it is relevant to note that in his discussion of how to extend the principles of liberal justice to the 'society of peoples', the great liberal theorist Rawls identifies policy influence, not distributive justice, as the means under conditions that are likely to include 'oppressive government, corrupt elites and the subjection of women abetted by unreasonable religion . . . with overpopulation' (Rawls 1993, 64). The ultimate goal is that 'each society now burdened by unfavorable conditions is to be raised to, or assisted towards, conditions that make a well-ordered society possible' (Rawls 1993, 62). A clearer statement of the moral philosophy of the liberal motivations of Western aid cannot be imagined.

We turn now to look more closely at the relationships of domination and compliance that underpin the subsistence crisis contract. We focus on why the identity of that elite and their position within Bangladeshi society and with respect to the international community was so critical to the formation and defence of that particular contract. And we look at how those relationships have changed, in key respects, towards less blatant forms of domination, more diffuse exercises of power, and more complex modes of interdependence.

3.2 A 'Middle-Class' Elite

Perhaps the defining characteristic of the Bangladesh elite is that it has not, until recently, been particularly 'elite':

> The word 'élite' begins to lose its meaning when it is applied to the middle-income professional and business petty influentials who, under Sheikh Mujibur Rahman, carried the message of the Awami League to the rural people of East Bengal.
>
> (Nicholas 1973, 145)

Elites are groups among whom power or influence over decisions is concentrated; national elites tend to be identifiably wealthier, culturally superior, socially and sometimes racially or ethnically distinct from the masses.[1] By contrast, the Bangladeshi elite has closely resembled the masses and been comparatively close to them, socially and spatially. The contemporary elite is mostly from Bengali-speaking Sunni Muslim stock, without important inherited or cultural status. Until independence from Pakistan, few of this group held great economic or political power. Compared to groups which have ruled the region in the past, and to contemporary elites elsewhere, the Bangladeshi national elite has been marked less by its distance and difference from the masses than by its affinity to them.[2]

This relative affinity has influenced the conception of the national project of development (Hossain 2005). Many Dhaka elites have recent peasant origins and associated ties. The nationalist political leadership and other elites are chiefly from recent peasant stock, families that entered the professions or had formal education in the past generation or so (see Siddiqui et al. 1990; Barua 1978; Sen 1986; also Sobhan and Sen 1988; Rahman 1991). The new nation-state of Bangladesh was an 'intermediate' regime, dominated by middle-class professionals, small businessmen, and wealthy peasants, rather than landed or large industrial interests (Sobhan and Ahmad 1980; Bertocci 1982).

Until recently, that group was close-knit, and multiply connected by ties of kinship and location. That connectedness comes with intertwined personal histories: 'batchmate' university friendships created some enduring ties that cut across sectors and ideologies within the present generation. A respected NGO leader once described to me a youthful friendship with a business leader whose own public profile was, shall we say, more ethically ambiguous. Past friendship trumped present differences, however, and the unlikely pair were seen side by side on pro-democracy platforms, demonstrating the importance of unity on issues of national importance. Such unlikely connections were once surprisingly common.

[1] The classic account remains Mills (1956). Despite contextual differences, the sample frames used to study 'elites' are often similar (Verba et al. 1987). Most political science focuses on national elites, based on positions within institutional structures and networks.

[2] The key text remains Ahmed's *The Bengal Muslims* (1996). It is not that there were no important social distinctions: Bengali Muslim society had its elite–mass distinction in the form of the *ashraf* ('foreign' aristocratic families claiming Central Asian extraction from way back in history) and *ajlaf* or *atrap* (local peasant and artisan converts) (Eaton 2001); it also had its own versions of castes, with well-defined occupational groups and rules. But while hereditary in theory, these were never entirely rigid. Economic change and religious fundamentalism meant these were declining by the late nineteenth century (Ahmed 1996). They have little current resonance (also Van Schendel 1982).

3.2.1 *A Flat and Fluid Society*

The elite has been comparatively close to the masses partly because Bangladesh has been comparatively equitable in economic terms.[3] Bangladesh probably started life with the lowest levels of economic inequality in the region (excluding 'foreign' business elites), but income inequality rose after independence, particularly in the early 2000s. Since then, there has been a slight improvement in the share of income going to those at the bottom, particularly since higher agricultural commodity prices raised rural wages after 2007.[4] Bangladesh now has similar levels of income inequality as India or Nepal, although (surprisingly) higher than those of Pakistan; it compares favourably with neighbours Thailand and Vietnam and low-income comparators such as Kenya, Uganda, Rwanda, and Zambia.

But standard inequality measures provide no sense of how economic inequality actually works to protect and reproduce itself.[5] For Bangladesh, it is obvious that small economic differences translate into minute but vital gradations of social hierarchy and status; there can be few contemporary societies so mindful of personal status and standing, perhaps the cultural manifestation of an acutely clientelistic society. But the ritual enactments of privilege and status that are so striking to the outsider are not the same as economic or political power.[6] It is often argued that the relative flatness of Bangladeshi society is not the point: small differences in wealth—in particular in land ownership—have been leveraged into large differences in class power (Wood 1994, 45–8). Inequality is so striking a feature of social organization in Bangladesh that a wave of village studies in the 1970s challenged assumptions that 'class divisions within the "peasant economy" were structurally insignificant' (Wood 1994, 137). These generally failed to replace myths of social harmony with evidence of hard and wide class-type differences,[7] but they

[3] Despite its popular image. A recent Bloomberg Businessweek article entitled a story about US Congressional district inequalities 'The U.S. Has Higher Income Inequality Than Britain. And Bangladesh. And Ethiopia', the surprise being that the US was more unequal than the least desirable places in the world (Chemi and Green 2014).

[4] See World Bank (2008); World Bank (2013). On rising rural wages, see in particular Zhang et al. (2013), who tell a remarkable story about the rapid changes in the rural economy.

[5] Among their other failings; see Wade (2013) on how the Gini measure underestimates inequality.

[6] A member of the Bangladeshi elite (or the Bengali *bhadralok*) would not traditionally carry heavy or bulky items, even their own bags. In the most progressive of NGO offices, an assistant will ferry the senior executive's briefcase from car to desk. This aversion possibly reflects the lingering effects of a Bengali cultural worldview that glorifies mental and disdains physical labour, no doubt also the source of the 'effete *babu*' of British imperial racism (Rosselli 1980). Disdain for manual work (particularly agriculture) was a feature of the *ashraf* worldview (see Eaton 2001).

[7] See Jannuzi and Peach (1980), 17; Jansen (1986), 300–1; Van Schendel (1982), 293–8. There were cases in which class-type structures were identified around irrigation infrastructure (e.g. Arens and Van Beurden 1977; Hartmann and Boyce 1983). See Adnan (1990) for an overview of the village studies literature.

drew attention to how small advantages of wealth empowered and enriched local landed elites. This group then used the opportunities of social and economic development to diversify into agro-business, local politics, and the aid industry. Bangladeshi land values have increased so dramatically in the past decade that people who simply sat on medium-sized landholdings for the past thirty years are now rich by world standards (Mahmud 2013).

While by no means an egalitarian society in everyday practice, political culture favours egalitarianism in theory, expressed as acceptance of upward mobility via educational and business success. For the 'intermediate classes' after independence, success in business was associated with exploitation by non-Bengali Muslims and trade and industry were socially inferior compared to the attractions of state employment. Distaste for business has now dissipated; leading business houses are from established families, and make it a point to promote philanthropy and high culture.[8]

The elite faith in meritocracy through education represents it as a society that rejects the unfair advantages of inherited wealth and position, rewards hard work and effort, and believes mass education is a solution to poverty and underdevelopment. It also relates to the formative experiences of elites who themselves experienced upward social mobility. In the 1950s and 1960s, stellar academic performance by sons of the rich peasant and lower-middle classes in East Pakistan village schools granted a special few entry to the prestigious Civil Service of Pakistan. One political leader whom I interviewed in the late 1990s recalled how 'in our day, bright boys could come out of remote villages'. A highly respected former civil servant had 'joined the civil service in Pakistan in 1967 through an open competitive examination... Twenty of us were selected for this cadre from all over Pakistan that year, out of several thousand who took the written and oral examinations' (Chowdhury 2009, 1). The importance of this route to upward mobility helps to explain the urgent power of the language movement of the 1950s: for the upper peasant and middle classes of East Bengal, the imposition of Urdu would have closed off one of few channels of advancement.

The possibility of social mobility, however unlikely now, resonates with nationalist emphasis on the homogeneity of Bangladeshi society. Faith in social mobility helps affirm a sense of social cohesion between rich and poor by highlighting the ways in which Bangladeshi society is egalitarian. It gives it a modern quality compared to caste-bound India, feudal Pakistan, or royalist Nepal. Social historians note that upward mobility was always theoretically possible, citing the optimistic proverb: 'last year I was a weaver (Jolaha), now

[8] Most notably the Bengal Foundation, which hosts the highly popular Bengali Classical Music Festival as well as fine arts exhibitions and other events. See http://www.bengalfoundation.org/about-us/ (accessed 29 September 2015).

I am a sheikh, and next year, if the crops are good, I shall be a Syed.'[9] An emphasis on the absence of rigid social distinctions stresses the absence of a basis for class conflict, which in this region has had a strong but not exclusively communal character (see Bose 1986; Cooper 1983; Custers 1987; also Hashmi 1988; 1994). The protracted, two-part struggle for national independence meant liberation from 'foreign' oppressors—from the British and Hindu landlords and moneylenders, and then from non-Bengali Muslims. Since we have all become 'Bangladeshi', the social differences to which it was once possible to attach class conflicts have been less salient.[10]

3.2.2 *New Money*

The new political salience of social and class distinctions has much to do with the rise of the industrial elite, the prime beneficiaries of the booming export sectors. Their rise has made the national elite distinctly more capitalist. The same policies of economic liberalization and privatization that unleashed economic growth made it possible to accumulate capital, including from 'bargain' sales of state-owned enterprises and industrial debt default in the 1970s (Sobhan 1991; Sobhan and Ahmad 1980; Sobhan and Sen 1988; Alam 1993; Quadir 2000). Compared to before independence (Kochanek 1994; Sobhan and Sen 1988), the captains of industry are now more likely to be Bengali Muslim, and Nicholas's 'middle-income professional and business petty influentials' have been transformed into a business–industrial class. We see this in the changing composition of parliament. In the first parliament of independent Bangladesh, businessmen comprised 24 per cent of MPs compared to lawyers' 27; a quarter-century later, in the seventh parliament, the figures were 48 to 17; in the last contested election, in 2008, it was 56 to 15 per cent. Business and politics have become symbiotically related, such that success in one is likely to lead to success in another:

[9] Cited in Van Schendel (1982), 295; Jansen (1986), 750; see also Ahmed (1981), 21–2. A 'syed' was at the top of the socio-political and economic hierarchy, associated with land-owning and possibly aristocratic status, and a 'shaikh' could be a local religious leader, with independent landholdings.

[10] For Bengali-speaking Muslims, that is. Note that 'Bangladeshi' (as opposed to 'Bangalee' or 'Bengali') is itself a political intervention, a neologism of the Zia regime to distinguish from the 'Bangalee' label of the nationalist struggle and from Hindu Bengalis (Chowdhury et al. 1996). It has been pointed out to me that discussion of the homogeneity of Bangladeshi society is offensive to the many millions of citizens (and denizens) whose primary identification is not as Bengali Muslim and who face multiple modes of exclusion, marginalization, and repression as a result. Among them are the indigenous or *adivasi* hills or plains communities, including the Chakma, Garo, Hmong, Mro, and other groups; the twenty million or so Hindu citizens; and the Buddhists, Christians, and Urdu-speakers still now dismissed as 'Biharis' or Pakistanis. My point here is that the numerically and otherwise dominant majority of Bengali Muslims is internally relatively undifferentiated, that the dominant elite group is very similar to them, and that this comparative homogeneity is highly politically salient.

> A new breed of politicians has emerged who have parachuted into parliament from a business, bureaucracy, or military background without any prolonged apprenticeship in party politics. (Jahan 2015, 259)

Party nominations are a business, and a seat in parliament an investment: in one view, 'You can now buy yourself an MP nomination the same way as you buy an air ticket to Singapore: pay up and off you go!' (Amundsen 2014, 140). Organized business interests need to align or partner with ruling party men to get anything done, just like everyone else (Hassan 2013). But the business of making money is different and arguably above mere politics. In the more mature 'limited access order' of Bangladesh in 2013, Hassan finds that far from being competitors, political rivals were commonly business partners: this, they had learned, was the best way of hedging against the uncertainty of political transitions (2013).

The business orientation of the main parties has harmonized over time. Elections to the tenth parliament were boycotted by the traditionally pro-business BNP, but the declared occupations of the Awami League, Jatiya Party, leftist (JSD and the Workers' Party), and independent MPs suggest that business predominates in these parties too, with 52 per cent declaring it among their occupations. Career politicians and lawyers are still important (17 and 15 per cent respectively), and other professionals such as journalists, former civil and military bureaucrats, doctors, and professors make a respectable showing (12 per cent altogether). Interestingly, forty-one MPs declared an interest in agriculture or some form of agro-business; at 12 per cent, this is more than women, non-Muslims, or ethnic minorities (see Figure 3.1).

There have never been rigid divisions between the vernacular elites—the landowners, agro-processing industrialists, mill- and brickfield owners, rural politicians—and their national counterparts, who are mainly different because they made the transition a generation or so earlier. National elites generally retain both landholdings and rural connections. Uniquely in East Bengal, the relationship between the state and the rich peasantry became closer in the twentieth century, as first the British and then the neo-colonials were removed from the equation. Independence ultimately strengthened the local landed class in its pole position between the state and the rural masses (see Van Schendel 1982, 278). Despite efforts to decentralize power (or sometimes because of them—Crook and Manor 1998), the line between the centre and the *moffusil* or rural areas remains short and direct, a characteristic of a compact, monolingual territory. The return to multiparty parliament in the 1990s drew local elites even closer to state and party political power, as block grants for constituency development encouraged MPs to focus on local more than national matters (Amundsen 2012). And the rural economy has become

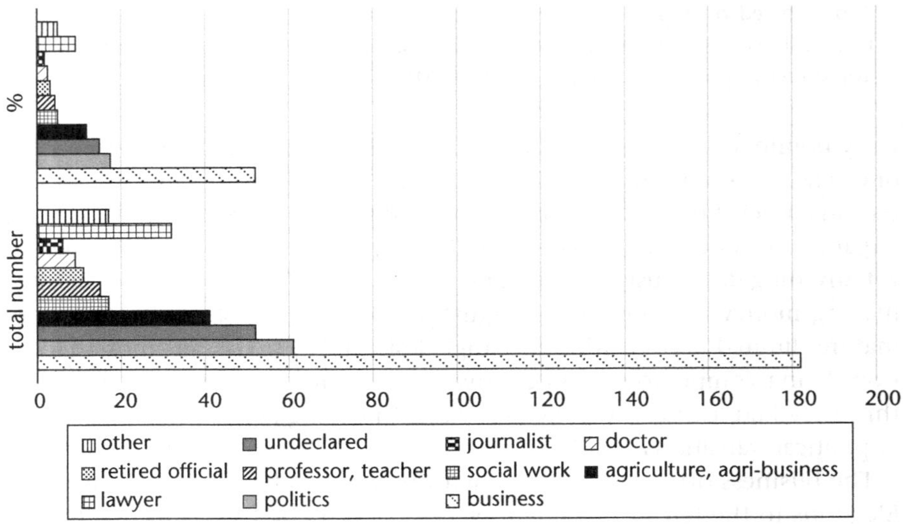

Figure 3.1. Occupations of Members of Parliament in tenth parliament

Note: multiple occupations permitted; n = 443; total MPs = 350

Source: Author's compilation from list of MPs in tenth parliament, http://www.parliament.gov.bd/index.php/en/mps/members-of-parliament/current-mp-s/list-of-10th-parliament-members-english (accessed September 25–28 2015).

more important. The 'blue revolution' saw frozen-food exports averaging around USD 600 million (2.6 per cent of total exports) in the 2011 to 2013 period, and the rapid growth and diversification of the rural domestic economy in the 2000s, including rising food prices, gave agro-industrial interests stronger motivations to seek political representation.[11] New rural wealth can only increase the mutual interest between national and rural elites.

New money from agro-processing and non-farm rural industry pales into insignificance compared to the wealth from labour and garments exports. In 2013–14, woven and knitwear exports earned Bangladesh USD 24 billion, around 80 per cent of all exports in recent years; a further USD 14 billion was earned in expatriate remittances, and migrant workers earned between 7 and 10 per cent of the country's GDP in the past decade (MoF 2015a). It is worth stressing that Bangladesh's growth industries built on its human resources: 8.6 million workers, a fast-rising proportion of whom are women,

[11] On the freshwater shrimp export industry, see Ahmed, Allison, and Muir (2010). Export figures are from MoF (2015a). On rural economic diversification and development, see Nargis and Hossain (2006) and Toufique and Turton (2002). On growth in the rural economy since the global commodity spike of 2007–8 see Zhang et al. (2013). There does not appear to be any published analysis of the political salience of the agro-processing and frozen food industries to date.

were estimated to be working abroad in 2015; at present, the readymade garments (RMG) industry employs four million workers in more than 4,000 factories, mostly women. The rapid turnover of workers in that physically demanding industry means that several million more workers will have contributed to that growth.[12]

The country's wealth may have been earned by the toil of its masses, but the owners of the woven garments, knitwear, and 'man'power industries have profited handsomely. The display of this new wealth is contentious, set as it is against evidence of neglect and abuse of migrant and garment workers' rights, including of their basic survival.[13] It is instructive for its insights into how society is changing. An unmissable example is the flamboyant figure of Dr Moosa bin Shamsher, who founded a labour recruitment company, DATCO, in 1974. 'Prince Moosa', as he is known locally, is reportedly an arms dealer with USD 7 billion frozen in Swiss bank accounts; his offer of a GBP 5 million donation to the British Labour Party was declined by Tony Blair, and he currently faces corruption charges at home (despite close links to the political leadership). Dr Shamsher has been the subject of a Japanese television documentary and a *Sunday Telegraph* magazine article, and is described as[14]

> the fountainhead of a vast business empire operating in more than 30 countries... Along with arms dealing, his main interests are in the construction industry, manpower services and the hotel trade. He bathes every day in rosewater and owns 3,000 suits. 'One can't expect him twice to be seen in the same very apparel.'... He looks a dandy... in his finely tailored Italian suit and ruby rings. His belt buckle winks with clusters of diamonds. There are rubies and diamonds, too, on his gold Rolex, and when he notices me squinting as my retinas adjust to their brilliance he tells me that it is the most expensive watch in the world. That it cost $1 million. (Farndale 2013)

With their *bhadralok* sensibilities, the old elite frowned on conspicuous consumption as a sign of insensitivity to the plight of the poor. With such lavish

[12] BBS (2014). Factory and worker numbers are from the Bangladesh Garment Manufacturers and Exporters Association (BGMEA) website (http://www.bgmea.com.bd/chart_test/factory_growth_in_bangladesh), accessed 5 October 2015. See also Bangladesh Bank (2015).

[13] On the RMG workers' wage struggle, see Muhammad (2011); see also Khanna (2011) and Hossain and Jahan (2014). There is no shortage of reports of migrant workers' rights being abused and of the role of recruitment agencies: the Refugees and Migratory Movements Research Unit (RMMRU) at the University of Dhaka has been documenting these issues since the mid-1990s (see, for instance, Siddiqui 2005). For a recent example see McGeehan (2015).

[14] I could find neither, but refer here to an article by Nigel Farndale (a *Sunday Telegraph* contributor) based on an interview with Prince Moosa (Farndale 2013). The Labour Party donation story is from Timmins (1994).

displays, the new rich jeopardize the social peace, in the words of a former senior civil servant turned politician in 1998:[15]

> Maybe we are largely shielded because our poor are not so violent. If they were violent it would affect us very very much, because they are the majority... we are not terribly insensitive. We do care. There are of course the super-rich and the defaulters who do not care. But by and large I think we do care. (Hossain 2005, 91)

Less than a generation later, the lavishness of a Prince Moosa is constructed as a matter of nationalist pride—a challenge, no less, to the 'basket case' epithet:

> Date-line mid 70s when the newly born at the same time the war torn country was devastated by millions of problems like famine, poverty as epidemic the whole nation was eclipsed by the darkness of distress humanity and untold misery. As the world's poorest country it was defamed by the world media as bottomless basket... But suddenly news sparked worldwide and that become a bolt from the blue to each and every Bangladeshi and helped to hope to see the light at the end of the tunnel i.e the meteoric rise of a young aspirant man in Asian foreign trade in competing with the giants in the field astounded all in the East. The world media showed keen interest in this rising star and cast their searching sights on a least developed country like Bangladesh.
>
> It is a matter of pride at least that one of our close comrades has occupied a prestigious position in this world of immense wealth and unlimited power. He has added extraordinary qualities to his personality characterized by firm commitment to righteousness and genuine sympathy for mankind...
>
> He is highly respected as the pre-eminent architect of man power export to whom the nation shall remain ever grateful. During the last few decades' natural calamities that befell the nation one after another, he came out in a big way to provide supports to the afflicted people.[16]

Beyond the paeans to Prince Moosa's diamond-encrusted fashion sense, this vanity journalism says something interesting: that a biography of business success must adopt the sentiments of development nationalism to resonate. Shamsher's achievements are set against the dark post-independence days, and charity for those afflicted by natural calamities show that he has the vital quality of care for those in distress, the glue that keeps the nation together. His success demonstrates that a citizen of benighted Bangladesh can rise to prestige and power on the world stage in a technicolour version of the rise of the business classes in Bangladesh.

[15] Social media offer a whole new virtual world in which to conspicuously consume. I have been told (I have also seen the evidence) that some wealthy Bangladeshis have dispensed with 'selfies' altogether, in favour of professional photographers who follow them around to record their social activities for Facebook, etc.

[16] From the online business paper, businessnews24bd.com (S. A. Hossain 2013).

3.3 Elites and the Masses

As the elite has changed since independence, so too have the masses, and the relationship between them. It is still a strongly clientelistic set-up, but it is not as informal, farm-based, or infused with ideas of benevolence as was the case a decade or two ago. What has changed is as follows: in the political relationship between the ruling elite and the masses, we hear a change in tone from the grateful masses to an increasingly sophisticated political society. In the economic domain we see a marked shift towards real structural interdependencies with business depending on the labour of the masses. It is here that conflicts of a class nature are showing up, arguably for the first time since the *tebhaga* agrarian rebellions of the 1930s. In the social relationship, we see a shift away from interpersonal patronage to a more organized and public form of charity, a professionalization that marks the growing detachment from semi-feudal relations and the need for elites to create and demonstrate social status.

3.3.1 *The Spirit of '71*

There are also continuities in that relationship. Despite growing economic distance, the elites and the masses share important beliefs and cultural practices. For the Muslim majority, this includes adherence to a customarily private, moderate, and tolerant form of Islam. For the middle and upper classes, newer forms of religiosity are more assertive and more reflexive. In their rising use of the *hijab* or *burka*, educated and affluent women come to resemble their *moffusil* sisters whose mobility has always been limited or licensed by Islamic modesty in their dress.[17] Compared to the secular leftism of the progressives in their parents' generation ('Frantz Fanon and all that', as one nostalgically recalled), the post-'71 elite generation arguably takes more interest in the intellectual and cultural history and practice of Islam, so that faith connects them to their Muslim-majority fellow citizens.

But it is a complex religiosity that competes with cultural identity and political values and does not imply rejection of secular (or non-communal) values within the nation-state. Values of pluralism and justice can be consistent with faith (Huq 2010). The complex relation between Islam, national identity, and political values—an identity crisis older than Bangladesh[18]—reemerged in the Shahbag movement of 2013. This campaign occupied the city centre for weeks, with up to half a million people reportedly involved.

[17] See for instance Huq (2010, 99) who identifies a growing tendency for 'a brand of Islam that is more thought through and is disseminated from extra-familial sources' among women across the class divide. Rozario (2006) discusses the rise in veiling among educated women.

[18] See R. Ahmed (1996) on 'The Crisis of Identity–Muslims or Bengalis?', chapter 4.

Shahbag cut across classes but also generations, bringing people from all walks and stages of life onto the street in support of the delayed 'transitional' justice for the war crimes of 1971. Paradoxically, given the bloodthirst of a campaign demanding the death penalty for Jamaat-i-Islami politicians convicted of war crimes, the movement was a brief reprisal of the unity of the painful but glorious nationalist struggle, a sign that 'the spirit of '71' lived on.[19] This movement has now been reduced—or inflated—to a struggle of Western-oriented middle-class moderns against vernacular traditionals seduced by militant Salafists (adherents to extreme text-based orthodoxy).[20] Yet Shahbag should be interpreted as continuity with the past, as a broadly shared demand for justice overdue.

3.3.2 *The Emergence of 'the Public'*

In the quarter-century of its ferociously competitive democracy, ideas of political freedom, rights, and the mandate to rule have started to displace notions of benevolence and mutual obligation in popular political culture. The rhetoric of political leadership is still tinged with maternal affection, but this language is ornamental: the people now *expect*, they no longer pray for crumbs from the table of the rich. But then the population has become accustomed to the idea of itself as a political force, perhaps because until 2014 (an election boycotted by the main opposition) it had evicted the incumbent each time it went to the polls.

The public did not reject client status or turn into autonomous political actors overnight: there remains 'contract all the way down', as Carole Pateman puts it (1988). But patron-clientelism is resilient and flexible, and adapts well to democratic cultural forms: in this more competitive political market '[t]he how of giving... becomes as important as the what' (Devine 2006, 92). Ruud argues that ordinary citizens embrace the 'mechanisms of democracy' because they give them influence over who is in power, but do not expect to take it themselves (2012, 46). Kabeer (2011) finds that for urban folk the state is malign or absent, but rural people do not feel 'imprisoned' by local power structures (Wood 2000). Instead new forms of political consciousness and practice suggest political change from below (Sobhan 2000, cited in Kabeer (2011)). People mobilized by organizations like *Nijera Kori*, with its class-struggle theory of social change, recognized the sources of their problems and saw their relationship to

[19] Although some of those who were there in 1971 struggle to see the connections—see Zeitlin (2013). There may be more detailed accounts in Bangla, but analyses in English include Murshid (2013); Lewis (2013); Zeitlyn (2014). The leftist blog *Alal o Dulal* features the best of the progressive political events analysis: http://alalodulal.org/2013/03/19/paltan-to-shahbag/ (accessed 7 October 2015).

[20] Murders of 'atheist bloggers' by fundamentalists solidified the clash-of-civilizations thesis and introduced a transnational dimension, with British–Bangladeshi fundamentalists claiming the killing (Hammadi 2015). Zeitlyn's (2014) article about how the politics of Shahbag and the International Criminal Tribunal were being viewed by British Bangladeshis seems prescient in light of this development.

the state and political power changing: 'barriers to citizenship were spoken of in the past tense, suggesting that at some significant level, there has been a real shift in the balance of power. Rural respondents... saw themselves as citizens, or in transition to citizenship' (Kabeer 2011, 352).

If the hard facts of power have changed little, there is a stronger grasp of political possibility and the underlying power dynamics. The change registers as tone more than content. We hear it in the shifting language with which ordinary citizens speak of themselves as political actors, less often as *jonogon*, a word suffused with moral meaning, than as *public*, with its implications of collective, if usually latent, power (Ali and Hossain 2006). Perhaps the loan-word *public* was necessary because vernacular terms for relations of power are too contentious[21] or the political relation itself is new: never before have the masses been the political masters of the elite. Possibly television talk shows popularized the word, since the liberalization of broadcast media in the 2000s spread the habit of political debate.[22] Whatever its source, *public* suggests citizens who deliberate about their common affairs in the public sphere (Fraser 1990, 57); it suggests formalization and a degree of withdrawal from the private role of the client.

How and whether mass political power can countervail against entrenched political power is not obvious. But political culture is shifting towards greater awareness and a powerful sense of citizenship on which all else hinges. An otherwise 'shy and hesitant' woman told researchers, when asked if her husband told her how to vote, 'No, I decide my vote. Voting is freedom [swadhinota]. To vote for the candidate you like best. If you cannot vote for him, then there is no freedom' (Ruud 2012, 54). Polls of political attitudes tend to find that the majority of Bangladeshis prefer multiparty elections to other ways of choosing their leaders (Barman et al. 2002). There is a difference between deciding who can decide and being the group on whom decisions are benevolently enacted, even if that difference remains theoretical for now.

3.3.3 *Material Interdependence*

In *Elite Perceptions of Poverty in Bangladesh* (2005) I argued that poverty was not an urgent concern for the Bangladesh elite because—unlike the elites of now-developed countries at similar stages of economic development—they were

[21] For terms used in the Bangla press for protests during 2007–12, see Hossain and Jahan (2014).

[22] Note that 41 per cent of households owned a television by 2006, compared to only 8 per cent a decade earlier, and 65 per cent of adults watched television in 2006, of whom 16 per cent watched talk shows and 66 per cent the news (Rahman 2011).

insulated against its adverse impacts (Swaan et al. 2000). There were three reasons for this:

1. urban crime was a concern, but not one closely associated with poverty;
2. epidemic health threats were not a worry, because of modern medicine and the greater threat from non-communicable diseases;
3. the quality of the population, a significant concern for early twentieth-century elites in industrialized countries, did not adversely affect the interests of the Bangladeshi elite: the main industries relied on cheap and plentiful rather than productive labour. Garments factory owners spoke of workers in tones of benevolent patronage, not as employers with stakes in their productivity (see also Kabeer 2002).

The first two points remain valid, but in respect of the third, the situation has changed. Export manufacturing and labour services were already vital for economic growth and foreign exchange when I was researching elite perceptions in the late 1990s, but the elite view of the masses did not then conceive of the relationship as one of self-interest (enlightened or otherwise) (Hossain 2005). It is now the case that the collective material interests of that group (and the country as whole) are directly affected by the behaviour and productivity of workers in labour-intensive sectors. Given that demand for the reserve army of Bangladeshi women export workers is growing, the 'man'power industry is insulated against pressure for welfare standards and skills in the short term. But in the RMG sector, industrialists have been facing acute pressures to raise wages and improve working conditions and standards because of periodic labour unrest since 2005. It is relevant that this unrest peaked in the period 2008–11, a period of global food and financial crises, highlighting again the exposure of the Bangladeshi economy and livelihoods to global volatilities. The chief impact of ongoing industrial unrest has been a trebling of the minimum wage rate in less than five years; by December 2013, it was BDT 5,300 (USD 68). Despite wage gains, Bangladeshi RMG workers are the lowest-paid in the world (Moazzem and Raz 2014).[23] Since the 2012 Tazreen factory fire in which 112 workers died and the Rana Plaza factory collapse that killed 1,134 workers, worker safety and working conditions have been under the glare of the international media: the US withdrawal of trade privileges under the Generalised System of Preference (GSP) in the wake of the Rana Plaza disaster highlights how directly workers are increasingly able to materially affect the interests of employers (USTR 2015; Kibria et al. 2014).

[23] High inflation over the 2000s probably means RMG workers have not actually achieved real wage rises (Shibli 2014). Wages are still far below the BDT 8,200 calculated in 2014 as the appropriate level taking into account ILO minimum wage-setting principles (Moazzem and Raz 2014). Workers' organizations are continuing the struggle.

This interdependence is not necessarily acknowledged. Basic labour rights abuses are recognized as a problem. But labour unrest is viewed with suspicion, as either criminal extortion or as a conspiracy to sabotage the successful Bangladeshi industry (to persuade garments buyers to move to India, etc.). Workers' grievances are seen as stirred up by outside troublemakers rather than as genuine problems, and the response is policing and blocking labour organizations through which they might negotiate. Alongside rises in the minimum wage and (since Rana Plaza and the withdrawal of the GSP) stronger emphasis on compliance with safety regulations, a key shift in industrial relations has been the Industrial Police force set up in 2010, whose mission is to 'ensure safety and security of industries. To uphold the rule of law for the owners & workers. To take necessary measures to prevent any labour unrest in the industrial area'.[24] Workers' rights are mentioned in this mission, but the central purpose is '[t]o increase the production as well as to develop our national economy for better future of Bangladesh'.

A sign of a functional interdependency between the classes would be recognition that upward pressure on wages entails the need for higher productivity, and that in turn requires investments in the quality of labour. The trade journal set up by the BGMEA, the owners' association, started just after Rana Plaza, indicates a focus on investing in training and upgrading, particularly with regard to safety, and on building 'brand Bangladesh', presumably to repair damage to the international image of the sector after Rana Plaza and the Tazreen fire. Research on the connections between the RMG sector and women's empowerment in Bangladesh is also showcased. There are stories about charitable and philanthropic efforts, including work with people with disabilities. But given the emphasis in the policy research on the need for higher productivity, it seems striking that the industry leadership does not appear to connect issues of worker productivity to broader public policies influencing worker wellbeing. Neither in the trade journal nor in other forums is there evidence that employers of millions of workers consider their housing, public health, education, safety, or social protection to be matters of common interest. When it comes to lobbying government on behalf of the sector, the emphasis remains on tax breaks and subsidies. Marking its second anniversary, the editorial notes that:

> We have always been very quick to write about issues that nag the RMG industry. For example, Budget 2015–16 FY. Though the budget for 2015–16 FY does have a number of business-friendly steps, some proposals have raised concern in the RMG sector. Among them the proposal for increasing source tax to 1 percent from 0.3 percent was instantly written about in our magazine. We delineated the

[24] From the website of the Industrial Police, http://www.industrialpolice.gov.bd/aboutus.php#/section-2 (accessed 8 October 2015).

> impacts of such decision on the RMG sector. The government later reduced the source tax to 0.6 percent. (BGMEA 2015, 6)[25]

The contemporary BGMEA discourse suggests that while the industrial elite has real reasons to be concerned about the wellbeing of workers and about public investment that might enhance the quality of the workforce, it remains loyal to an old model of benevolent patron-employers, and does not view itself as a business elite whose relationship with its workers is informed by enlightened self-interest.

3.3.4 *From Private Patronage to Organized Philanthropy*

In the 1990s, despite the successes of the huge NGOs and 'social enterprises' like Grameen Bank, BRAC, and ASA, private action for the poor was seen as ideally about personal charity. Assistance to the known poor—particularly those closest to the core of the concentric circles of patronage (poor relatives; needy kin; folks from the home village, district, or region; the deserving poor more widely)—was ideally benevolent and kind, and the personal touch was favoured. There was a strong gender dimension to this, as elite women were particularly expected to perform personal acts of charity, but also to be involved in charitable groups and efforts. This 'Lady Bountiful' style of private charity was part of older Bengali modes of clientelism, but it also made a particular statement about high culture and good breeding (Hossain 2005).

More recently, that relationship has become more institutionalized and professionalized. Private giving no doubt still goes on and patronage networks are characteristic of the environments of the rich and powerful. But there has also been a flourishing of new types of charitable organization that aim to dispense with the old inefficiencies and inadequacies of private giving in favour of more rational modes of charitable assistance that do not, for instance, breed dependency. They are licensed and organized; some, like the highly regarded Jaago Foundation, depend on social media and youthful idealism (Hossain 2014). The Jaago Foundation is one of the organizations through which the students of the elite International School Dhaka get involved in social service. The change is also notable in the rise in corporate philanthropy and corporate social responsibility. There is much goodwill and enthusiasm for social justice in these new modes of charitable action. They nonetheless reflect a society in which the gap between the richest and the poorest, undetectable by measures of inequality such as the Gini coefficient, has become far wider, and in which it is increasingly through the medium of an organization's bureaucracy that the relationship between them will be mediated.

[25] Examples here are from the second anniversary, July–August 2015 issue of the BGMEA's English language bimonthly trade journal, *The Apparel Story*. http://www.bgmea.com.bd/media/newsletters/July-August-2015/July-August-2015.pdf (accessed 8 October 2015).

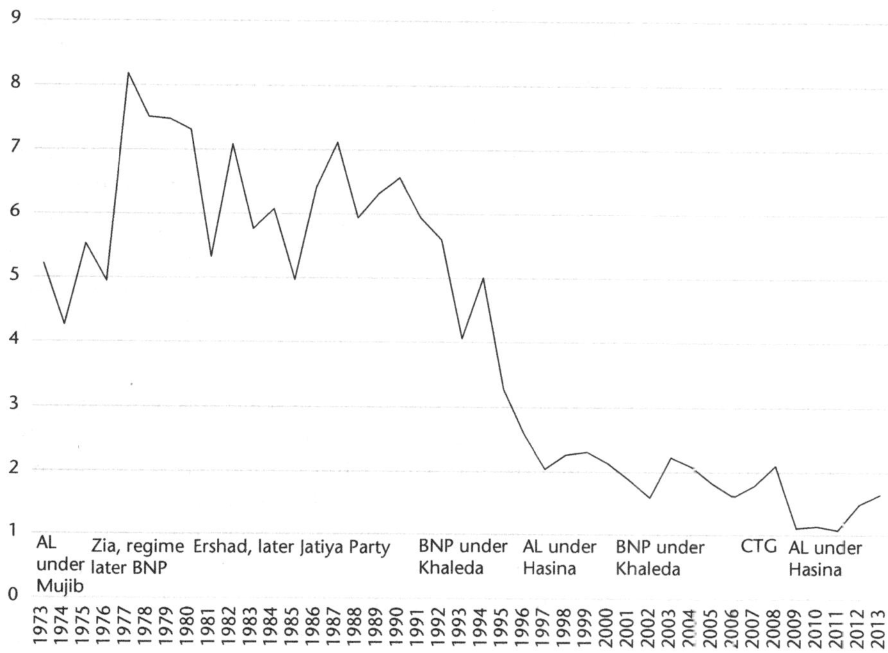

Figure 3.2. Aid as a percentage of gross national income, 1973–2013
Source: World Development Indicators. Accessed 14 October 2016. http://databank.worldbank.org/data/reports.aspx?source=world-development-indicators.

3.4 Elite–Donor Relations

Aid no longer defines the relationship between Bangladesh and the rest of the world, but the early dependent years permanently shaped the political economy of development. Aid continues to contribute a significant chunk of government expenditure, and even more of that of the NGOs whose spending is assumed to be comparatively more concentrated on services to people on lower and more precarious incomes.

Figure 3.2 shows that the relative importance of aid has fluctuated over time, suggesting aid flows could not have been entirely reliable; also that there are distinct periods, more or less coinciding with political regimes, in which aid flows were absolutely and relatively higher or lower. This appears to reflect the amenability of different governments to particular areas of economic reform, and more generally the relationship between donors and governments at particular moments of their rule (see Quadir 2000; also Guhathakurta 1990). Overall, aid has become a smaller contribution to gross national income over time, and this has altered the relation between donors and elites beyond recognition. This owes partly to the declining relative importance of aid as a result of relatively rapid economic growth from the 1990s, but also (and not coincidentally) to the fact that aid relations were always easier, from the point of view of donors, under authoritarian regimes.

That aid has influenced the pathways of Bangladesh's development does not need to be re-established.[26] It is beyond question that pressure from aid donors explains some of the key turns in macroeconomic, trade, and social policy in Bangladesh's development history. We will look at some of those turning points in more detail, but here our focus is on understanding how donors feature within the relationship between the elite and the masses. There appear to have been three distinct stages to that relationship:

1. The immediate post-war period 1971–5, in which aid was dominated by the UN-managed reconstruction and recovery programme and the modalities of the aid relationship were being figured out. The continuities with how aid donors viewed the country before and after it achieved independence were discussed in Chapter 2. Under first the elected Awami League Government and then the single-party BAKSAL regime, public policy took an increasingly socialist-statist turn, at least in intention. Western aid donors disapproved of the policies, the political direction they implied, and the corruption and mismanagement that were evident by 1975, and were openly lobbying for economic reforms. At the height of the economic crisis, Mujib was assassinated and the series of military coups that put General Ziaur Rahman in power took place.
2. The military era, dominated by Zia and his successor, General H. M. Ershad, 1975–91. Partly to appease donors and partly to win popular legitimacy, this period was marked by acquiescence to the aid donor push in most directions, but in particular under Zia on food security and population, and under Ershad on privatization and economic deregulation, credit and other support for the manufacturing industry, basic health and education, and flood prevention. Aid-financed NGOs began to grow large and significant in the long Ershad decade, performing the functions played by progressive politics or a functioning bureaucracy in other settings, but which were absent or weak in the Bangladesh of the time.
3. The democratic period, from 1992 onwards. The first decade in this period was the golden era for Bangladesh's success, building on the foundations of food security, disaster prevention, macroeconomic stability, and a growing set of governmental and other institutions geared towards human development. As a proportion of national income, aid

[26] Sobhan's (1982) study makes the point in significant detail; see also Islam (2003); Guhathakurta (1990); Khan (2014); Quibria and Ahmad (2007).

fell sharply in this period. By the 2000s, aid donors arguably needed Bangladesh more than Bangladesh needed them. Certainly this was true enough of the mega-NGOs like BRAC. But it was also increasingly true of the major human development sectors, for which Bangladesh had won so many laurels: any serious donor needing to show 'impact', 'results', or 'value for money' had to try to fund some health, education, or anti-poverty initiative (preferably one with a female face) in Bangladesh. The country still had large numbers of poor people densely and therefore accessibly located, and it was increasingly clear that skeptical taxpayers and charitable donors back home could get the best bang for their buck if they backed Bangladesh.

3.4.1 *Masters and Servants*

There is no love lost between the elite and the aid donors in Bangladesh, but the mutual animosity between the elite and their donors can be surprisingly intense. Sobhan's view that 'the psychology of dependence on donors has become ingrained in the psyche [of elites] such that... the goodwill of the donors is an important political resource in the domestic politics of Bangladesh' (1993, 5) has been influential. But you will be hard-pressed to meet a Bangladeshi national, however invested in or dependent on the aid industry, who does not hold nationalistic views on self-reliance. This development nationalism is more than surface-deep. On one occasion, the director of an NGO had described equitable partnerships with his donors during an interview, only to change tack once the tape recorder had been put away and start a lengthy discourse on how aid sustained imperial domination. A retired senior government official whose job was to advance the donor position with the government described an encounter when his employers felt the government had broken all the rules. He agreed that the government's behaviour had been outrageous and regressive, but he nonetheless described with satisfaction how donors had been put 'back in their proper place... the idea that they can dictate terms has to some extent been nullified' (see Hossain 2004, 18).

It is a commonplace that the aid relationship is an ill-concealed extension of colonial rule; aid flows are seen as either rightful restitution for historical imperialism or as evidence that the extractive relationship never ended, aiming to make Bangladesh safe for global capitalism. The global social compact of Rawlsian liberal justice theory is nowhere in sight. A telling analogy was that of the 'master–servant' relationship, a phrase that speaks of the acute personal discomforts of the aid relationship in which members of an elite are forced into the role of international beggar. Struggles against colonialism are grand and noble but the master–servant dynamic is only ever about petty humiliation.

The language speaks of reversals in the status hierarchies to which elites are accustomed, a sense of powerlessness within the larger web of international relations.

The elite might find it annoying or even humiliating to need aid, but the animosity seems to run deeper than that, reflecting gross inequalities of power enacted in the aid relation that have been worn into psyches over time. Social relations run along those grooves, like it or not, and on both sides. Aid officials who behave acceptably in London or New York are different in Dhaka. A Northern aid official whom I believe is a progressive-minded individual elsewhere told me that malnutrition meant Bangladeshis were unfit for democracy and 'verging on the cretinous'. (In my shock, I failed to produce a retort and so no doubt confirmed this view of the intelligence of Bangladeshis.) It is hard to imagine such an extraordinary statement being made in another setting. It is no coincidence that the sociologist Sarah White, who broke an aid industry taboo when she wrote about race and white privilege (White 2002), is a long-term observer of development in Bangladesh.

3.4.2 *The International Trade in Ideas*

Against the obvious shortcomings of a system that grew out of colonial policies and Cold War politics, the proximate—and paradoxical—reason for prickly aid relations is that in Bangladesh aid has been a 'pure gift' (Stirrat and Henkel 1997), given without expectation of comparable material. It is this absence of material reciprocity that gives it its power. Because it is not returned, has no element of transaction in it, it always carries some part of its donor with it. Aid donors are 'incumbents of status positions and do not act on their own behalf' (Parry 1986, 456); but that status is one of immense power, leaving the recipient indebted and marked by the motives of the donor (Stirrat and Henkel 1997).

What are these motives in relation to Bangladesh? Guhathakurta's study of British aid to Bangladesh through the 1970s and 1980s finds 'no *strong* economic or strategic motivations involved', but politics were never absent: the motives of long-term aid giving were not simply developmental but 'determined and negotiated at state-level politics' (Guhathakurta 1990, 302). The significance of aid in a context where its gift has no material benefit for the donor must be intangible. Certainly, as Guhathakurta points out, the significance of aid to Bangladesh must be judged against its influence on the policy process, rather than either its volume or its contributions to growth.

In relation to the history of development in this country, the significance of aid can only be found in the domain of ideas. The motivation (and perhaps the post hoc justification among progressive-minded donors) has been untinged by commercial or economic interest, yet powerfully shaped by the need to persuade. The elite of Bangladesh needed to be persuaded to pursue market-friendly policies deemed pro-poor in the Western liberal traditions of public policy.[27] But partly because of the notoriety of Bangladesh as the 'basket case of the world', the world needed to be persuaded that there were no hopeless cases; that the judicious application of generous aid could ultimately guide even the most challenging countries towards progress; that the technologies and techniques for doing so were available and sound. However, over time, its having become the poster child for results, aid donors started to need Bangladesh more than the elite needed aid donors. That phase of the social contract in which the elite depended on donors for the capacity to protect against crises of the most basic subsistence is now over, in the main. Yet donors now continue to invest in Bangladesh because after forty years of investment and aid donors and projects and NGOs, development has become an art that they do exceptionally well.

[27] As distinct from social democratic.

Part 2
The Basket Case

4

The Breaking of the Patriarchal Bargain and the Emergence of the 'Woman Issue'

The human-development advances of the first forty years could never have been possible if the mass of rural women had stayed as secluded, excluded from paid work, unschooled, and without control over their fertility or health, as they were before independence. But the crisis events of the 1970s brought about an abrupt break in the already weakening patriarchal bargain.[1] Out of the devastation of the period, and partly in an effort to demonstrate the modernist credentials of the new state, 'the woman issue' came to be viewed as both an urgent and an actionable problem. The ideological space and resourcing generated by this new view of women allowed state, market, aid, and civil society actors to dream up new ways of working with them, many of which were later exported elsewhere. Some of these ideas and interventions were coercive and controlling; many aligned with or actively shaped women's own interests and desires.

By recognizing women's issues as matters for public policy, Bangladesh was relatively advanced compared to other low-income post-colonial states. The demands of foreign aid helped draw political elite attention to the connections between gender and the reproduction of poverty (Nazneen et al. 2011, 31) and to making public finance at least partly dependent on attention to matters of gender (see Nazneen 2009). But in key respects, aid agencies were pushing on—or walking through—a door that had already been opened by the crises of the 1970s:[2]

[1] This chapter grew out of conversations with Naila Kabeer about the effects of the early 1970s on gender relations in Bangladesh. Particularly important for me have been her insights into the way in which the shock to Bangladeshi society disrupted customary gender norms and women's behaviour, paving the way for challenging new approaches to 'women's needs'.

[2] The 'woman question' had already been raised in previous generations of nationalist political discourse in colonial Bengal at the turn of the twentieth century, typified in the *Ghare-Baire* ('home and world/outside') dichotomy of Rabindranath Tagore's nationalist novel of that name. Women's liberation was dropped from nationalist political concerns as customary gender relations came to

> The first half of the seventies in many ways marked a watershed in attempts to deal with women's issues... a gradual dawning of awareness among women themselves of the unequal social relationships in which their lives were embedded. For poorer women, the upheavals which marked the early years of the decade (the cyclone of 1970, the War of Liberation of 1971, the famine of 1974) may have merely confirmed what they already knew: in times of crisis, women are the earliest casualties. (Kabeer 1988, 110)

The old patriarchal bargain had worked well enough so long as the rural economy supported livelihoods secure enough to protect women against hunger, disaster, and exposure. Kabeer points out that the series of crises showed that the women of Bangladesh were no longer (if they ever had been) guaranteed such protection, shifting middle-class attitudes so that the women's movement in particular came to see the concerns of the average Bangladeshi woman as inseparable from its own (1988).

The events of the 1970s did not cause the break, but they dramatized the slow-onset crisis engulfing the agrarian system on which customary patriarchy depended, hastening the inducement of institutional change in gender relations (Kynch 1998; Kynch 1997; also Ruttan and Hayami 1984). On the ruins of the old bargain, Bangladeshi women were gradually incorporated in a more public, citizen-like role, included within the social contract in their own right instead of via the borrowed citizenship implied by the sexual contract (Pateman 1988). The enlargement of the customary domains of women's lives not only brought them out of *purdah*; it also brought problems of security and survival out of their familial and reproductive domains and into the public sphere, complicating the boundaries of politics and government. Women's citizenship rests largely on their status as mothers of the nation, current or future, but this nonetheless means they are seen as citizens with substantial and important interests, concerns, rights, and political leverage (Werbner 1999). Like other states in an era of globalization, Bangladesh needed to transform the population to make it more amenable to government; in this the interests of mothers and the state had to align, so that bodies and behaviours could be measured, monitored, and transformed to meet the needs of the national project.

4.1 The Weakening Agrarian Basis

The patriarchal bargain had been in decline for some time before the crises of the 1970s so dramatically highlighted its breakdown (Kabeer et al. 2011).

be emblematic of Indian difference from the West, such that 'the home was the principal site for expressing the spiritual quality of the national culture, and women must take the main responsibility for protecting and nurturing this quality' (Chatterjee 1993, 126).

Across their lifetimes, the women of this part of Bengal had customarily moved from father's house to husband's, depending entirely for protection and support on lifelong good relations with in-laws and bearing sons who survived into adulthood (Kabeer et al. 2011). The ideal-typical patriarchal bargain in the Bengal Delta had exchanged protection of women against hunger, exposure, and violence for their reproductive and rice-processing labour, as well as their adherence to social norms of seclusion and sexual purity. Women were—and still are—married as minors.[3] They all but universally moved to their husband's house and lived in extended family arrangements where they cared for the present and produced the next generation; they also supplied the extensive but invisible labour for post-harvest paddy processing. In return, women expected to be fed and protected against violence and insult; higher-status women could expect to be withdrawn from physical labour and secluded within the house; when widowed (as was common, because husbands were much older), or divorced, women hoped to be looked after by sons or brothers. Daughters relinquished their claims on paternal property in return for the promise of being cared for by brothers, if their husbands failed to protect them. Practices of seclusion and veiling, glossed as *purdah* or 'curtain', ensured women's sexual purity by curtailing their movements and delimiting their relationships.[4]

4.2 Negotiating *Purdah*

The patriarchal bargain never covered all women. Poor widows and others without male protection were always given latitude to labour for wages, albeit at the starvation wages afforded by labour-market segregation and gender

[3] The practice persists on an almost universal basis, reflecting the continued priority of female sexual purity, the extreme personal insecurity faced by or feared for girls and women, and the institution of dowry or payments to grooms' families since the twentieth century, a reversal of the direction of marriage transactions that historically applied (Lindenbaum 1981; Ahmed 1987). These appear to be the main reasons Bangladesh has the second highest rate of child marriage in the world, although its 'outlier' status continues to present a puzzle. Almost three-quarters (74 per cent) of women aged 20–49—that is, who came of age since Bangladesh's independence—were married before they reached eighteen, the legal age of marriage (UNICEF 2014). The situation does not appear to be improving: 65 per cent of women aged 20–24 had been married before 18, according to most recent figures—a level that has stayed fairly constant since the mid-1990s (NIPORT 2013). However, recent evidence suggests that at least some of these 'early' marriages occur later than girls' actual birthdates would suggest, because the premium on female youth means parents would prefer to lie and break the law on marriage age than to admit that girls are over 18 at the time of marriage (Streatfield et al. 2015).

[4] Kandiyoti's description of classic patriarchy applies here (1988). For accounts of Bangladeshi forms of patriarchy specifically, see Adnan (1993); Cain, Khanam, and Nahar (1979); Kabeer (1988); Feldman (2001). Greeley (1983, 43) examines the implications of changing agricultural technology for the economic basis of patriarchy, and Feldman and McCarthy (1983b) detail the new symbolic and spatial forms taken by *purdah* against these shifting economics.

seclusion.[5] But impoverishment, landlessness, and the commodification of paddy production[6] undercut the material basis of the patriarchal bargain for even those women who could have expected male protection; these processes, we saw previously, had been underway since at least the mid-twentieth century, and probably far longer. Population pressure and landlessness (Greeley 1983), nucleation of the peasant family (Cain et al. 1979), ecological disasters (Feldman and McCarthy 1983a), and the immiserization that accompanied a precariously commodifying agrarian economy (Adnan 1993; Feldman 2001) contributed to a situation in which it became impossible to hold men to the bargain:

> The kinship, political, and religious institutions that support male dominance and authority remain strong and intact, while the associated sanctions that ensure that males carry out their responsibilities to women have weakened. With the pressure of increasing poverty, this outcome is predictable, since male authority has a material base while male responsibility is normatively controlled. Normative control, while powerful, is nevertheless relatively malleable in the face of economic necessity. (Cain et al. 1979, 410)

Poor, unprotected women had little recourse in this context of broken bargains. But the relative malleability of normative control gave them one weapon: they could break *purdah* if that were necessary to survive, by reference to the 'natural laws' of necessity. As one woman summarized the corollary of the broken bargain: 'If my husband/family/community cannot feed me, who are they to say I cannot work?' (Feldman 2001, 1115). Statements of this kind can be found in much of the literature on *purdah* and poverty (for instance, World Bank 2007).

There are several aspects to the manipulation or renegotiation of the institution of *purdah*. First, the case had to be made to establish a norm respecting women's rights to bare survival. The pioneering early twentieth-century North Bengali feminist author Rokeya Hossain wrote of the obsession with *purdah* in her stories of *The Secluded Ones*, where she observed the fatal irony that to Muslim society, women's bodies were worth less alive and unveiled than dead but covered. Even in arguing for the right to 'come out' on grounds of bare survival, Bangladeshi women were pushing boundaries. It had to be demonstrated that the failure to protect women was more socially costly than

[5] In one of my earliest research projects, a study of women-headed households, I realized that the norm of extended family care of elderly women was probably a middle-class ideal when a destitute widow we were interviewing made it clear she had never expected her son would take her in: he had a hard enough time keeping himself and his wife and children alive (Hossain and Huda 1995).

[6] And probably the rise of jute production, although I recall no examples where reliance on jute production has been analysed as a reason for the decline in the material basis of East Bengali patriarchy.

the effects of broken *purdah*. These were among the lessons of the rape, destitution, and social breakdown of the 1970s.

Second, while the bargain was often broken, no better system of protection replaced it. The social protection and poverty reduction programmes since the 1970s represent aspects of that system under construction. But these are at best a patchy system that could never match the total protections (and affections, and controls) of a financially solvent father or husband. Few Bangladeshi women are able to entirely dispense with male protection, so even when the bargain was so fundamentally broken, women still adhered to some version of the norms of seclusion that afforded 'symbolic shelter' (Papanek 1973).

Third, when broken en masse, it became necessary to reinterpret the norm, to make paid work outside the home compatible with good womanhood. Within a generation or two, an apparently rock-hard patriarchal principle was perceptibly softened. By the 1990s, women threw a *dupatta* or sari *anchol* over their head as a nod to modesty norms, and it was enough to permit them to move about their business with only the aggravations of sexual harassment to deter them. Many now invest in the apparently orthodox, but in fact mobility-enhancing, *burka*; middle-class professionals adapt this further by wearing a white jacket that mimics a lab-coat and clearly signals professional-woman-at-work. The adoption of the *hijab* probably signals the global politics of Islam more than a renegotiation of *purdah*, but it nonetheless lets women combine personal freedom with the respectability that comes with overt religiosity (see also Rozario 2006). Many Bangladeshi women now talk of *purdah* as an internal condition that governs personal behaviour, but has little to do with outward appearances. Elora Shehabuddin detects a 'subaltern rationality' in how women define *purdah* as 'a state of mind, a purity of thought, something that they carry inside them rather than an expensive outer garment, [which] permits these women to present and even see themselves as pious Muslims yet leaves them free to meet the basic needs of survival' (2008, 4). In this remarkable feat of ideational engineering, the contemporary practice of *purdah* seeks the symbolic shelter of personal modesty, while confidently carving out a feminine public space. Rokeya Hossain's stories of *burqas* that strangulate their wearers read now as tragicomedies of an almost unimaginable past.

4.3 Rape, Masculinities, and the 'Spectral Wound' of Nationhood

Women may well have stayed bound by the terms of the broken patriarchal bargain had the crises of the 1970s not dramatized its failures so powerfully.

The spectre of large numbers of poor women who had been displaced, widowed or abandoned, raped, or made destitute as a result of cyclone, war, or famine highlighted the need for a new social contract in which women had alternatives to reliance on male relations. This created the space for public action to promote livelihoods and protect against the risks inherent in the lifecycle. It also eased the proscription of women's mobility and paid work, even if the stigma of physical labour and male resistance to women in public space has not disappeared. For better or worse, it implied a transfer of last-resort responsibility for protection of women from family and community men to the state.

Mass wartime rapes both dealt a blow to the presumption of women's sexual purity and set a precedent in state intervention into the private domains of women's bodies and reproductive capacities. An accepted estimate is that between 200,000 and 400,000 women were raped during the war of independence in 1971, from which 25,000 forced pregnancies resulted (D'Costa 2014a).[7] Most were by Pakistani soldiers, but other men also took the opportunity to rape during the upheaval (D'Costa 2014b; Saikia 2011; also Mohaiemen 2011; Mookherjee 2015). Unknown numbers of women and children, possibly in their thousands, were kept in rape camps during the conflict, but most were attacked at home, some in front of their families and communities. Some were later killed, but there are reasons to believe that the Pakistani army internally justified its campaign of rape—an unusually excessive episode of mass sexual violence during war—with the ethnic-cleansing or genocidal intent of 'improving'/Islamicizing the bloodline of Bengalis. The total stigma of rape in a sociocultural system centred on women's sexual purity meant women tried to conceal the crimes they had endured, or face rejection by families unable to cope with the shame. Some hanged themselves with their own hair (D'Costa 2014a).

The effects of this deep psychic trauma have often been seen as a 'spectral wound' (Mookherjee 2015) to the national body rather than harm to the women themselves: 'Women's experiences of sexual violence during the war were, until very recently, largely depicted in the language of loss or harm to the nation, and an assault on the community's *izzat* (honour)' (D'Costa and Hossain 2010, 332).

The campaign of war rapes signalled that women's bodies were 'territories to be occupied, marked or claimed for masculine rule' (D'Costa 2014b, 469), and

[7] The war rapes have been analysed in detail by Bina D'Costa (2011; 2014b; 2010), Nayanika Mookherjee (2015; 2008; 2012), and Yasmin Saikia (2011), and I rely on their work for the facts and for understanding these events in their context. On the points about the genocidal intent of the rape, see D'Costa and Hossain (2010). Gerlach (2010) disputes that 'genocide' was intended, but then he disputes the concept of genocide entirely. He does, however, note that the sexual violence in the Bangladesh war of independence was unusually extreme. See also Sharlach (2000).

were accordingly emasculating for Bengali men (also Mookherjee 2008). The ambivalent public discourse of the war rapes stems from the wounds they inflicted on Bengali masculinities. The Mujib government attempted to rehabilitate the survivors by declaring them *birangona*[8] or war-heroines, encouraging society to see their 'sacrifice' as equaling those of men on the battlefield. They were honoured and shamed, silenced but graphically displayed, euphemized and 'aestheticized'. Rape victims were depicted as despoiled beauties, with 'loose hair, threaded [groomed] brows and large eyes' (Mookherjee 2011, S79). The ambivalence extended to the governmental domain: the rapes were enumerated and the numbers used politically, yet records were destroyed so that verification was impossible. Sheikh Mujib's reported statements that rape pregnancies should be aborted or adopted abroad to keep out their 'polluted blood' contrasted with (what was on the face of it, and in intention) a progressive effort to valorize rape survivors to integrate them into the nation, going against prevalent social norms to do so (D'Costa 2014a).

These 'aestheticizing' tendencies depicted women's rapes as the rape of the nation, so that the recovery and rehabilitation of raped womanhood became equated with national reconstruction. With the nation as the raped mother, the state was transformed from jackbooted authoritarian to benevolent patriarch; the public discourse of the war rapes was operationalized in nation- and state-building agendas around the protection of women as bearers of future citizens:

> The imagery of the mother as the innocent victim, caring, nurturing, compassionate, desexualized, of whose pure womb sons are born to further the cause of the nation, provides a powerful underpinning for the state to see itself as a caring parent, concerned for the fate and future of its citizens. It is this concern that makes it necessary for the state to rehabilitate and 'normalize' the raped women—to recover the mothers of its future citizens. (Mookherjee 2008, 49)

> Imagining the nation as a mother figure further provides a powerful underpinning for the state to see itself as a patriarch, responsible for its citizens. The state in this sense is essentially masculine, but also welcomes tenderness and emotion.
> (D'Costa 2014b, 463)

The mass wartime rapes were one-off crises[9] from which gender relations could, in principle, have recovered, and there are signs that the immediate

[8] As well as widows, women freedom fighters, and those who sacrificed and risked their lives by staying behind and supporting or caring for the fighters and the wounded (D'Costa and Hossain 2010).

[9] Although rape by the Bangladeshi military of indigenous women as part of the settlement of the Hill Tracts and other *adivasi* community territories continues this theme and tradition of sexual violence as military conquest/genocide of 'the other' (see D'Costa and Hossain 2010).

post-war period was a time when old patriarchal controls were, or were trying to, reassert themselves. In *Our War*, a documentary about women's experiences of 1971 by historian Afsan Chowdhury, one woman commented that the war should have changed men's attitudes towards women because they saw what women were capable of; instead they got worse—behaviour she would protest till she dies, she said (Chowdhury 2001). If men wanted to try to reestablish their old rights in that moment, then they had women's hard-won new awareness to contend with.

4.4 Institutional Legacies of Wartime Rape

Beyond the public discussion of the erstwhile unspeakable crime of rape, itself a profound change in a closed and private society, the violence of the war left two institutional and programmatic legacies. The first was that many hundreds of thousands, and very likely millions, of women and children were left without male protection or support. We know this because of the million or more who died or were disabled in the conflict, a high proportion would have been adult men (see Curlin, Chen, and Hussain 1976). Many of the thousands of women who 'came out' to work on public works schemes after the famine were probably widowed or became household heads as a result of the war. Afsan Chowdhury's film documents the tough lives led by women in this situation, recording their assessment that little was done to help them and their sense that someone, preferably the state they sacrificed to bring about, should have acted to support them. The war left a discernible population of women without reliable male support—a group for whom the old patriarchal bargain had, visibly, nothing to offer. These women had expectations of the new state for which they had sacrificed so much, and were disappointed by what the new state had to offer.[10]

Despite women's disappointment with their state, the war rapes saw the start of public services that intervened specifically on the ground of the old patriarchal bargain. In the immediate aftermath of the war these were a limited range of emergency services related chiefly to the rapes. They included schemes under the National Board of Bangladesh Women's Rehabilitation Programme to get women re-integrated into society through marriage or by equipping them with skills to earn a living. Unsurprisingly, given the social

[10] Shehabuddin makes a similar point when she notes the state is an important actor in the study of women's lives in Bangladesh more 'by virtue of its limitations and absence' than because it is felt to have done much for women (2008, 16). I disagree that the state has been absent from women's lives, but that there remains vast room for supporting and enabling Bangladeshi women through more and better state action is without doubt true. That women have expectations of their state is itself, I would argue, a sign of their growing sense of citizenship.

stigma of rape, few women came forward to claim the privileges accorded those with official *birangona* status (compared to the thousands who claimed to have been *muktijoddha* or freedom fighters). But this was a sign that the 'newly formed state became responsible for making these women available to the nation, "returning" them and "protecting" them from the assumed prevalence of "Muslim" traditions and taboos' (Mookherjee 2007, 342). There was a temporary suspension of the law against abortion to permit a programme of abortion on an almost industrial scale, in part about 'protecting' women 'from the emotions of motherhood so that they could return to society' (Mookherjee 2007, 339). A temporary law (the Bangladesh Abandoned Children (Special Provision) Order of 1972) permitted international adoptions of the babies from pregnancies too advanced for abortion, or for other reasons brought to term but not kept by the mother (Mookherjee 2007). This last was also about protection, this time of children who were otherwise vulnerable to abandonment or trafficking (Chowdhury 2015), but it was also about ridding the country of the offspring of Pakistani rapists.

Each of these actions reversed the old logics of the patriarchal bargain. The first authorized women's independence from (family) men; the second prevented women from mothering; the third removed children from their society. The laws on abortion and adoption were temporary—as Mookherjee observes, a classic example of Agamben's 'state of exception', operating as 'the legal form of what cannot have legal form' (Agamben 2005, 1). No written law permitting abortion was possible as the constitution was not ratified till October 1972, and the lack of written law and the destruction of documentary records reflect the fact that later-term abortion is again illegal in Bangladesh.[11] But while these events took place within the state of exception, their effects have been enduring in their implications for society. These are most direct for the individual members directly affected, but also evident in how they shaped institutions and inclinations of the state to intervene in 'family' matters, and therefore in the relationship between women citizens and state.

The effects of the overall effort to reintegrate the survivors of rape were mixed. The interventions are often seen as having been disempowering, intended to force women back into some kind of socially acceptable settlement by 'taking away women's agency, transgressing their humanity and transforming them into bodies that were manipulated so that men would

[11] Although 'menstrual regulation', a 'procedure that uses manual vacuum aspiration (MVA) to safely establish nonpregnancy after a missed period', is legal (Guttmacher Institute 2012). USAID's population programmes in Bangladesh experimented with the production of cheap devices through which untrained users could facilitate early stage abortions, sometimes through the medium of feminist NGOs and marketing technologies. Some of the organizations at the forefront of this technology were involved in the large-scale abortion programmes in the post-war period (see Murphy 2012).

not have to deal with the unhappy reminders of the past' (Saikia 2011, 168). The ambivalence with which the efforts were made reflects the fact that this was more than merely a matter of rescuing citizens from harm: in symbolic terms, the foundational institutions of family, private property, and inheritance ultimately rested on women's sexual purity. Practically and conceptually, the social order depended on the restoration of sexual order (see Ortner 1978). But Bangladeshi society could never return to its pre-war condition, and the rape rehabilitation interventions required something new of the beleaguered state. It responded as well as might have been expected under the conditions. To the extent that these interventions marked a transfer of the responsibility to protect from society to state, and certainly within a liberal political framework, they can be regarded as progressive. Efforts to valorize and rehabilitate women were intended to signal modernity and progressive thinking (Mookherjee 2008); and in some respects these efforts were pioneering. D'Costa and Hossain argue that the 'interventions were ahead of their time, providing women with much needed support and solidarity and critical material assistance which helped them rebuild their lives' (2010, 342). In a continuing theme of the export of ideas and technologies of government, the legal provisions for dealing with the aftermath of the rapes have been seen as precursors to international legislation on forced pregnancy after wartime rapes in contexts like 1990s Bosnia (Mookherjee 2007, 342). Naila Kabeer (1988) argues that although in practice in the early years after independence, policy on women was mainly limited to conventional instrumental treatment of women's bodies as sites for fertility control, the commitment to secularism created more ideological space for a struggle for women's rights than had been possible before.

It could even be said that Bangladesh's role as the world's aid lab started in the effort to handle the wartime rapes. Several international NGOs and agencies got their start working on the sensitive matter of reproduction in Bangladesh at this time. 'Travelling' methods of abortion like menstrual regulation were developed under these sad 'laboratory' conditions, and later used elsewhere.[12] Without the desperate need to rehabilitate women after the war, the poverty and social protection programmes and fertility control and reproductive health schemes for which the Bangladesh government and NGOs are now seen as pioneers may not have had such a receptive environment.

[12] Murphy (2012) documents how the experience of wartime rapes came to be institutionalized in fertility control programmes after the war, including through 'USAID's approach to fertility control, which knitted together reproduction, economy, and experts in a way that harbingered later neoliberal forms of development' (Murphy 2012, 168). In another connection between the war rapes and the experimental fertility programmes through which the aided state sought to make Bangladeshis, Mookherjee notes that 'a large number of women raped during the war received professional training . . . and worked as these lady village workers' distributing family planning advice and devices (2007, 346).

4.5 'The Woman Issue' in Development

While Bangladeshi society was struggling with the implications of post-war devastation in the 1970s, the world of aid was starting to discover the potential role of Women in Development. Just as the country served as a testing ground for experiments in development, it has been on Bangladeshi women's bodies and in their lives that technologies from reproductive devices to financial services and modes of public service delivery have been devised and refined in the name of development. In its early years, the concerns of the aid industry could seem oddly disconnected from the visceral pain of a society putting itself back together after a bloody struggle, depicting Bangladeshi society as

> a strange political void where the concern became to teach village women to read, write, sew, embroider, knit, weave, appreciate the value of eating low-status vegetables and fish, and become small-scale agricultural entrepreneurs, even while the country was busy abandoning thousands of innocent rape victims, victims of the 1971 War of Liberation in the notion that they were 'polluted'.
>
> (Alam and Matin 1984, 2)

In how it presented issues of women and gender in the early post-independence years, much of the literature is, as Alam and Matin argue, oddly detached from history and politics and focused on understanding how women can be made to do development faster and better, or at all. Abdullah and Zeidenstein's well-known study of rural gender relations, undertaken to inform a programme to 'integrate' women into rural development via credit and livelihood activities, is guilty of just such a disconnected view. They note that the women they study consider social change to have been very rapid in the recent past, but say little about how the traumas of the conflict may have shaped their worldview or adherence to older customs (1982). One of their key conclusions is that 'projects or services intended to reach rural women are more likely to take hold if they address the *priorities* of rural women and their families and the village' (1982, 216), presumably reflecting the fact that development approaches that did not do so were common. Despite its limitations, the study showed that new space had been created in which to discuss issues of gender. Knowledge about rural women turns out to be crucial to development practice: in her foreword, no less than Ester Boserup notes the key lesson that 'experts must first learn from the rural women before they can teach them' (Abdullah and Zeidenstein 1982, viii). And the study challenges the idea of the intractability of the 'woman issue', showing that rural women and their men were both more favourably inclined towards women's involvement in development projects than urban educated men in aid agencies and government.

A key and enduring critique of the dominant representations of women in Bangladesh is that they often take a 'utilitarian and manipulative stance towards women which seeks to reduce women to the status of means of social policy', chiefly to encourage them to have fewer children or to be 'harnessed to the cause of development' (Alam and Matin 1984, 9, 3). Social-scientific and public policy interest in women starts and ends with their contribution to development, such that development policy 'appears like a super ego in virtually every work on women in Bangladesh' (White 1992, 18). White further argues that the

> changing imagery of Bangladeshi women—from a 'backward' sector 'left out' by development, through 'human resources' or 'resource managers' to the passive 'target' of programmes aimed to reduce their fertility and draw them into capitalist production—originates in the aid community, rather than in Bangladeshi society itself. (White 1992, 19)

It seems unarguable that the specific language and concepts used to define and describe women and their material and social concerns start with the concerns of aid. But it is worth asserting again that the history of the emergence of women's issues suggests that aid was applying its own projectized language and categorizations to a setting of social decline and profound human crisis about which little could be understood, let alone changed. Into the platitudinous blandness of some of this early aid research on women we can read an understandable effort to sanitize the horrors and pain and render them, literally, manageable.

4.6 Implications of Women's Citizenship in the Emerging Social Contract

In later chapters we will look in more detail at how public policy has transformed the lives of women and girls and the roles they have played in their country's transformation. But for now, we explore two examples of the changing terms of the social contract between women, society, and the state. The first is the strength, firmness, and multiplicity of opposition to violence against women in social movements and in the law. Levels of violence are high in absolute and relative terms, and a significant minority remains supportive of patriarchal norms: for instance, a third of women of all ages agreed it was acceptable for husbands to beat their wives for infractions of the wifely code (burning dinner, going out without permission, refusing sex; NIPORT 2013). Almost three-quarters of men report having been violent towards their wives (World Bank 2007), between a quarter to two-thirds of Bangladeshi women experience violence from husbands in their lifetime, and women and girls routinely face violence, threats, and harassment from non-family men in public spaces.[13] Violence against women is relevant here not because its levels or forms have changed, but because of the institutionalized and powerful resistance it has engendered. Prominent, powerful, and organized sections of Bangladeshi society no longer accept male authority over women's bodies to the extent of violence, and have successfully organized their state to reduce the impunity, if not the prevalence, with which women experience violence. In this, they appear to have the support of the general population. This is a movement taking place at different levels, involving coalitions of actors across levels, classes, and sectors: community groups, national women's organizations like Mahila Parishad and Nari Pokkho, development NGOs, parts of the mass media, the state machinery, and international human rights mechanisms and networks.[14] Resistance to violence signals a growing assertiveness to refuse patriarchal rights to commit violence against women, whether wives or women who transgress patriarchal norms by being in public spaces (and are therefore 'legitimate' objects of violence).[15]

A second example of the growing citizenship of Bangladeshi women is in the institutionalization of social protection against the crises inherent in the life-cycle. Again, this displaces old patriarchal responsibilities that were largely honoured in the breach. The institutionalization of what in Bangladesh is known as the social safety net has been noticeable in the wake of the global food, fuel, and financial shocks of the early twenty-first century (see, for instance, GoB 2012). But recent changes to the state safety net build on a system that has developed over the decades, partly motivated by democratic–clientelistic political competition, partly by the drive to absorb more and use aid better, and partly, too, because these imperatives align with state policy to protect the poorest. This has been present across regimes, but most expansionary and explicit under Awami League majority rule in the democratic period since 1991. It is early to say whether recent efforts to strengthen the social safety net will foster women's citizenship, but programmes set up in the post-famine period set the stage for the transformation of the relationship between women and the state, and indeed organized non-state action. Chief

[13] See Table 7.1 in World Bank (2007, 90–1).

[14] See for instance, the 8th official submission to CEDAW, the Convention on the Elimination of all forms of Discrimination Against Women (GoB 2015).

[15] There is a large literature examining the distribution, sources, and character of violence against women in Bangladesh. These include cross-country comparative analyses of prevalence by the World Health Organization (García-Moreno et al. 2005; Garcia-Moreno et al. 2006). Ruchira Naved has produced an exhaustive body of work on the nature, extent, and correlates of violence experienced by women in Bangladesh (e.g. Naved and Persson 2010; Naved 2013). Much work is also devoted to exploring the relationship between women's involvement in paid work, micro-enterprise, and other 'non-traditional' activities (Schuler et al. 1998; Heath 2014).

among these has been the Vulnerable Group Development[16] (VGD) programme, known locally as the '*dustho mata* (destitute mothers') card'. This was a World Food Program (WFP)-supported scheme through which rural political representatives channel a regular ration of foodgrains to cardholders supposedly selected as the most needy. As need far outstrips supply and there is no formal accountability in the process, the card is among the rents which local political patrons distribute among the lowest layers of their client-base. In fact, although the bureaucratic governance of the programme is weak to non-existent, the political incentives to ensure the cards mostly reach poor women are fairly strong; the programme is a prime example of an intervention that succeeds by 'going with the grain' of local political power arrangements (see Hossain 2007a). In variations to the core food transfer scheme, there have been training and other initiatives by NGOs and donors to 'graduate' these women into micro-finance schemes, frequently in a bid to reduce their dependence and integrate them into the market.[17] But at its core, the programme protects a large number of vulnerable women from absolute destitution. It also gives them a recognizable stake in 'getting on the list'—seeing and being seen by the state (see also Chatterjee 2004; Corbridge et al. 2005).

The VGD programme was established under military rule in 1975, immediately following the economic and political crises in which the assassination of the nationalist Sheikh Mujib sparked off a series of coups, the last of which installed the military leader Zia Rahman in power, where he remained until his assassination in 1981. VGD was a product of both its time and the aid 'tilt' of the Zia regime. The 1974 famine taught donors that government food stocks were precarious and in need of further donor support, and that food aid needed to be targeted to the poor. The new regime was by no means on the left, despite having come to power on the back of a leftist coup; but the particular political context and constraints lent it a discernibly pro-poor tendency (discussed further in Chapter 6). Zia was a pragmatist rather than an ideologue who submitted to international donor community pressures (Sobhan 1982). These directions included market orientation, against the statist economic management that had characterized Awami League 'socialism', as well as interventions targeted to the poor. The Vulnerable Group Feeding (VGF) (as it was originally called—not to be confused with an existing intervention that now takes that name) came about as part of this wider reorientation, and it reflected the beginnings of a move away from universalist

[16] Originally the Vulnerable Group Feeding programme, not to be confused with the current Vulnerable Group Feeding programme which has a somewhat different purpose and means.

[17] See Matin and Hulme (2003) for an analysis of the lessons of the long-running BRAC extension of the VGD programme. Also Lewis (1993) for a critical view of the preference for integrating poor Bangladeshi women into markets rather than building welfare systems.

rations programmes which, despite their rhetoric, had favoured the politically organized urban middle classes at the expense of the rural poor (see Chowdhury and Haggblade 2000).

VGD is not a progressive programme by contemporary standards. Very poor women are required to queue for hours for deliberately public handouts that highlight their destitution and dependence, often to receive foodgrains of inferior quality. There are no effective grievance mechanisms, and the rationing of the cards means that there is no effective right to such protection: if you get a card, you are lucky. But if you are unlucky, no matter how severe your need or deserving your case, there is neither a formal rights basis on which to demand it nor a formal legal basis through which to claim it. Informally, however, a local political leader who fails to provide a card for visibly destitute elderly women will lose political capital, and, worse, may even be subject to public shaming or, if particularly egregious, to threats (Hossain 2010b). The programme works despite weak systems of command and control because of how society and politics are configured: local elites are not so detached or distant from the poor people they are supposed to serve that they can routinely afford to neglect them.

These are not the only and they may not be the best examples of the feminization of citizenship in Bangladesh, nor of development 'success'. But each adds an angle to the argument that the patriarchal bargain broke because women could no longer afford to rely on their men to provide and protect, they have been pushed into laying claims on the state, and (partly to attract aid) the state has taken up some of that slack. It has done so for better and for worse, and women and girls in contemporary Bangladesh experience new and different disciplines and controls to those that constrained them under the old patriarchal bargain. But although the process has not been unambiguously empowering for women, there can be little doubt that their incomplete release from the customary patriarchal bargain to be reincorporated as citizens has been crucial to the advances of human development in Bangladesh. There should also be no doubt that the state has been foundational in permitting and enabling these new incorporations, as it extends its reach into the most personal (but no longer private) domains of homes and families, bodily practices, and sexual relationships.

The mandate to address gender was by no means accepted with alacrity by the society or its governing elites in the first instance. Several of the truths that needed confronting and the new ways of being that a recognition of women entailed amounted to attacks on deeply personal and private matters of sex and sexuality; marriage, family, home, and kin; honour, shame, and status. But the extremes of destitution and desperation that became unignorable in the wake of the war brought the joint issues of gender and poverty to the policy table. Once women had been recognized as citizens and development agents in their own right, it was a short step to operationalizing the knowledge that gender relations held the key to the human-development challenge in public policy and social action. Somewhat later, the interest in the nimble fingers of an endless stream of apparently docile female workers gave the pay-off to an ideology of women's economic empowerment—an ideology that perfectly accommodates the spirit of globalized capitalism.[18]

There has never been an important challenge to the national development ideology of women's economic empowerment: to the extent that this succeeded, it was a classic example of strong winners (public policymakers seeking donor approval and funding; NGOs seeking the same but also winning formulae and replicable models; a strong, cross-class women's movement with useful coalitions across other civil society actors; industrial elites benefiting from effective subsidies from state and society) and weak losers (the dispersed power of the local landed elite, who gained as much or more than they lost from women's advancement; the Islamic right—weak and localized to date, with little to gain ideologically or materially from opposing the economic advancement of extremely poor women).

In the forty years since independence, women have mostly consolidated and extended the terms of their engagement in the social contract, becoming the objects of both protection and control. We will explore this further as we look at how women have increasingly pushed for and are being treated by the state as citizens in their own right, with their own concerns; the growing extent of gender equality in the middle classes, particularly as a result of public service employment; and the priority given to social protection, which primarily serves women at vulnerable stages of the life-cycle. Progressive forces and organizations, including civil society organizations and NGOs, have played a major role, often with the backing of aid. And there have also been backlashes at local and national levels against women's mobility and freedom in particular, but also against women's rights to organize as workers. These changes have frequently been viewed as evidence of women's empowerment in Bangladesh, but it may be more appropriate to see them as evidence of the declining relevance of the traditional patriarchal bargain, and its replacement with a social contract between citizen and state. This may loosen the domination of one set of patriarchal institutions, but the terms on which the state, the market, and global institutions contract with Bangladeshi women come with their own controls and domination—as well as benefits and sources of power.

[18] On which, see (Fraser 2012).

5

1974

5.1 An Eloquent Silence

By the best estimates, one and a half million Bangladeshis—2 per cent of the population at the time—died because of the 1974 famine.[1] And yet the fortieth anniversary of this event passed without marker. There were no newspaper articles or documentary films, no commemorative artworks or calls for memorials or commissions of inquiry. There were no statements in parliament. The exception, as ever, proves the rule: the critically acclaimed 2013 novel *The Black Coat*, the only recent and first fictional account of the famine of 1974, met a muted response in the country in which it was set.[2]

It is easy to read this lack of public discussion as neglect or indifference. The famine is not part of public discourse or official history. But it is privately

[1] There is no official history or account of the famine to my knowledge, but the figure that 27,000 died, based on the recorded statement of Sheikh Mujib in 1974, appears to serve as an official statistic. It is most likely derived from *langarkhana* (feeding camp) records, but as these were under extremely weak administration, there is no reason to believe they are credible estimates. As deaths attributed to the famine according to conventional methodologies continued well into 1975, and the 1974 famine is considered to be one of the best-documented famines of all time due to the study by M. Alamgir (Devereux 2000), I refer to the more conventional assessment of famine mortalities, which is that 1.5 million people died from starvation or (as is more usual in times of famine) of starvation-related illness. The famine victims were already weakened by displacement, war, and the longer processes of impoverishment which they had faced and so were highly vulnerable. The floods and food crisis of 1974 should probably be understood to have contributed in part to these deaths, serving as triggers rather than supplying the full causal explanation: if these people had not already been very poor, undernourished, and in bad health, the effects of the famine are unlikely to have been so catastrophic. See Currey (1978) on the 'famine syndrome'.

[2] Personal communication with the author, Neamat Imam, in 2014. Other observers agree that the book has probably been deliberately overlooked; see http://www.livemint.com/Opinion/BoMfueB5Vp6FDYWJUfxGCP/POLITICAL-ANIMALS-An-authors-lament.html (accessed 10 December 2014). Although it was favourably reviewed in the *Daily Star*, Bangladesh's leading English language daily, the reviewer was Indian. Imam has yet to be invited to the Hay Festival of literature in Dhaka, which usually includes published writers of Bangladeshi origin working in English. I have no way of knowing if this oversight is deliberate or the effect of the middle-class avoidance of the famine that I discuss above or some other factor, but it seems significant nonetheless.

remembered by Bangladeshis of a certain age, with, I think, a mix of shame and guilt. The episode occupies part of the collective memory of that period, and for some tarnishes the glories of the liberation war victory. Far from being forgotten, the tragedy has left a heavy imprint on public policy and politics. We know this not because it is discussed widely and deeply—not since the early 1980s has there been much scholarly examination of the famine, and (unlike 1943) it has rarely been represented artistically and culturally—but because every so often governments face tests like those faced by the government of 1974, and in the responses of political elites and officials we can hear the repetition of the hard lessons of 1974. We hear them, too, in popular expectations of government. Occasionally, public figures refer to 1974 as a turning point in their life story. More often it is a silent signifier, the point that no one needs to make.[3]

Two factors shaped how the famine influenced the future direction of development. The first was acceptance that preventing famine was crucial to the legitimacy and power of rule; the second a more personal moral imperative at work in how the elite came to conceptualize their responsibilities as rulers, closely shaped by the relative affinity between the elites and the masses, a relationship that had been politicized by the contentious historical differences between (oppressive) ruling classes and ruled masses. That the famine meant the loss of legitimacy of the heroic nationalist leadership is common knowledge. It is well known that protecting Bangladesh against food shocks has been a policy priority since 1974, and the reasons why are no secret, either: no government could sustain rule over a population of this size and fractiousness without its consent. And that consent has come to rest, at a minimum, on action to prevent death by starvation. It seems a minimal commitment, but in an economy and ecology as fragile as that of Bangladesh, the assurance of protection against acute hunger has mattered, again and again.

What has not been appreciated is that it was in the aftermath of—and arguably because of—the famine that Bangladesh set out on its distinctive development pathway. It is the famine that added several vital elements to the Bangladesh success story, specifically a pioneering approach to the gender–poverty nexus and an early (compared to other LDCs) emphasis on food security and social protection for the poor and vulnerable. Underpinning these shifts in public policy was a tacit renegotiation of the political settlement. The experience of the famine crafted a political culture of accountability between ruler and ruled, which meant that whatever happened, and at whatever cost—whether to ideology, longer-term planning, short-term political

[3] It seems the same is true of the Irish famine of 1848–52, which 'until recently was publicly invisible while, paradoxically, remaining part of most Irish people's consciousness' (Kinealy 1994).

expedience, the interests of the middle classes and the elites—action had to be taken to make sure poor people were not left hungry.

The political culture of accountability for hunger did not mean a rush to embrace neoliberalism in public policy, although a shift in that direction did follow. Nor did it mean the ideological opposite—greater control of the economy—although there were signs of that, too, in the food economy after the famine. What 1974 did was create a moral economic restraint on public policy, in which its pursuit of economic growth was tempered by distributive concerns, and its effectiveness in achieving national development goals judged against what was happening to the poor. Another way of saying this is that after 1974, policy and political elites knew they had to find a way of making it work for the poor, and this imperative opened the policy space up to a range of alternative approaches and innovations that were not on the policy table elsewhere. We will look at the effects of 1974 in Chapter 6. Here we focus on understanding what happened.

5.2 Accounting for 1974

> Naturally, the government of the day bore the greatest responsibility as famine always brings discredit to any government. It is considered a mark of a government's failure that in its watch people died for want of food i.e. the most basic necessity of life. (Islam 2003, 221)

> Famines occur because they are not prevented; they are allowed to happen. Most food crises have a long gestation period—not days or weeks, but months or years—so failures of public action must be incorporated into the causal analysis of all famines. (Devereux 2000, 27)

The conditions in which the famine unfolded were exceptionally difficult. The room for manoeuvre by the government of the time was constrained by financial, practical, and domestic and international political factors, and the removal of the crutch of the post-war relief operation revealed that Bangladesh could not yet stand on its own (Maniruzzaman 1975a, 117). Unique though the circumstances were, the Bangladesh experience had much in common with other famines in this era, a time when technical problems of food production and supply had been solved yet post-colonial conflict and geopolitics were turning food into the ultimate weapon of war (Devereux 2000). All famines are a one-off concatenation of circumstances, but the Bangladesh famine could only have happened because of processes of socio-economic and political rupture and adjustment that were also at work in Ethiopia, India, the Sahel, and Biafra.

There are four main explanations of the famine, and we look at each in turn.

5.3 'Natural Calamities'

> In some places this happens, but we have our open free kitchen everywhere, people are welcome to come there. And they have come. We have camps, still we have not closed all our camps . . . people have started working in the fields now. But of course, this trouble is there. Such a serious flood, serious famine. We have not . . . we have not suppressed the news. We have already declared in the Parliament that about, round about 27,000 people have died by starvation. And of, by disease. We have not hide anything from anybody. It is a fact, natural calamities.
>
> (Sheikh Mujibur Rahman, interview with John Pilger in 'An Unfashionable Tragedy', 1974: Pilger 1975 6:23–7:06)

> First the floods, then the famine. So runs the capsule story of the Bangladesh famine of 1974. (Sen 1981, 131)

The floods were severe in 1974, and had the Jamuna River not burst its banks six times between June and August, 1.5 million Bangladeshis may not have starved and sickened to death. But natural calamities are never purely ecological: there is a politics to who is afflicted, and a politics to how they are managed. As the common views blame either government mismanagement or Cold War politics, it is important to recognize that the 1974 floods were extremely serious. One observer noted that although lower than the devastating floods of 1955, the 1974 floods were more destructive: the Jamuna was above danger levels for longer, and the Teesta, the main tributary to join the Jamuna from the Himalayas, was above the danger level for twenty-nine days in 1974, whereas in 1955 it never reached that peak. The erosion rate along river banks with population densities of 2,000 per square mile 'would have suddenly imposed 24,000 people without homes or lands on the already run-down rural infrastructure between June and October 1974' (Currey 1978, 90–1).

Natural disasters are frequent in the region, and mass starvation has also happened episodically. But these had rarely come at once (Alamgir 1980). The cyclone of 1970, the war and displacement, and inflation meant most people living in poverty had already been under-nourished for five or more years, so that millions of Bangladeshis were already physically weakened by the time food prices spiked in August. A 1975–6 nutrition survey found that dietary intake and calorie intake levels had worsened in the previous twelve years—fully 59 per cent of the rural population were now eating below the 2,122 recommended minimum calories—and that *every member of every family* with less than three acres of land was found to be deficient in calories, vitamins, and minerals (Franda 1981b). Many people are extremely poor and under-nourished in present-day Bangladesh, but the severity and scale of the problem in the 1970s are hard to imagine, even with the benefit of contemporary accounts (some of which will be included below).

In such a setting it may be correct to view famine as the logical conclusion of impoverishment, triggered by specific events, but not in itself a discrete occurrence (Currey 1992). But even if the famine was a low point in a cumulative process of shocks and decline, the floods marked the point of no return. In the most authoritative account of 1974, a study based on survey work and personal observation, floods were assigned a causal role:

> It would be premature to attribute the 1974 Bangladesh famine entirely to the flood, but there is no denying that the flood accentuated human suffering that was already in evidence, and all those families who were living well below poverty level, finally succumbed to the pressure. By the end of July, the scenario in all flood-affected regions of the country, was flood leading to loss of human and cattle life, loss of agricultural land and crops, loss of homestead, and loss of employment, all of which combined to lead to starvation and outbreak of epidemic diseases (particularly cholera), the situation being further compounded by shortage of fresh drinking water and prevalence of high prices of all essentials . . . By the beginning of August reports of excess deaths poured in from all over the country, particularly from the areas severely hit by the flood, such as Rangpur district. Our field investigator in that area learned that by the middle of July, the death began to rise sharply. (Alamgir 1980, 126–7)

The 1974 monsoon floods gave the government a figleaf to cover its failure to protect the most vulnerable, and an excuse to seek help. Foreign aid was crucial at this moment, when a worsening balance of payments and low foreign exchange reserves were more than matched by problems of food supply both domestic and international, as commodity prices shot up with the fuel-price crisis. But the patience of the aid donors was wearing thin after nearly three years of independence, as the government showed willing to settle into a habit of living hand-to-mouth, relying on food aid and relief operations from the international community.[4] The floods—for which no amount of official incompetence or corruption could be blamed—got the government momentarily off the hook, but at a price:

> In 1974 the government ignored indications of possible famine early in the year. When severe floods were experienced in July, August and September, however, it was facing pressure from donors and a foreign exchange crisis. The government assisted foreign journalists in their coverage of the floods and they made the most of the crisis to increase foreign aid. Some observers formed the impression that the government was 'crying wolf' and exaggerating the flood damage. As the flood waters receded, foreign interest and the government response waned. Then, through September the first waves of migrants started arriving in the cities and

[4] For the aid donor perspective, see (McHenry and Bird 1977). For the position from within the government, from the vantage point of the Planning Ministry, see Nurul Islam's account (Chapter 10, 'What was it about the 1974 famine?' in Islam 2003).

> when journalists again visited the countryside in October famine was obvious, severe and unstoppable. The death toll had mounted and stayed high throughout the following year. (Crow 1984, 1757)

Having made capital out of the floods, the government was left to fend for itself when the wolf finally came. Repeated pleas for help and images of destitute and desperate Bangladeshis had 'immunized' the international community by late 1974. We can recover that sense of Bangladesh-fatigue from John Pilger's impassioned introduction to 'An Unfashionable Tragedy', his film about the famine:

> I saw four dead children this morning, heaped on a stretcher. One of them was about 18 months old, and I could tell this because his feet were about the same size as my own son's. The rest of him was so thin and tortured that he no longer looked human. I'm told that he died from diarrhoea after eating poisoned leaves, because there was nothing else to eat. In other words, he starved to death. Of course he didn't have to die. But unfortunately the cost of keeping him alive was inflationary. Some milk powder and a handful of grain everyday would have cost at least twenty pence.
>
> I must apologize. This really isn't appropriate New Year television, is it? Especially with all our own problems of inflation in Britain. Indeed, before I came here I was told, many times, don't do Bangladesh, people won't watch it. They'll switch over. And of course, I can sympathize with people who do switch over. Because I realize that I and other reporters have helped to immunize people against Bangladesh, by reporting their horrors, year after year.
>
> ('An Unfashionable Tragedy' 1975; transcription by the author)

Popular opinion in the West was ready to 'switch over' and donor officials were increasingly restive. A valid concern was that humanitarian assistance would feed domestic political competition and corruption, and not the starving rural masses. Food and other aid was regularly converted into budget support, a practice which dated back to the cosy relationship between the Pakistan government and the US, the main food donor.[5]

In mid-1974, there were no good reasons to believe that emergency food aid would be used to feed hungry people fleeing floods. Confidential cables from the US Embassy briefing the Secretary of State, Henry Kissinger, on what to expect on his visit in October 1974 noted that:

> WITH THE ONSET OF THE UNUSUALLLY (sic) HEAVY MONSOONAL FLOODING IN JULY, [the Bangladesh Government] QUICKLY BEGAN A CAMPAIGN TO OBTAIN CONTRIBUTIONS FROM THE INNTERNATIONAL (sic) COMMUNITY

[5] During the 1970 cyclone, for instance, the US took the 'unusual' (by a USAID staffer's assessment) step of supplying food aid in the form of Title II; this meant it was possible for the government to sell the aid on the open market, rather than directing it straight to those in need (McHenry and Bird 1977).

> FOR FLOOD RELIEF. HOWEVER, IT WAS SOON EVIDENT THAT THE BDG [the Bangladesh Government], WHILE CONCERNED OVER THE DAMAGE WHICH WAS BEING DONE BY THE FLOOD, ALSO CONCLUDED THAT A CAMPAIGN FOR RELIEF OF HUMANITARIAN GROUNDS COULD WELL SUPPLEMENT ITS EFFORTS TO OBTAIN BUDGET SUPPORT, PARTICULARLY IF RELIEF WERE TO TAKE THE FORM OF FOOD SUPPLIES... (US Embassy Dacca 1974b).

In preparation for Kissinger's one and only visit to Bangladesh, a quick stop-off en route to somewhere more important, the 'basket case' epithet looked increasingly accurate.

In September, another, less serious flood hit six northern districts. Although it quickly receded, disease and hunger were by this time widespread, and official starvation figures showed an upsurge. The government made an emergency appeal for food aid and on 24 September the Prime Minister acknowledged the existence of famine and opened 4,300 *langarkhana* (or feeding camps) to feed up to three million people per day.

5.4 Entitlement Failures and Famine Economics

The floods gave the Minister for Food a reason to recalculate the food gap to at least three million tons, up from an already alarming 1.7 million tons (Alamgir 1980, 129). But was it because there was not enough food that people starved? This point is unresolved. Sen notes that crop production of rice and wheat was higher in 1974 than in 1971–3 or 1975, and that the worst affected districts (Mymensingh, Rangpur, and Sylhet) saw increased output in the year of the famine: '[w]hatever the Bangladesh famine of 1974 might have been, it wasn't a FAD (food availability decline) famine' (Sen 1981, 141). Yet looked at closely, the picture is mixed: Alamgir argues that production was one thing, availability quite another. Regional differences, decimated infrastructure, and fears about forcible procurement meant food was unevenly available. Smuggling to India was probably a major factor in uneven food availability and price rises, so that 'one cannot altogether reject the hypothesis that the 1974 famine in Bangladesh was partly caused by foodgrain availability decline' (Alamgir 1980, 239).

Economists may not agree on the role played by food availability, but they agree that people could not command the available food. This is the foundation of Sen's entitlement theory, and it is no surprise that this theory cut its teeth on the famines of this region—these were episodes in which the human misfortunes of natural events were compounded by the failures of markets and public authorities to respond. Sen argued that many famines occurred not because food was unavailable, but because people suddenly lacked entitlement to it—because they could not exchange labour for food or wages, or because other entitlements—public relief or charity—were unavailable. Why people suddenly lose their entitlements is a larger question, and one which Sen, neither a political scientist nor a sociologist, has answered less well (Devereux 2000; Dowlah 2006).

Wages and prices explained the economics of lost entitlements: real wages were hit hard by the floods, particularly because labour-intensive jute production was down that year. Agricultural wage labourers, the hardest-hit group, saw their real wages decline by 40 per cent between 1969 and 1974, and the wage in rice equivalent by 60 per cent (Alamgir 1980; Osmani 1991). The real agricultural wage declined by 43 per cent in the year between the monsoons of 1973 and 1974 alone (Alamgir 1980, 311).

While the floods may have triggered a sudden drop in wages, it was probably longer-term decline and overall poverty that led to people starving in such large numbers (Ravallion 1997). This sudden drop came on top of an extended period of declining real wages, the result of a fast-growing rural population, the decline in the jute trade (global factors again), and new 'Green Revolution' technologies. Osmani takes a long view, explaining that the asset base or endowments of people facing famine had been eroded so substantially over such a long period of time that they had little with which to cope when the floods came, prices rose, and wages and work were suddenly entirely inadequate for feeding families:

> [I]t is possible to argue that entitlement failure in 1974 turned out to be as precipitous as it was mainly because of severe entitlement contraction that had occurred in the preceding years, partly through natural calamities and partly through the destructions and dislocations caused by a prolonged war of liberation. The destruction of assets (houses, cattle, etc) caused by these events was a direct dent in the 'endowment set', especially for the rural people. Endowment contractions of this kind must have accentuated the gravity of the famine.
>
> (Osmani 1991, 332)

The sharp rise in the average rice price (see Figure 5.1) raises questions, particularly as food shortages appear to have been highly localized. But like declining real wages, the food price rises in 1974 came on top of an extended period of inflation, at least some of which was rooted in inflationary pressures from the global economy (Hossain 1999). The wholesale price of coarse rice ranged from (in prices per maund/37kg in Bangladesh *taka*) the high 30s to the high 40s from 1968 until 1972, when it rose to nearly 80, reaching 105 the next year and peaking at 223 at the height of the famine period (Alamgir 1980, 260). Like the sharp decline in real wages, the spike in food prices does appear to have been connected to the floods—not because they caused food shortages, but because of expectations that they could.

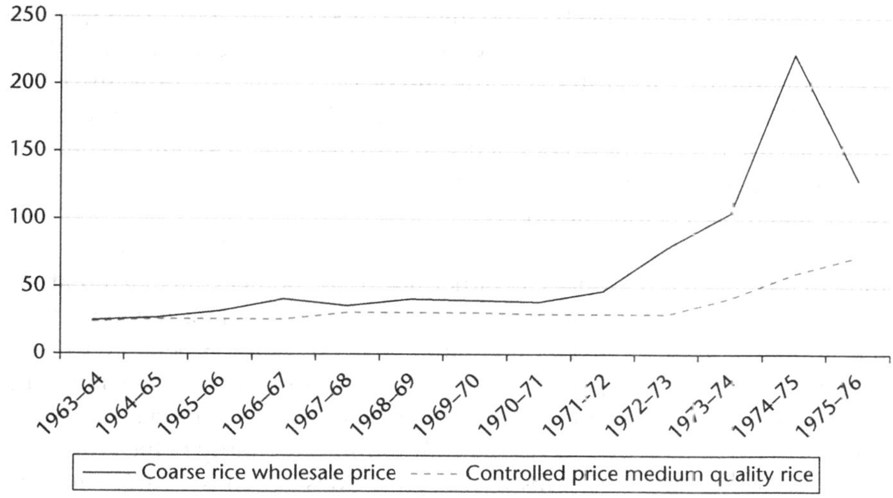

Figure 5.1. Rice price rises in 1974 (in Bangladesh taka)
Source: Calculated from Alamgir (1980, 260, Table 7.1).

Why then did prices spike in 1974? Public opinion was strongly behind the explanation that illegal speculative hoarding and smuggling were at work. The Prime Minister himself said that 'a group of sharks, hoarders, smugglers, profiteers and black-marketeers were trading on human miseries' (from *The Bangladesh Observer*, 23 September 1974, cited in Ravallion 1985, 15). A generalized suspicion of the grain trade and strong support for food commodity market regulation in Bangladesh comes from the belief that sudden food price spikes are the result of speculation and other 'sharp practices' through which food markets are manipulated, by well-connected businesspersons, to profit from dearth; these views continue to be an important part of the popular political ideologies (or moral economy) of food crises.[6] In 1974, fears of speculation were most likely true. Evidence indicates that grain traders speculated that prices would rise far higher than they eventually did, because of exaggerated predictions of massive crop damage from the floods (Ravallion 1985; Del Ninno, Dorosh, and Smith 2003; Quddus and Becker 2000).

[6] This dates at least to the famine starting in 1943, but may pre-date even that famine. Suspicion of the grain trade and its role in creating 'artificial' famines (that is, those not caused by aggregate declines in food availability) is probably found further afield than Bengal, but it appears to have a particular power in this area because of its history. For anthropological and sociological accounts of 'moral economy' understandings of the grain trade in this part of Bengal, see Greenough (1982); Greenough (1983); Hossain and Kalita (2014); Hossain and Jahan (2014). Participatory research in 1979 found that people who had experienced famine made detailed analyses of the local political economy of foodgrain marketing, including its impacts on the poor and connections with political power (BRAC 1992).

(Note the further tragic effects of 'crying wolf' about the floods.) This speculative behaviour built on years of feared food shortages, brought to a head by the steep drop in public food stocks at the end of 1973, after six consecutive bad harvests from 1971 to 1973, and 'a drastic reduction in public distribution . . . [which led to] the collapse of confidence in the government's ability to stabilise the price situation in the coming months' (Islam 2003, 223). Prices started to rise in March, well before the floods.

Smuggling also played a role, but how significant cannot be established. One study that compared rice prices on either side of the border concluded that the differentials were not big enough to signal large-scale smuggling, but its findings were critiqued on methodological grounds, and smuggling is believed to have taken place on a very large scale.[7] The army's diagnosis—that smuggling on a scale that threatened national security happened because politicians not only turned a blind eye but also turned a profit—almost certainly helped rationalize the series of military coups a year later (Mascarenhas 1986). And the personal interest that the Deputy Chief of Staff (later President) Zia Rahman took in this matter says something about the impact of the famine on first-hand witnesses (Islam 2003). As we will see, food security, or the avoidance of food-price shocks, became a priority in the Zia regime. The economists could not prove it, but smuggling on a large scale probably contributed to the famine, enabled by political support at the highest levels. Food prices dropped dramatically after Sheikh Mujib's assassination, when private grain traders and dealers dumped stocks to avoid being caught for smuggling or hoarding, in recognition of the fact that they had lost their political protection (McHenry and Bird 1977).

5.5 The Politics of Food Aid

Food aid played a role, but perhaps was not the smoking gun it is often assumed to be. The impacts of food aid were at once less serious as a direct cause of the famine, and more so among the structural factors that made it inevitable. Food aid was vital to the Bangladesh economy, as it had been to that of East Pakistan, ensuring donors significant leverage over government. Since 1971, food aid disbursements (excluding loans) averaged USD 143

[7] Alamgir was among those who argued that it was possible, indeed likely, that smuggling circuits started not in border districts, which were policed, but in more central areas, and transported by riverboat. When the borders were effectively closed in 1975, the rate at which domestically grown foodgrains were absorbed into the national economy (i.e., not smuggled to India) improved (Alamgir 1980, 237). McHenry and Bird make a similar point with respect to the price of rice after 1975.

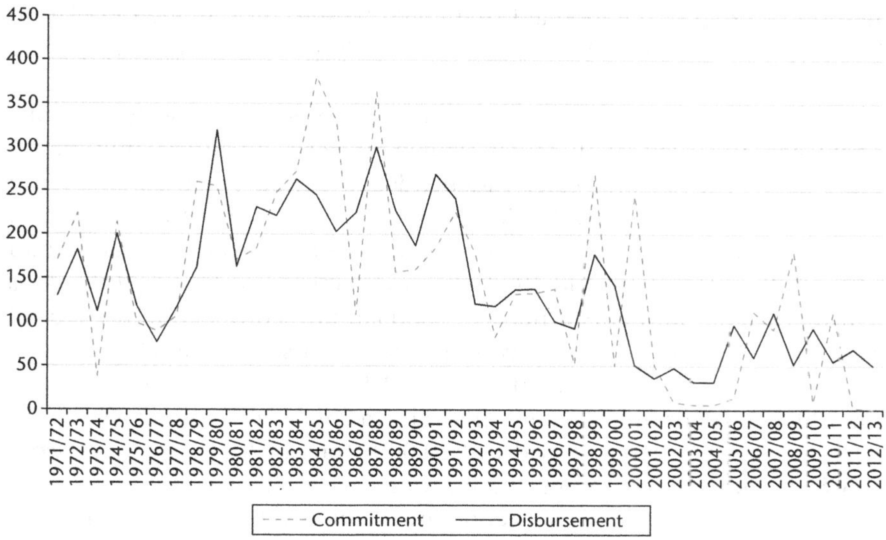

Figure 5.2. The value of food aid (USD millions)
Source: Flow of external resources into Bangladesh 2012/13 (ERD 2014).

million per year (see Figure 5.2), declining steadily after the 1970s; recent figures totalled USD 50 million, chiefly earmarked for poverty-focused schemes.[8] Of the USD 60 billion of aid disbursed to Bangladesh to date, nearly USD 7 billion has been food (ERD 2014). US food aid provided one-third of food imports and 40 per cent of food aid well into the 1990s. Until 1987, food aid distributed under the US Public Law 480 (PL480) alone was the equivalent of 10 per cent of export earnings (USAID 1997).

In the 1950s, the key purpose of PL480 was to offload US grain surpluses and create markets for American foodgrains, a strategy that was so successful in food-insecure East Pakistan that it was credited with permanently changing Bengali food culture by introducing wheat bread. Remarkably, relieving hunger only became an objective of PL480 in the 1960s (Atwood et al. 2000). In a poor country like Bangladesh, the volume of food aid meant it became vital to the operations of the government—and therefore to maintaining the terms of the political settlement. Its importance in helping structure and reproduce the political economy dated to pre-independence times, when food aid was used to finance rural development programming under the Basic Democrats programme. From the 1960s, food aid became an important source of budget support, sold and used as government revenue (Atwood et al. 2000). This was possible because some 71 per cent of PL480 was in

[8] Author's calculations from Economic Relations Division data (ERD 2014).

the form of programme food aid that could be sold on the open market to fill the government's coffers, rather than going direct to hungry people (USAID 1997).

Food aid was so extensive that it became an important subsidy to public sector wages (see Clay 1979), and is blamed for weak agricultural investment in the East Pakistan and early independence period (World Bank 1977; Franda 1981b; Ahmed, Haggblade, and Chowdhury 2000). In the first two years of independence, food aid was supplied mainly through humanitarian channels. But already by mid-1973, the government was having difficulties securing the commitments it needed. Food aid flows dropped in the crucial year of 1973/4 because of global commodity price rises, donor fatigue due to corruption and mismanagement, and the US withholding PL480 (Atwood et al. 2000). According to one insider, in mid-1973 the government requested 300,000 (later revised to 220,000) tons of food assistance from the US, 10 per cent of the estimated food gap of 2.2 million tons (Islam 2003). Even then, more than a year before the floods that triggered the 1974 famine, the government of Bangladesh appeared to have read the reluctance of the US correctly, as the request was repeated again that summer and again in early 1974.

World food prices were high at this time, and as its stocks dwindled, the Bangladesh government was forced to try commercial imports. But the government was in effect bankrupt, hit particularly hard by the global commodity price rises of 1973–4 and the need to pay hard currency for food imports it had hoped would be covered by aid. Two large grain contracts with US suppliers were cancelled because the government was considered insufficiently creditworthy (Rothschild 1976). Sobhan hints at collusion between the grain traders and US officials, aiming to 'bring Bangladesh to its knees' (1979, 1978).

Islam notes that the government of Bangladesh was still expecting US food aid when the US Ambassador dropped the bombshell in May 1974: because Bangladesh had agreed to sell Cuba jute sacks worth USD million, it could not have food aid under PL480, which bans trade with communist countries by recipients. Why the US government chose that moment to remember this rule, apparently ignored for other (more geopolitically important) countries like Egypt (Hossain 1999; Dowlah 2006), is not recorded. Islam recalls that even when the government of Bangladesh cancelled any future trade, the US government lawyers stalled, arguing that Bangladesh was technically still trading with Cuba. The jute sacks were shipped in October 1974, after which the food aid agreement was finally signed, a year after the initial request. 'This grim drama', recalls Sobhan, 'was being transacted in the capital city in the full view and knowledge of the US embassy as to the nature and gravity of the crisis' (1979, 1979).

Whether or not the timely shipment of PL480 would have made the difference is contentious, as it is not clear how much would have gone to the relief effort in any case (Islam 2003).[9] This is because food aid would have entered the Public Food Distribution System (PFDS), the official system for distributing subsidized or free foodgrains that had been in place in the region since 1943, and the PFDS had neither the mandate nor necessarily the administrative machinery with which to prioritize the needs of the rural landless poor. The organization of the PFDS will be discussed in more detail presently. But in order to assess the difference a more timely shipment of PL480 might have made, it is important to understand that in 1974 food aid would likely have been absorbed by the Modified Rationing channel reserved for rural populations. This was the channel that got what was left after the main beneficiaries under the Statutory Rationing channel (covering government servants and the main urban populations) had been served. Although directed to rural areas, Modified Rationing never targeted the landless rural poor effectively, and much of what they were supposed to get never reached them because of corruption (Chowdhury 1988; Chowdhury 1986). So it seems unlikely that more grains pouring into the Modified Rationing channel would have made a significant difference in alleviating the distress of the starving rural population. Sobhan's view that 'as far as it is possible [Modified Rationing] represents a conscious attempt to reach the poorest segment of the population' is either disingenuous or uninformed (1979, 1975); after 1974, the government and its partners did find ways of reaching the poorest, and it was not through Modified Rationing. Nevertheless, Sobhan is correct in principle, because the timely arrival of PL480 food would have eased pressures on food prices, in particular by alleviating fears that the government was unable to intervene—fears that speculators exploited to good profit.

Why did the US government delay signing a food aid agreement, even when death by starvation was visible to US embassy officials? Sobhan seems clear that the Cuba-PL480 crisis was little more than an attempt to call Bangladesh to heel. The 'tilt' to Pakistan had endured in a generalized hostility to 'the Bengalees' which spilled over into food aid policy. US officials took the opportunity of a Washington DC visit by Finance Minister Tajuddin Ahmed to press for Bangladesh to stop war crimes proceedings against Pakistanis, presumably the quid pro quo for food aid, while Rothschild notes the US attempt to create a 'despairing chorus line' of food aid recipients to lobby OPEC to cut oil prices (1976, 295).

[9] Dowlah argues that it would not have mattered, but as he refers to an amount of 20,000 rather than 200,000 tons, it seems he underestimates the quantitative significance of the shortfall (Dowlah 2006).

Sobhan is clear that food aid was being used as a weapon against a regime whose overall agenda the US government did not approve of:

> Its decision to suspend PL-480 shipments to Bangladesh against pre-committed food aid on grounds of Bangladesh's miniscule exports of jute goods to Cuba should thus be seen not just as an attempt to constrain the regime's external relations, but as a direct assault on the viability of the regime. The political motivation underlying this embargo may be derived from the fact that at that time Kissinger sought a special dispensation for Sadat's Egypt to continue exporting cotton to Cuba while receiving US PL-480 commodity aid. Whether this assault on the stability of the Bangladesh regime, through creating a crisis in the local food market, was itself the prelude to the dislodgement in August 1975 of the post-liberation regime in Bangladesh remains open to fuller enquiry, though there is some circumstantial evidence to suggest that such might have been the premise to US economic policy towards Bangladesh in 1973–5.
>
> (Sobhan 1991, 104)

Sobhan is no doubt correct that the US government treated food aid as a source of power over a disaster-ridden, war-torn, broke Bangladesh (see also McHenry and Bird 1977). But it may have been less the pursuit of hard-headed strategic interests than the lack of interest—the low priority of these events in far-off, unimportant Bangladesh—that stalled US food aid. US officials thought the teeming millions of a third world hotspot had 'a "power" to let millions of children starve on television'; an Assistant Secretary of State responsible for US food policy found it '"hard to think of any real purpose when it comes to the Indian subcontinent"'(Rothschild 1976, 294). Declassified official cables suggest the US feared being embarrassed by their failure to help with famine relief. Negotiations around the Cuba issue went on in secret, because both sides wanted it that way. But once noticed, the regulations regarding Cuba could not be un-noticed; lawyerly attention to detail in Washington DC somehow took precedence over humanitarian disaster in Dhaka, partly because PL480 was law and not policy. It would have taken an executive order or legal amendment for USAID to have permitted the signing of the agreement. All of this suggests that the diagnosis of a bureaucratic 'bungle' is close to the mark (McHenry and Bird 1977).

Part of the story, then, appears to be Bangladesh's low priority in the geopolitical order. An executive order had been forthcoming to permit Egypt, whose people were not starving, to continue to receive PL480, but not Bangladesh, whose people were. A likely motivation for such discrimination is that an ideology of 'triage'—in brief, that resources should be concentrated on those likely to survive rather than those destined not to—was at work in the minds of at least some US policy types. Triage theory, or 'lifeboat ethics' in Garrett Hardin's formulation (1974), was popularized by a book-length prediction that the world as we knew it would come to an effective end with mass worldwide famine in 1975 (Paddock and Paddock 1968). The Paddocks' *Famine—1975!* now reads as a faintly amusing anachronism. This breathless account of the impending world food crisis is almost parodic in its Malthusian descriptions of copulating brown masses being fed by idealistic, misguided Peace Corps-types. And yet triage theory and lifeboats were deadly serious ideologies (Singer 1972). And the Paddock brothers were in key respects accurate when it came to Bangladesh, where 2 per cent of the population was lost to famine in 1974–5. The extent to which triage theory helped make its predictions come true is not known, but it was among the ideological baggage with which the US government addressed the Bangladesh famine (Rothschild 1976; Tweeten 2001).

The politics of food aid in 1974 may in fact not be that the US pursued important political objectives, but something more insidious, because the only interest served was ideological. At least some of its officials appear to have been inclined to let mass starvation occur because they were possessed of an ideology that told them that Bangladesh anyway had more people than it could do with, and here was as good a laboratory as any in which to see what might happen if the US did not act.

5.6 The Political Economy of Famine Relief

If adequate relief had been available, one and a half million Bangladeshis may not have died in 1974–5. But relief was not provided until it was too late, or it was inadequate to avert large-scale disaster. It is because of its failure to provide adequate relief that the Awami League government of the time is so widely blamed for the famine.

What was the source of this failure? The task was not impossible: both before and after 1974, major food crises were averted. In 1972 and 1973, despite harvest failures, the aftermath of war, the displacement of at least ten million people, and sharply rising food prices, mass starvation was avoided chiefly because relief was distributed to those who needed it, with the support of foreign food aid and non-governmental agencies. However, if, as some argue, famine was 'exported' to India in 1971–72 and not averted at all (Bose 1972; Chen and Rohde 1973), this helps to put the 1974 famine into perspective: barring a miraculous upgrade of administrative capacity, unprecedented donor generosity, and reliable weather, a food crisis was inevitable in those early years. As Khondker notes, '[t]he famine which was feared in 1971 arrived in 1974' (1985, 87). In 1979 and 1984, serious floods meant food shortages threatened again, but in those years mass starvation was avoided by managing public food stocks to keep prices steady and reaching those in need (Ahmed,

Haggblade, and Chowdhury 2000; E. Clay 1985; Crow 1984; Cutler 1985; Del Ninno, Dorosh, and Smith 2003; Osmani 1991).

5.6.1 *The* Langarkhanas

The government must have been aware the rural masses were starving before they announced their relief programme, because people were dying in the Dhaka streets by August:

> By the end of August, the whole of Bangladesh turned into an agonizing spectacle of confusion and human suffering. With the addition of the flood, it was 1943 re-enacted. Streams of hungry people (men, women and children), who were nothing but skeletons, trekked into towns in search of food. Most of them were half-naked. Events such as husbands deserting wives and children, or wives doing the same, parents trying to sell children, mothers killing babies out of frustration and anguish, man and dog fighting for a piece of bone, women and young girls turning to prostitution became very commonplace. (Alamgir 1980, 128–9)

By September the situation was worse: Anjuman Mufidul Islam recorded a fourteen-fold increase in the numbers of unclaimed bodies on the streets of Dhaka, to 700 each month till the end of 1974 (cited in Currey 1978). But it was a full month after Alamgir reported the spectacle of famine in plain view that 'near famine' conditions were officially declared, and that only after an attempt to conceal the situation by pushing beggars into camps on the city outskirts (US Embassy Dacca 1974a).

The immediate action by the government was to set up 4,300 *langarkhanas* or feeding camps, one in each union of the country. Alamgir's (1980) extensive work gives vital insights into the government relief programme. Most *langarkhanas* operated from early October to the end of November, and at their peak some 5,792 camps gave food to 4.35 million people, 6 per cent of the total population—a remarkable feat by any reckoning (Alamgir 1980).

'Indoor relief', as feeding camps are known, is acknowledged to be far less effective than other forms of relief, but in this instance the shortcomings of the relief programme were serious enough to undermine the assistance being provided. First, although the government declared it would aim to provide wheat flour of around 113 grams (a cup in US cooking measures) per head per day,[10] the allocations were meagre and variable. *Langarkhanas* were put in every union,[11] even though hunger was concentrated in some districts,

[10] Calculated from information in the US embassy's cable on the subject, the day after the announcement was made.

[11] The union is the lowest level of the rural political and administrative system; there are currently 4,550 unions.

and—unbelievable though this seems—corruption was reported to be a major problem. Observers tell grim stories. In Dewanganj, wheat of the value of 414 to 640 calories was given to two or three thousand people each day. In Mymensingh, the *langarkhana* operated for only one month, and between two and three people got food worth between 212 and 324 calories. In Sunamganj, only 37 grams of wheat flour was allocated each day to the 500 inmates, so that '*langarkhana* assistance by itself could not possibly have saved many lives during the 1974 Bangladesh famine' (Alamgir 1980, 174). The economist Anisur Rahman reported that:

> The typical picture of a langarkhana is one where utterly inadequate quantities of eatables or semi-eatables are distributed to hundreds of men, women and children by persons with lathis (sticks) in their hands. The city langarkhanas have relatively more to give than the country ones for various reasons: the former got priority in the distribution of official supplies because of nearness to headquarters, and also because foreign visitors, journalists and television photographers are taken to these centers for overseas publicity, private contributions are also greater in the city centers than in the country ones. In the unions of Rangpur, I have seen langarkhanas where hundreds of starving people came from four, five, six miles afar and wait all day, finally to get only one chapatti (hand made bread) the weight of which varies according to daily relative supply of Ata (wheat flour). These are not residential kitchens, and the journey to and from the langarkhanas back to the village may cost more calories than the langarkhana supplies. The starving people naturally expect and want more. Indiscipline results, and I have seen the management literally beating them until these once-human beings sob and weep into submission and discipline is restored.
>
> (Anisur Rahman, cited in Alamgir 1980, 176)

The official relief response may have actually been counter-productive: the feeding centres drew the hungry in, yet failed to nourish or to protect them against disease. Beyond its poor design, the relief effort simply did not distribute enough grains. Deterioriating terms of trade and rising food prices on the international market had left the government short of foreign exchange and scheduled imports of foodgrains were cancelled because US commercial exporters refused the government credit: public food stocks were known to be low, and speculators took advantage of the knowledge that public intervention was unlikely to hoard and push prices up further. Donors delayed sending food aid and efforts at domestic procurement had been counter-productive (Ahmed, Haggblade, and Chowdhury 2000; Clay 1979; Dowlah 2006; McHenry and Bird 1977; Sen 1981; Sobhan 1979).

For all of these reasons, public food stocks were low in 1974. But they were almost twice the levels the year before or after the peak of the famine (Alamgir 1980, 198). Through this period, the government continued with its Public Food Distribution System (PFDS). Despite its name, this was probably the single greatest obstacle to an effective emergency relief programme. The massive PFDS, which by 1977 covered twenty million Bangladeshis (World Bank 1977), originated in the aftermath of the 1943 famine, and grew after independence from Pakistan (Chowdhury 1986). At the time of the famine, the main channels for public food distribution were the Statutory (SR) and Modified Rationing (MR) channels. SR chiefly benefited better-off urban people, in particular public sector workers and 'priority groups' like industrial workers, while MR theoretically catered to the needs of the rural poor—but only after other needs had been met.[12] Sobhan argues that a key factor in the famine was that the floods, low imports and lack of food aid meant there were not enough grains to supply through the Modified Rationing channel, never entertaining the possibility that Statutory Rationing could have been cut or diverted towards relief (Sobhan 1979). Urban bias, distorted incentives in the administration, massive corruption, and leakage meant that only a small proportion of the rural poor ever benefited from Modified Rationing anyway (Chowdhury 1988).

Whether or not the government could have channelled food to the rural masses, in 1974 it chose to protect Statutory Rationing and other 'priority' groups while directing what was left to MR and relief (see Figure 5.3). Nearly 60 per cent of government rationing went to urban people in 1974–5, although less than 9 per cent of the population was urban (Muqtada 1981).[13] All of the urban population was officially covered during 1973–5, compared to around 6 per cent of rural people (Chowdhury 1986). The subsidy was so generous that ration cardholders paid only one-quarter of the market price for medium-quality rice (Chowdhury 1986).

Why were such meagre efforts made to reallocate foodgrains towards relief? By September of 1974 the rural poor were visibly facing starvation en masse, and the political leadership knew this. Sheikh Mujib's speech at the United Nations acknowledged the situation to the world:

> Lately, in the face of this economic crisis that has hit the entire world, we need to take immediate initiatives in order to create a just international financial system ... I am speaking on behalf of a country that tops the list of countries affected by this economic meltdown. I would like to talk a little bit about how severe this loss is. Bangladesh was born in the rubble of war. Ever since we encountered a number of natural disasters in sequence. The last one is this unprecedented flood ... Natural disaster has not only prevented the economy from growing but also

[12] The PFDS has been a large and complex system since before Bangladesh's independence, with numerous aspects that are beyond our present scope. For detailed historical and political economic analyses of the PFDS, see Adams Jr (1998); Ahmed, Haggblade, and Chowdhury (2000); Chowdhury (1986); Chowdhury (1988); Franda (1981b).

[13] 1974 census figures available from the Bangladesh Bureau of Statistics.

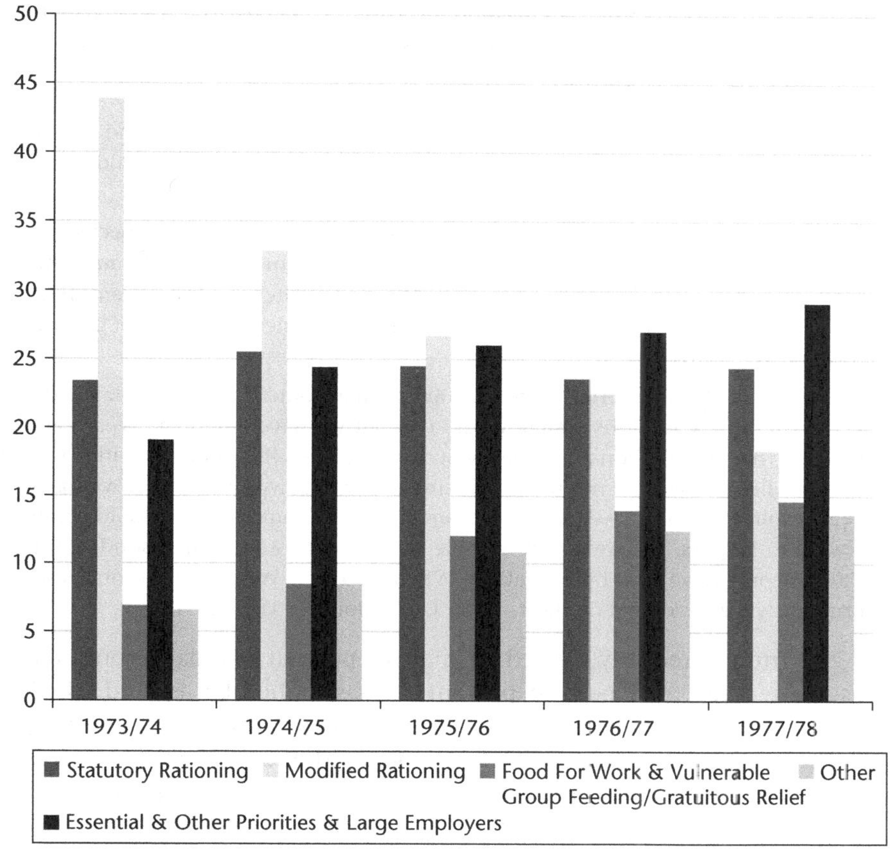

Figure 5.3. Share of PFDS schemes 1973–8

Notes: 'Other' includes FM (allocations to selected flour mills) and OM (open market sales); FFW & VGF were started after 1975/6 so before then this figure represents Gratuitous Relief and related channels.
Source: Chowdhury (1986), based on Food Directorate data.

created almost a famine situation. At the same time a country like ours has been facing a million dollar deficit in terms of paying debt due to the global inflation. People's living standards have gone down even below living conditions. Those who have a per capita income of less than 100 dollars, their condition is more miserable. According to the World Health Organization, people who are having less food than the minimum requirement of food intake to survive are now starving. The future forecast about countries that are poorer is very disappointing. Continuous price hike takes food price beyond the purchase capacity of poor countries...

(Bangabandhu Sheikh Mujibur Rahman at United Nations, 25th September, 1974, 2013)

Also in 1974, Sheikh Mujib acknowledged that 27,000 people had starved to death in an interview with John Pilger, a figure from which the government appears to have taken comfort:

> Sheikh Mujib: We have already declared in the Parliament that round about 27,000 people have died by starvation. And by disease. We have not hide [sic] anything from anybody. It is a fact. Natural calamities.
>
> John Pilger: It seemed when—it seemed much worse than I had expected in August. I have seen outside relief camps, people being turned away because the camps are full. Granted that you have set up these gruel kitchens, but it seems that many many people, or perhaps tens of thousands of people are simply not getting food in this country.
>
> Sheikh Mujib: It is not correct. Then 27,000 people would not have died. People expected that few millions people would die, but we have fought it. Everybody expected that few millions will die by starvation, after the flood and after the inflation. Because we had not the foodgrains in our godown at the time. We have tried to collect from all over the world. And that time some people should come forward to help us. But we in our humble way, we have tried. And round about 27,000 people have died by starvation. Which is a fact. We have tried our best, consciously we have tried our best. ('An Unfashionable Tragedy' 1975)

Any government recently elected by massive popular mandate would have 'consciously tried their best' to prevent a catastrophe of this kind. Sheikh Mujib and his government would have known that the 1943 famine had been the nail in the coffin of the British Raj and a factor in the politics of partition (Bose 1990; Mukerjee 2010), as well as that the callous neglect of the Bhola cyclone victims similarly killed the fantasy of Pakistani integration. They had the grains to feed more of the rural poor, but they were going to the urban middle class. So why did they not 'consciously try their best' to reallocate foodgrains from the urban middle classes and formal sector workers? One possibility is that re-orienting food supplies towards relief from Statutory Rationing was administratively and logistically infeasible.[14] The flood relief effort earlier in the year had been token, under-resourced, corrupt, and mismanaged (Schwartz 1974). The lack of administrative capacity was compounded by demoralization, lack of authority, and politicization and 'by the end of 1974, there was not any civilian institutional group in Bangladesh to implement Mujib's program of national reconstruction' (Maniruzzaman 1975b, 125), let alone famine relief. This is no doubt part of the reason why the official response was too little and too late. By September, it was too late to stabilize prices or to increase relief through the rationing channels. The

[14] And possibly illegal, or at least requiring legal changes as Statutory Rationing was a statutory provision. But emergency conditions would very likely have made it possible to override this provision, so this seems an unlikely barrier.

administrative challenge was already to feed hundreds of thousands of people who had left their homes in search of relief, so that feeding camps were by then the only option. The numbers fleeing hunger in their villages were likely swelled by those of the ten million Bangladeshis displaced by the war who had not yet re-settled. The civil administration was not up to such a task. The post-war reconstruction and relief programme was led by the United Nations Relief Operation in Dacca (UNROD) with collaboration from UN agencies and NGOs, but the government appears to have been largely on its own in 1974. Despite being demoralized by the political wranglings of the post-war period (Mascarenhas 1986; Khan 2013), the army was the most likely agency to manage the logistical demands of a flood and famine relief programme. It was already handling the anti-smuggling effort, but without success. It is possible that Sheikh Mujib's fear of the army, well-founded as it turned out to be, influenced the decision not to involve the military more centrally in the relief programme.

Whether or not the administrative capacity could have been stepped up, there was no political will to re-allocate foodgrains away from the urban and middle classes. As Sobhan put it, the PFDS had 'its own politically determined rigidities' which made reallocation of grains away from the (themselves tightly stretched) politically important urban and middle-class groups 'too politically hazardous for a regime already under severe political attack for the sharp escalation in prices' (Sobhan 1991, 101). A US official in Dhaka said that the problem was that the food went to 'the wrong people' (McHenry and Bird 1977, 75). As the major food aid donor and a staunch critic of the ration system, the Americans saw the failure to reallocate foodgrains as a simple political calculus about which groups were most dangerous for the government to neglect:

> THE STARVING ARE A CONCERN AND AN EMBARRASSMENT TO THE GOVERNMENT, WHICH CAN BE PARTIALLY ALLEVIATED THROUGH THE FEEDING PROGRAM, BUT THESE EXHAUSTED, LISTLESS PEOPLE ARE NOT A POLITICAL THREAT. OPPOSITION EFFORTS TO MOBILIZE THEM CONTINUE TO BE FUTILE...THE POLITICALLY VOLATILE ARE THE WORKING AND MIDDLE CLASSES OUTRAGED BY RISING PRICE OF RICE AND OTHER FOODS. THE PRICE JUMP THIS WEEKEND WAS MET WITH ALSMOST (sic) UNIVERSAL ANGER BY PEOPLE WHO CAN FORESEE THEIR FAMILIES GOING HUNGRY, NOT FROM LACK OF FOOD BUT FROM THEIR INABILITY TO BUY ENOUGH AT CURRENT PRICES. REPORTEDLY ONE RATION SHOP WAS LOOTED THE OTHER NIGHT AND THERE HAVE BEEN ALTERCATIONS AT OTHER SHOPS IN BOTH DACCA AND THE COUNTRYSIDE
>
> (US Embassy Dacca 1974a, 3–5).

The implication is that the government protected the urban and middle classes out of the more proximate fear of political unrest. Certainly the regime's credibility with the politically engaged urban middle classes was already under threat. Mainstream and radical leftist opposition groups were successfully challenging the Awami League's leadership. In April 1974, a United Front of opposition parties came together under NAP (B)'s Maulana Bhashani, who was arrested before a planned rally in June. The challenge from the left was even more threatening, as the Jatiya Samajtantrik Dal or JSD, a front for the Bangladesh Communist League, was among the radical organizations that considered the Bangladesh revolution incomplete, and was mobilizing youth and in rural areas (Maniruzzaman 1975a). The Supreme Court had declared government actions to clamp down on opposition groups through its Special Powers Act of February 1974 illegal, and the JSD responded with strikes and rallies, signalling its growing support. Meanwhile the Awami League itself was fragmenting, with its student wing attempting to lead a breakaway faction. The year ended with a State of Emergency, highlighting the fragility of the government's authority (Maniruzzaman 1975b).

Few opposition groups had mass membership, but many had made food security for the masses an explicit concern. The United Front's four-point charter included the introduction of nationwide rationing and control of profiteering. The JSD was mobilizing around the rising costs of essentials and had its cadres take direct action to release stored foodgrains in the rural areas, both to distribute among the hungry and to prevent hoarding and speculation.[15] It was clear that it was not only the poorest rural people who were affected by the famine: urban recipients of Statutory Rationing such as the industrial workforce and low-paid public sector workers, and even the middle classes, struggled to meet rising living costs in the early 1970s (Sobhan 1979). So this politicization of food security may have inadvertently drawn political attention away from the masses, fixing it on the politically engaged urban groups.

The failure to reallocate food aid to the starving poor has been depicted as a simple choice to sacrifice the poor 'to feed the better-off urban middle class population and prevent any urban unrest which might undermine the Dacca government' (McHenry and Bird 1977, 74). But there is one final reason why this was never a realistic choice. During this short-lived political settlement, rationing had come to form part of the overall package of public service benefits service, 'the means by which subsistence wage goods were guaranteed to politically essential elements of society and government, through a period of increasing instability of supply and rapid price inflation' (Clay 1979, 130).

[15] Many Bangladeshis of a certain age have stories about the famine. The founder of an NGO I met in 2014 recalled his student days of forty years past, when he and his JSD comrades 'liberated' grain from his own uncle's storehouse in Gazipur, after warning the local elite that this would be the result if they failed to feed their local poor. After that, he recalls, they never had a problem getting grain for the local relief kitchen again.

In other words, rations comprised part of wages. There was never any question of re-allocating urban rationing to relief: that would have been literally taking away wages—and a portion of their wages which inflation was making increasingly valuable—from the urban and middle classes (see also Rashiduzzaman 1977, 795). From a political economy perspective, the protection of Statutory Rationing through the famine period was part of a structural class bias that had been relatively newly operationalized in the form of rations for the urban and middle classes since independence (Chowdhury 1988; Chowdhury 1986; Franda 1981b). That the Awami League government, an 'intermediate regime' if ever there was one, put in place structures to prioritize the middle classes was entirely consistent with who it was and how it came to power (Bertocci 1982). Food aid provided the resources on which this short-lived political settlement rested, financing a significant portion of the public sector benefit package at the time. Food aid made it possible for the Dhaka government to keep the politically important urban and middle-class groups appeased. It is no surprise, then, that the food aid that had been implicated in the creation and maintenance of political authority and support was not reallocated to protecting the politically unorganized rural masses from starvation.

5.6.2 *Famine in a Democracy?*

The 1974 famine tests the Drèze–Sen thesis that famines do not occur in democracies with a free media, and finds it wanting. Some have argued that in the Bangladesh of 1974, 'the institutions were democratic and liberal in name only' (de Waal 2000, 11), so that the thesis holds. But others have defended the state of democracy, arguing:

> [T]his was the best year, from a democratic perspective, during the entire period of the Mujib regime (1972–1975), when growing opposition and the press raised their voices against government mismanagement and corruption as well as the impending famine. (Dowlah 2006, 353)

There were few food riots to raise the political temperature, but as we saw, by June 1974 the leftist United Front was demanding universal food rations (Maniruzzaman 1975b). And it was not until after the peak of the famine that Sheikh Mujib declared a National Emergency, arranging a constitutional amendment to declare himself President under the one-party BAKSAL (Bangladesh Peasant and Workers' League) system. So to all intents, this was box-fresh democracy, led by a party with a massive popular mandate which nevertheless failed to protect the most vulnerable people from catastrophe.

Famines have occurred in democracies and been prevented in authoritarian regimes (Plümper and Neumayer 2009; Rubin 2009). Indeed, democratic practices of political competition may exacerbate failed responses to famine, as happened in Bihar in 1966 (Rubin 2009). Certainly for the 1974 Awami League regime, competing demands on food aid from a non-elite electorate made reallocation to the poorest very difficult. What matters, hypothesize Plümper and Neumayer, is the extent to which a regime's political support depends on it protecting the masses—instead of just the elite—from a food crisis. The presence of a good flow of international food aid influences this calculation because it insulates the government against the need to make zero-sum decisions about the use of public foodstocks (Plümper and Neumayer 2009). In the 1974 famine, the distribution of food aid was already integrated into the political calculus, providing the resources on which the political settlement rested. US political games over PL480 meant food aid provided no additional insulation. The Plümper and Neumayer hypotheses draw attention to the fact that in a relatively ethnically and religiously homogenous, politically engaged nation which had only just won its independence in a hard-fought struggle, the fate of the starving rural masses mattered enough for the government to recognize the political significance of its failure and to try to act. The famine was one of several factors behind the assassination of Sheikh Mujib, but it is a key reason why the great nationalist hero lost his legitimacy. Nevertheless, between the rock of the starving masses and the hard place of the squeezed and politically sensitive urban and middle classes, the short-term calculus was that the ration-wages could not be diverted to the poorest.

In addition to the balance of resources and power within the political settlement in explaining the famine, then, we need also to recognize the technocratic features of the administrative failures of timely knowledge and capacity for rapid response, and the influence of the wider Cold War political settlement, in which Bangladesh was a negligible player. After 1974, the apparatus to plan, detect, and respond to food shocks and natural disasters were gradually improved, and the political elite became acutely sensitive to the food insecurity of the masses.

Much remains to be understood about the famine of 1974; with existing sources it is impossible to reconstruct the logic of the time, to gain a picture of the fire-fighting in an increasingly complex, crisis-prone, and aid-dependent setting. We can end this discussion with a suggestion that there may be a powerful psychological dimension to the 1974 famine. Middle-class Bangladeshis with whom I have spoken recall both the sufferings of the masses of destitute people and, with shame and sometimes horror, their own relative degree of comfort. Ferdous Jahan, my long-time collaborator in research on the politics of food in Bangladesh, with whom many of the ideas in this chapter were formulated, was a small child at the time, but recalled that 'they died because we ate'. Other friends and colleagues have expressed a sense of class guilt, recognition that 'those who ate' bear some collective responsibility for the famine, even though many personally tried to help the poor. We should also acknowledge the state of shock or trauma in which many Bangladeshis probably lived at this time. One colleague reflected that 'we just let it happen', a recognition that middle-class Bangladeshis, including Freedom Fighters, progressive intellectuals, and leftists, were complicit, or compliant, in the famine. I suspect that part of this apparent acceptance relates to the trauma of the war and its aftershocks, which cut across class groupings, and which included disillusionment with the regime in power by early 1974. I have often found there is a momentary blankness in many people's responses to references to the famine. This blankness suggests an effort of the will to dredge these matters up from memory, and some discomfort in having done so. To some extent the forgetting has been successful: the famine has been more or less thoroughly expunged from public discourse. Many of the *Midnight's Children* generation born in and around 1971 have but the vaguest knowledge of the famine; those that came after, none at all.

Part 3
The Test Case for Development

6

Never Again

The Long Shadow of Famine

6.1 An Enduring Contract against Subsistence Crisis

> [T]he occurrence of a famine so soon after independence caused a massive crisis of legitimacy for the then government whose violent overthrow a year later was seen as an expression of the loss of this legitimacy. The crisis of legitimacy due to a failure to contain the famine appears to have become for subsequent governments a crucial political concern. (Rahman 1995, 278)

6.1.1 *2008: The Food Riots that Never Were*

'Because of the famine', we were told, when colleagues and I set out to understand why Bangladesh has relatively robust protection against subsistence shocks—relative, that is, to other low-income countries and to the horrible history of the region. The moment of our investigation was the global food crisis of 2007–12. The country had been hit hard by the price spike of 2007–8, a time when India banned rice exports to demonstrate political commitment to preventing famine at home; on the heels of relatively serious floods, and sandwiched between Cyclones Sidr (in 2007) and Aila (in 2009), Bangladesh risked a major food crisis, at a tricky moment of political transition back to multiparty elections after a period of military-backed caretaker rule.[1] There were portentous echoes of the global commodity crisis of the early 1970s, but this time, domestic rice prices stayed below world prices (World Bank 2010). Low-waged urban workers protested rising living costs and the international media duly reported 'food riots', but these scattered outbursts

[1] On the context, see BRAC University and Institute of Governance Studies (2010) and World Bank (2010).

reflected expectations that the government should and could act more than a generalized sense of its failure to do so: the world expected poor, populous, import-dependent Bangladesh to have food riots, but they did not materialize (Hossain and Jahan 2014). And act the government did: the Awami League government elected in late 2008 took the credit for stabilizing the food situation in a turbulent period.[2] It shopped further afield for grain imports, expanded open market sales of cheap food, widened the social safety net, and built warehouses for expanded food reserves.[3] Tackling food prices took top billing on the election manifesto that won the party its largest mandate since the 1970s, signalling its intention to handle the crisis at all costs (BRAC University and Institute of Governance Studies 2010). When world food prices spiked again in 2010–11, Bangladeshis were better insulated than many of their neighbours—and than their grandparents would have been.

That famine—any episode of dearth or sudden price rise that might presage famine—is acutely politically sensitive is no secret (Islam 2012). A popular political theory heard around the 2008 crisis was that the government was responsible for protecting its people against food shocks; it would do so not out of great love for its people, but because of simple democratic pressures—exerted, if necessary, through direct action. The tenure of the caretaker government (January 2007–December 2008) coincided with the rising rice price, losing it popularity and confirming the idea that military governments were inherently less capable than 'political' governments of protecting against food crises (see Islam 2012). As it had (somewhat ineffectively) banned political protests, the sound of popular discontent was muffled.

As if to prove the unelected government had a tin ear, Army Chief General Moeen U Ahmed advised Bangladeshis to replace costly rice with the versatile potato, then enjoying a bumper crop. This was an attempt to subdue fears that the country was enduring a 'silent famine', as claimed by the government advisor, respected historian Akbar Ali Khan. In an episode dense with irony, the *Daily Star* newspaper reported the story from Rangpur, the epicentre of the 1974 calamity (also the home town of General Moeen) (Unb 2008). And so a 'let them eat potato' moment was due not to detachment from the masses but to the sensible fear of a military ruler who lacked the skill of a seasoned politician to reassure the population and cool the markets, demonstrating at least the intention to try their utmost. Food prices dropped sharply just after the Awami League government took power in early 2009, giving credence to the idea that political government responds faster than military

[2] Marked, in addition, by a bloody uprising by sepoys in the Bangladesh Rifles (BDR) battalion, located in heart of Dhaka, in which seventy-four people were killed, fifty-seven of whom were officers. See BBC (2013).

[3] Against the advice of the World Bank, which had encouraged reliance on international food trade rather than domestic stocks.

(even though the success reflected the global commodity slump and a bumper harvest more than action by the new government[4]). In general, the failures of the caretaker government were overstated in popular opinion, and the successes of the Awami League government in 2008 slightly lucky. But the popular theory was reaffirmed.

6.1.2 *The Political Costs of Famine*

Bangladeshi governments do their damnedest to prevent famine because there is an established 'anti-famine contract' (de Waal 1996; 1997; 2000), an agreement forged through 'a popular movement successfully articulating a new right, and forcing a reluctant government to comply with its claims' (de Waal 1997, 11).[5] I prefer to think of the Bangladesh version as a 'subsistence crisis contract' because that better expresses the scope of what successive governments have sought to protect against, and what the people of Bangladesh expect of their government: a meaningful effort to prevent and relieve death and destruction from natural disasters and other external shocks.

De Waal's anti-famine contract is a codified right to subsistence. It is an explicitly politicized version of the 'moral economy', the customary political culture around subsistence rights that provided the theory for food rioters in modern Western Europe. The moral economy—or the idea that people have a right to subsistence that supersedes that of profit in times of dearth—was the ideological counterbalance to the political economy of Smith and Malthus, which informed a 'politics of provisions' through which the masses negotiated entitlements in the crisis-studded transition to capitalism.[6] In functioning contracts, wrote de Waal, 'famine is a political scandal. Famine is deterred. The contract is enforced by throwing out a government that allows it to happen or otherwise punishing those in power' (1997, 5). In Bangladesh, that 'popular movement' for subsistence rights occurred before the famine, when liberation struggle established protection against life-threatening crisis as within the mandate of the Bangladesh state. The year 1974 was a crucial moment in the negotiation of the politics of provisions because the contract was broken.

Although political sociologists such as Hossain Zillur Rahman and Habibul Hoque Khondker have recognized the significance of this event for politics,

[4] The point was made in research discussed in Hossain and Jahan (2014). One poll found 78 per cent of respondents were 'dissatisfied' with price rises in 2008 (BRAC University and Institute of Governance Studies 2009).

[5] A recent PhD thesis at the University of New South Wales argues that the 1974 famine has featured prominently in the politics of food security (Islam 2012).

[6] The seminal accounts of the moral economy are Thompson (1971); Thompson (1991). See Bohstedt (2010) on the emergence of the 'politics of provisions'.

public policy, and elite–mass relations, it has generally been downplayed or neglected in political science and political history. Most political histories of the country discuss 1943, but few discuss the 1974 famine (see, for instance, Sen 1986). In her evaluation of the early years of independent Bangladesh, for instance, Jahan notes in passing that a famine occurred, but this is chiefly in reference to 'the USA delaying US grain shipment which resulted in a sharp decline in food stock pile with disastrous consequences for the regime's ability to tackle the famine in 1974' (2005, 276). In her earlier essay on the background to the assassination of Mujib (written in November 1975), she does not refer to 'famine' at all, writing instead of inflationary prices which 'hit not merely the urban middle class [but also] the bottom 30 to 40 per cent of the population who were the worst sufferers' (Jahan 2005, 167). Although the magnitude of the calamity was not then widely known, this still remains a notable understatement (see also Rashiduzzaman 1977). Mookherjee notes that 'historians skim over the controversial period of Sheikh Mujib's rule from 1972 to 1975' (2015, 46). In China, similarly, while the Cultural Revolution has been much documented and analysed, the Great Leap Famine has been of less interest to an intellectual elite who were only indirectly affected by the disaster, or were themselves implicated in it (Yang 1996).

Whether such exclusions or neglect from the political historical record are due to the complexity of the matter or to disciplinary–methodological, class, or party political biases is unclear. Once the gravity of an episode that killed 2 per cent[7] of the citizens of this brand new nation is recognized, there is the risk of detecting its influence everywhere. I intend a more limited analysis here. By treating the famine as the critical juncture in Bangladesh's development pathway I aim to show the following. First, that the famine was an important part of the broader context of economic crisis and social and political chaos; this included popular disillusionment with the regime and its loss of legitimacy, as well as a mass dislocation and decline in law and order against which political authoritarianism was established, liberal economic reform initiated, and targeted social programmes introduced. However, other forces and events were also crucial, and it was partly in interaction with these that the effects of the famine were so potent. Second, the famine was followed by significant changes, and in some cases abrupt volte-face in domains relevant to food security, which reduced the likelihood of its recurrence; these suggested that

[7] There is no debate about the famine figures, but neither are they agreed. I follow Alamgir's (1980) mortality estimates on the grounds that (a) they are derived using standard definitions and methodologies for estimating famine mortality; (b) they are accepted by famine scholars such as Stephen Devereux and widely cited in the scholarly literature; and (c) the 'official' figures of starvation deaths in the thousands are not based on any recorded evidence. Nevertheless, several scholars cite the 27,000 figure, possibly on the grounds that these were the only recorded deaths from starvation (as distinct from other famine syndrome deaths); for instance, Khondker (1985).

institutional learning and cognitive change among the elite had taken place, from which reckoning it is unlikely (although possible) that the famine was absent. This learning included the hard recognition that Bangladesh was dependent on food and other aid for the immediate future. These changes are unlikely to have happened, or to have happened so early, had the famine not prompted rethinking about the priorities and means of public policy. Third, key members of the political and social elite have invoked their witnessing of the famine as an influence on their worldviews, personal ideologies, and careers, so that there are good reasons to believe it triggered and directed individual, political, and organizational trajectories of wider national importance. The international community also came to be part of this contract. The problems of Bangladesh soon became archetypal of the problems of extremely poor and dependent nations facing disaster and overpopulation, the live example of neo-Malthusian fantasy. The horrors of the famine were being broadcast along with the World Food Conference of 1974, which set the stage for wider changes in global food markets (Gerlach 2015).

6.2 After 1974: Post-Famine Politics

'Elites have long accepted a moral obligation to relieve those most at risk during famines', from the pharaohs of ancient Egypt to the otherwise neglectful French *ancien regime* (Ó Gráda 2009, 197), so elite failure to meet their 'moral obligation' often produces wide social, political, and economic consequences (Torry 1984; Arnold 1988).[8] 'New famine thinking' has recently taken a political turn in its examination of how regimes, conflict, global economic adjustment, and the 'humanitarian international' (de Waal 1997) can exacerbate episodes of mass hunger (see Devereux 2006b). This new emphasis on politics fills a gap that Sen's entitlement theory, an essentially economic theory of famine causation, was unequipped to tackle.[9] Recent analysis has refined the broad association of democratic accountability with famine prevention by identifying the role of state legitimacy (Sutter 2011), state capacity (Burchi 2011), the 'selectorate' (Plümper and Neumayer 2009), and the insulating effects of foreign aid (also Plümper and Neumayer 2009) on the priority

[8] Theorizing of the effects of famine has largely focused on demography, health, and to some extent social relational change (for instance, Kynch 1997; Kynch 1998). Sociological literature predicts changes in individual and community social behaviour, but typically in the immediate aftermath. Some predict that social organization may become animalistic, 'pared down to satisfaction of nutritional needs, the most basic requisites of life' or turn to sociopathy, discarding or destroying social rules (Dirks et al. 1980, 31). People may withdraw from social participation or draw on 'contingency' rules hardwired as a result of natural selection and social learning, or depress vitality, operating at a lower level of intensity and activity (see, for instance, Sorokin 1975).

[9] See introduction in Devereux (2006b); also Devereux (1993; 2001).

given to famine prevention and relief. These new approaches analyse why and under what conditions governments fail to relieve famine, and with what implications for accountability (Edkins 2006; Devereux 2006a), helping to bring the effects of famine into view.

An examination of accounts of modern famine episodes suggests two broad political effects are common, both operating through the delegitimizing consequences of famine on the balance of political power.[10] This may be destabilized or challenged by a) the emergence of subaltern groupings and/ or a mass threat or b) elite challenges to political leadership through, for example, the prospect of a palace or other coup. In wartime Bengal, for example, the Communist Party focused on strategy rather than organizing the peasants and lost support after the war; by contrast, frontline Muslim League activists tried to help starving peasants, a fact that contributed to both their party's post-war provincial election victory and the (chiefly Muslim) peasant reprisals against (mainly Hindu) graindealers and moneylenders in the Noakhali riots of 1946 (Bose 1990). In the Indochina famine of 1945, members of the nationalist Viet Minh died alongside many of the Tonkin peasantry, but their strategy of seizing granaries to feed the starving became key to their support in the north (Bose 1990). In Ethiopia armed peasant groups fought long-running campaigns against the state after 1973, and Tigrayan separatism grew out of the unrest (de Waal 1991). The enduring effects of the famine in Tibet have featured in the political memories and popular grievances against Chinese rule in that region (Jisheng 2012).

Famines may also directly affect the terms of the political settlement if contending elites recognize in the crisis the possibility for regime change. Christopher Clapham has shown how the 1973 famine was implicated in the loss of peasant support for Haile Selassie's empire, but also that the middle classes and student population sympathized, and were critical of official inaction (Clapham 1990; see also de Waal 1991; Shepherd 1975). The Irish famine ultimately forced a divided political class to overcome its differences in a more unified articulation of interests against Britain (Kinealy 1994). In China, grassroots cadres made clear their dissatisfaction with the moderate reforms after the famine became known to the political leadership; Communist Party leaders like Deng Xiaoping were 'repulsed' by Mao's failures to acknowledge the famine, weakening his hold on the party leadership (Becker 1996).

[10] We focus mainly here on the Irish Potato Famine of 1848–52, the Bengal and Indochina famines of 1943–5, the Soviet Union famines of the 1930s, the Great Leap (or Chinese) Famine of 1958–62, the El Niño-triggered calamities across Asia and Africa in the late nineteenth century, and the Ethiopian famines of 1973 and 1984–5. The African and North Korean famines of the recent past are not discussed here because the longer-term consequences for politics, policy, and social relations have not been closely analysed or because (apart from North Korea) mortality levels were contained to a level that prevented these events from being seen as major catastrophes.

6.3 A 'Crisis of Legitimacy'

Wholesale social revolution, as in Ethiopia after 1973, is rare after a major famine. But before the June floods, Bangladesh in early 1974 was already ripe with revolutionary ferment, and the political agenda full of hunger, inflation, and corruption. Far-leftists (the Jatiyo Samajtantrik Dal (JSD)) in increasing contention with the ruling Awami League held rallies in January and February 1974, and *gheraoed* (besieged) the chairman of the notoriously leaky Red Cross, food aid relief committees, and the State Trading Corporation (responsible for foodgrain management) in March. The centre-left also mobilized around food security. In June, the Bhashani-led United Front launched a four-point programme including universal foodgrain rations and tackling corruption, smuggling, and speculation (Maniruzzaman 1975b, 121). The politics of food security in this dependent economy were inevitably internationalized: the economic and food crises were blamed on smuggling to India and the regime was criticized as overly pro-India (Khondker 1985). Hostility to the US meant foreign aid was resisted by the left. By late 1974 all foreign aid had effectively dried up, and the 40 per cent of the budget that depended on external assistance went unfinanced (as did the food gap, as has already been seen). The government took an aggressive stance against the underground far-left parties, for whom national independence was 'an unfinished revolution' (Maniruzzaman 1975a). By late 1974 thousands of Awami League workers had been killed by the regime's opponents, and far-leftists had been jailed, killed, or driven underground, mainly by the regime's paramilitary force, the *Rakkhi Bahini* (Karim 2005).

For upper- and middle-class idealists who had envisioned an egalitarian 'Golden Bengal', disillusion centred on members of their own class in power. Decades later, the former Planning Commission member (and famine researcher) Anisur Rahman reflected that

> The war and its aftermath were painful not only because of what happened, but because of the dream that has been shattered. So many things were promised and so much we have lost. And we lost that dream to a great extent because of the betrayal of the so-called nationalist elites... We ate together, starved together, suffered together and shared our lives. [But after independence] The elite rejected the people. (quoted in Tripathi 2014, 234)

Rahman was among a group of seventy intellectuals that publicly accused the regime of having caused the famine with their tolerance of smuggling and corruption (Weinraub 1974).

The 'lost dream of a shared nation' is a recurrent motif in middle-class memoirs of the period. A freedom fighter who remained in the army in liberated Bangladesh described his experiences with the anti-smuggling and relief effort:

> Bangladesh was on the brink of a famine. The euphoria and aspirations engendered by victory and the liberation of Bangladesh had turned into national despair. I returned to Saidpur after the completion of my assignment with the overwhelming thought of how my fallen comrades would have behaved in battle if they knew that the poor people who had helped the *Mukti Bahini* at great personal risk would starve in an independent Bangladesh. (Q. K. Khan 2013, 231)

Stories of women and children being abandoned by husbands and fathers dramatized the failures to provide minimal protection against death and exposure. A notorious image of a starved young woman, Basanti of Kurigram, draped in a fishing net (because she had no clothes) depicted bare life in a nightmarish echo of the wartime rapes.[11]

The masses write neither political manifestos nor memoirs, but some of their views—more often, middle-class and foreigners' views of their views—have been recorded. That the masses were disillusioned seems probable, but early political history is sensitive and polarized, making it difficult to read the signs with clarity, and there are few firsthand accounts from people who suffered. The international media typically quoted officials, glossing the views of the masses in general statements that veered wildly. A *New York Times* journalist noted in October 1974 that 'Sheik [sic] Mujib's popularity remains intact... he is still venerated by most people as the father of the nation'. By December, her colleague found the Prime Minister and ruling party were the subject of angry criticism and a common theme was that 'life was better under the Pakistanis' (Rangan 1974; Weinraub 1974). Perhaps popular disillusion had spread; perhaps people held both views at once.

One view is that the Father of the Nation had to date been excluded from the disillusion, and the famine was the turning point: 'the people now cursed not only the government but also Sheikh Mujib himself' (Mascarenhas 1986, 44); '[t]he year of the famine became the pivot of Mujib's decline' (Lifschultz and Bird 1979, 46). The emotional quality reported of public disillusionment suggests his fall was painful precisely because he had been so beloved (and, as Father, symbolically and literally responsible for feeding them). Other politicians were both more obviously to blame and demonstrably cared less. One widely loathed politico, Gazi Golam Mostafa, chairman of the Red Cross and party boss for Dhaka city Awami League, was described by an aid official as 'the most corrupt man in Bangladesh' (Lifschultz and Woollacott 1975), and

[11] The 'Basanti' image appears to have been staged in an effort to attract attention to the famine, although the distress it depicted and Basanti herself were genuine. The image appears to be a matter of some controversy, and (unusually for a controversial image) cannot be found online.

he was the regular target of leftwing protests and the media. In a fatal connection, Mostafa was also involved in an altercation with a Major Dalim, an army officer who had previously been part of the army's humiliating failed drive to curb foodgrain smuggling and was later part of the plot to assassinate Mujib (Mascarenhas 1986; Lifschultz and Bird 1979).

'Much has been made about the lack of public grieving over Mujib's death' (Tripathi 2014, 250), but how should this be read? Certainly there was disillusion. For the masses, the time of the famine is remembered as a time of great hardship: political violence, authoritarian rule, and blatant corruption outraged the Dhaka upper-middle classes, but across the rest of the society, the memory of hunger lingers.[12] Yet Mujib was still the leader of the victorious liberation struggle. As human rights activist Sultana Kamal points out, despite his failures (highlighted indefatigably until the return to democracy in 1991), Mujib retains broad popular appeal: 'people remembered what it meant to fight for a Bengali nation; what Sheikh Mujib meant for that struggle' (Tripathi 2014, 250). Even at the time, disappointment mingled with respect. In a rare contemporary account of village people's views of Mujib's assassination, Hartmann and Boyce reported mixed emotions on the breaking news:

> 'My brother died fighting for independence', [one man] said somberly. 'Now they have murdered the Father of our Nation.'
>
> 'Mujib was a thief,' [another man] retorted. 'He gave all our wealth to India.'
>
> By afternoon, the villagers' initial anxiety had given way to euphoria. 'No one is crying for Mujib,' [one woman] told us. 'He has got his due.' There was almost an air of celebration in [the village], as groups of villagers gathered to discuss the news.
>
> (1983, 240)

The response to the cold-blooded murders of the entire Rahman family suggests disillusion and betrayal by a beloved hero, but also a traumatized population inured to bloodshed. The extreme nature of the violence against Mujib and his family was deliberate, a tactic to pre-empt protest. Author of the constitution and Mujib-era minister Kamal Hossain explained that '[Mujib's assassins] succeeded in shocking everyone into a state of paralysis . . . They were worried about how people would react, and they correctly guessed that the more horrific their act, the more afraid the people would be' (Tripathi 2014, 251).

In any case, top leaders are often spared mass disapproval in such times. In China's Great Leap Famine, starving people blamed frontline officials rather than Mao: 'A distant entity called "the government" and a semi-god called "Mao" were on the side of good. If only he knew, everything would be

[12] In personal communication, the historian Afsan Chowdhury has told me that in a survey he was conducting about wartime memories he was surprised to find that researching memories of 1971, rural people recall the years after the war, not the war itself, as the time of hunger.

different' (Dikötter 2010, 229). Starving Chinese peasants believed Mao would save them and 'dragged themselves to the top of the nearest mountain, faced the direction of Beijing and called out aloud for Mao to help them' (Becker 1996, 310). It is unlikely that Bangladeshi famine victims would have had quite so much faith in the top leadership: Bangladesh in 1974 was an open, if violently fractious, polity. But there is limited evidence that the poorest blamed the government or Mujib personally. In one report from North Bengal, a starving man is asked what caused the famine. 'Allah', he responds, flatly. But the journalist adds: 'Others blame the Government—some even Sheikh Mujibur Rahman', with no evidence in support (Schwarz 1974b). In another instance, a starving twenty-two-year-old widowed mother-of-three responded to a question about who is to blame: 'I do not know who is responsible. I blame my own destiny'—a response roundly rejected as the ignorant fatalism of a village woman by people (not starving) who witnessed the exchange. 'She should blame the government', the audience pronounced. Middle-class disappointment that the Bengali masses did not rise up against their starvation is an old theme.[13] But starving people may not behave as intellectuals and leftists would have them do, for physiological as well as political reasons: the resources of even the most resilient people would have been depleted after the horrors of the 1970s.

Among the many tragedies of this time is that Mujib appears to have been personally distressed by the famine and aware that it could presage his own end. This was so even though Dacca never displayed a grasp of the severity of the situation and persisted in the view that 'only' tens of thousands of people had died, when the rigorous conservative estimate is more than fifty times that. In 1974 Mujib rarely made public appearances. In August he told a UN official: 'Country is fighting for survival. I am fighting for survival' (Gerlach 2010, 168). Video and witness testimonies of his mood at this time in no way suggest a political leader who was detached from or careless about his people. Unlike Selassie or Mao, for whom famine was an embarrassment or irritant, Mujib made little attempt at concealment. Swallowing his considerable pride, he went cap in hand to the international community. He even hosted Henry Kissinger at the height of the famine in an effort to save 'his people' from starving. This point is not to absolve Mujib for the failures of his administration, but to note that a sense of moral responsibility distinguishes the 1974 famine from others of the modern period: here was a political leadership that could not, politically speaking, afford a famine, and which had powerful historical and social affinities with the starving masses.[14] No such sense of

[13] There is a long discussion of this in Thompson (1991); see also Greenough (1982).

[14] These come through in the pained writing by elites about this time. A particularly thoughtful account of 1974 is by former head of the Planning Commission, Nurul Islam (2003).

moral responsibility is ever detected among ruling elites in accounts of the Irish, 1943 Bengal, or Ethiopian famines, least of all in the imperial British attitudes to the 'late Victorian holocausts' (Davis 2001). In China, Mao seemed unmoved except by the impact of the famine on his own power, and then-President Liu Shaoqi was reportedly horrified once he witnessed the devastation in his own home village (Jisheng 2012). It is one thing to tolerate famine among peoples who are different and far from the capital. It is quite another when they are your own people, and lie dying before your eyes.

6.4 The Balance of Power

Loss of legitimacy did not lead to a mass political formation in Bangladesh, but the series of elite and military coups that followed the famine were powerfully influenced by that possibility. Fear of a mass uprising and the loss of legitimacy of the elected government were threads running through the sequence of events that followed the famine. Fearful for his control of power, Mujib engineered an uncontested constitutional change that paved the way for the establishment of the single-party BAKSAL regime in early 1975, with himself as all-powerful President. A coup by junior army officers in August assassinated Mujib and his family in a gruesome attack, installing a right-leaning Awami League leader who was then displaced by a second and finally a third coup, the last a 'sepoy mutiny' of leftists in the military. By a twist of fate and treachery, this last installed General Zia Rahman (not a leftist) in effective power in November 1975. Political power finally settled for the next fifteen years on a pair of military or civilianized-military regimes that were able to assert some control over the army, hold off political opposition, appease international backers, and offer the prospect of some improvements in security, including of food, and which sowed the seeds for human development.[15]

For contending nationalist and leftist political elites, loss of mass support implied a loss of support for the statist socialist economic model that had been so briefly tested, and by implication for parliamentary democracy as a political system. The international community and the 'comprador' class of domestic business interests read the same signs differently. Both within and beyond the Awami League leadership, it was clear the regime needed to 'pull a rabbit out of an old hat', as Mujib's attempt to install a single-party system with himself as President was described (Lifschultz and Bird 1979, 143).

[15] The most detailed accounts of the means and motives of these coups remain Lifschultz and Bird (1979) and Mascarenhas (1986); but see also Tripathi (2014); Jahan (2005); Maniruzzaman (1988).

The 'year of the famine' was the 'real testing time for Mujib and his ideology' (Z. R. Khan 1996, 221):

> Mujib would appear to have become receptive to the idea of a radical change [away from multiparty democratic rule] only after the 1974 famine... it was only then that he became convinced of the need for a 'breakthrough' in order to build an 'exploitation-free' society. (Karim 2005, 345)

Ideological conflict was playing out in almost total anarchy within and outside the government: from ministerial resignations and palace plot and counter-plot to armed insurgency, repression, and murder (Maniruzzaman 1975a; Maniruzzaman 1976; Maniruzzaman 1975b; Karim 2005; Jahan 2005; Sen 1986). But—in a polarized world, with the left split along Moscow–Maoist lines, the aid pipeline dry, bankrupting the country—which way would Bangladesh go now? A folk song by a member of the leftist Krishak Shamity (peasants' organization) gives a flavour of the popular mood:

> It is time
> We ate them.
> Let's eat them, brothers,
> They are killers.
> It is time
> We ate them.
> We are many.

(Excerpt from *Song* by Nazu, performed at a pir's mazar (saint's shrine) in December 1974; recorded in Jahangir 1976, 261–2.)

From the local left through to the Cold War power elite, all saw the situation as ripe for revolution. The US and the USSR saw the famine as the main threat to the stability of this 'violent political tinder-box' of a region (Lifschultz and Bird 1979, 108) (Schwarz 1974a). There was little appetite for a social revolution within the political elite, but the crisis of 1974 had made the parties further to the left of essentially bourgeois Awami League a 'much more powerful force than they had been in the former East Pakistan':

> [T]he utter failure of the AL government to alleviate the sufferings of the people made it easier than before to believe that in a developing country socialism could not be achieved through western democratic methods and that the salvation lay in a social revolution engineered and led by a party of the proletariat.
> (Maniruzzaman 1988, 165)

If the revolution did not arrive it was 'because of betrayal in high places, rather than because conditions were not ripe for radical change' (Hossain 2005, 85). Under the Awami League, tens of thousands of members of underground parties on the left were allegedly killed or arrested, a process that continued into General Zia's regime (Maniruzzaman 1988).[16] Older, less popular parties of the moderate left survived or were co-opted. International and regional powers were universally unsupportive of a strong left, just as they had been of Bengali independence: the Indian government viewed radical groups as potential Naxalites, and the Chinese leadership had no interest in the small Maoist struggle in Bengal, enemies of their allies in Pakistan.

6.5 Policy and Institutional Change

6.5.1 *Policy Ruptures*

Amid the political convulsions of the famine, a series of ruptures in public policy shifted Bangladesh onto a development pathway from which no subsequent government, elected or otherwise, has substantially deviated. This period appears to have consolidated certain ideas about the essentials of development among the political, bureaucratic and business elites. Yang says the Great Leap Famine transformed the Chinese development project by wreaking 'drastic cognitive changes . . . among both elites and masses', most of whom had anyway been uncertain about the radical collectivization that caused the catastrophe (1996, 240). Something similar could be said here. The brief flirtation with socialism (and, for a time, with secularism and democracy) was now at an end; the ideology of the state emerged as a distinct form of 'Bangladeshi' nationalism in which beating the 'basket case' label was a motive force.[17] While both secularism and democracy have re-emerged among the political desires of (some) Bangladeshis, the ideals of 'socialism' have been replaced by a lightly pro-poor persuasion of globalized capitalism, notable mainly for the extent to which its emphasis on protecting the poorest is reconciled with its emphasis on economic growth through the exploitation of labour in international markets.

The development pathway on which Bangladesh set off at this time was the first steps towards the road it has now travelled for several decades, bordered on the right by an emphasis on the market principle as the means of unleashing growth and ensuring efficient distribution, and on what remains of the left by a safety net, a set of provisions to protect the poorest and most vulnerable from the worst consequences of unfettered global capitalism. This pathway is aggressively pragmatic, devoid of principle other than the imperative of

[16] Including the infamous jail killings of Awami League leaders including Tajuddin Ahmed, the first Prime Minister. In a well-known case, Colonel Abu Taher, the JSD former freedom fighter who led the leftist coup that installed Zia Rahman, was tried in camera and hanged by the man he had rescued, most likely from the firing squad (Lifschultz and Bird 1979).

[17] Like most Bangladeshis, Zia was said to have been incensed by the label and determined to turn the country from a basket case to 'a basketful of hopes' (Islam 1984, 571).

avoiding annihilation from the elements and the volatilities of a global economy. But at first it was an emergency exit, an early instance of Naomi Klein's 'shock doctrine', a world away from the deliberated, hopeful plan for just progress plotted by the early development planners.[18]

The first break with the leftism of the liberation government was the Awami League government's capitulation to donor pressures over macroeconomic management starting in 1974. Rehman Sobhan documents how Western aid donors held the country hostage till they adopted policies the World Bank deemed correct, in a textbook case of the use of aid as 'leverage' (Hayter 1971). Before the famine, under the intellectual leadership of the Planning Commission, the country had been all set to steer an independent path to development as a sovereign nation. In response to donor efforts to impose aid conditionalities in March 1973, Mujib supported the Commission, stating firmly that 'the nation may suffer but it would not die' (Sobhan 1982, 182). Donors were aware that this 'strident nationalist spirit could not feed Bangladesh' (p. 172) and kept up the pressure. The First Five Year Plan, the development plan for the new nation, was published under unpropitious circumstances: a moment of global commodity inflation, floods, and rapidly declining public authority. It was at this moment of acute vulnerability, when the fragile new state most needed the sort of external support it had received in 1972,[19] that 'donors tended to become much more eloquent about their various concerns over the development policies of the regime' and to push for currency devaluation, monetary stabilization, cuts in public subsidies, and in general market-friendlier policies (Sobhan 1982, 191).

In April 1975, the government agreed to devalue the *taka*; it had already conceded ground on investment policy by raising caps on investment, but through 1974 and 1975 the government continued to reverse reforms, and donors became clear that this was not a regime with which they or the Western interests they represented could do business. Donors kept 'Bangladesh twisting in the wind' through 1974 (Sobhan 1982, 193), cutting down on aid commitments at the moment of its greatest economic crisis. Given Bangladesh's dependence on external financing at this time, there can be little doubt that aid relations wittingly played a significant part in the political crisis that followed. A key point of contention between Bangladesh and the World Bank was that of the new country's share of debt accrued as part of East Pakistan. The government of Bangladesh contested its liability for loans from which the West had chiefly benefited, but eventually was forced to accept

[18] Klein (2007). Two firsthand sources on the twists and turns in the process of development planning in early Bangladesh are Sobhan (1982) and N. Islam (2003). For the World Bank/aid donor perspective on this period, see Faaland and Parkinson (1976).

[19] And which it received again in 1979, when the more aid-amenable Zia regime was facing floods and famine. See in particular Osmani (1991).

liability of $150 million for ongoing projects, as a result of intense lobbying on behalf of Pakistan by the World Bank (Sobhan 1982, 174–7). As a demonstration of power, it was gruesomely effective.

The second and more decisive break came with Zia. There was 'a radical change' in aid relations after 1975, as aid donors, particularly the World Bank, looked more favourably upon the new regime (Sobhan 1982, 196). Evaluating Zia's rule, Akhtar Hossain argues that the Awami League's economic mismanagement set the bar against which all subsequent regimes would be judged (Hossain 1996a; Hossain 1996b). Zia lacked the 'policy baggage' that came with Mujib, and borrowed ideas from 1960s Pakistan (see also Bertocci 1982; Maniruzzaman 1988). The basic facts of the Zia regime are as follows: it established an institutional culture of military–bureaucratic rule, including clamping down on protest or dissent (with declining effectiveness over time); overturned the progressive, pluralist constitution by removing provisions for secularism and socialism, including declaring Islam the state religion, rejecting the secularism of the liberation struggle; reoriented foreign relations towards the Middle East and Western aid donors; and shifted economic and social policy in directions favoured by the new external allies, notably towards greater market orientation with a visible pro-poor edge. The Zia regime brought a degree of economic stability and some improvements in security, presiding over a period without any major catastrophes from the environment or the markets. All of this was possible because the organized left were under siege; the Awami League in disarray, in hiding, or discredited; and even if the masses had organization or leadership, they would have been too traumatized and exhausted to resist. Eventually, Zia too proved unequal to managing contending elite demands, and was assassinated in yet another military coup—the final of a reported twenty-seven attempts in the period 1977–81. The old political settlement was quickly restored, however, under General Ershad, who ruled till he was unseated by a democratic uprising in 1990. But the building blocks of the national development project were by then firmly in place.[20]

Donor pressure for reform was undoubtedly heavy-handed, but it may not be correct to see these reforms as forced wholesale upon a recalcitrant ruling elite or accepted without resistance, whether in the Mujib or the Zia period. The options available to Bangladesh were always off a limited menu, and many within the Planning Commission and the regime recognized the need to stabilize the macroeconomy and accelerate economic growth (Sobhan 1982). It is telling that, nonetheless, on the priority matter of food policy, World Bank prescriptions to privatize public grain procurement and eliminate

[20] Authoritative sources on the 'Zia episode' include Islam (1984); Zafarullah (1996); Maniruzzaman (1988). See also Franda (1981c); Franda (1981a); Jahan (2005).

food rationing were resisted by successive governments of all stripes for several decades after the famine. Common fears were about the public perception of food security (or perhaps faith in the state's capacity to protect the population against food crisis), by the masses fearful of grain speculation and public sector employees resistant to the loss of their subsidies (Adams Jr 1998; Sobhan 1982; Franda 1981b; Clay 1979; Chowdhury 1988; Chowdhury 1986). Donors were using aid as leverage, but were mainly levering open a door that policy elites knew needed opening if they, and the nation-state, had a chance of surviving.

The political motivations for this policy shift were tactically diverse. While its external agenda was shaped by the material need to satisfy Western donors and the symbolic need to distinguish itself from Mujib's secularism for the Islamic world, internally the energy and resources of the new regime were absorbed by satisfying bureaucratic and industrial elites disempowered or discontented by liberation. The spoils of the state were once again divided up, this time with military spending shooting up from 7 to 20 per cent of the budget; civil servants disciplined for disloyalty under Awami League were reinstated with the benefits they had enjoyed in the Pakistan era; ceilings on investment and restrictions on trade were lifted and de-nationalization came under consideration (Islam 1984). Yet amid this elite jostling for a space at the table, from Zia's time onwards, a certain watchfulness emerged with respect to the needs and concerns of the rural masses. This included a tendency (borrowed from the 'Basic Democrats' approach of Pakistan authoritarian rulers) to engage them in local participation, through Village Governments and the Village Defence Force, set up as institutions for local order and development in lawless 1976.

Like economic policy, the participatory turn of Zia's rule was as pragmatic as it was programmatic. Like Zia himself, public policymaking in this period came to be characterized by opportunism, a certain ruthless expedience, but also caution, a tendency to see which way the wind would blow.[21] The famine and its aftermath had created conditions under which policies to protect against subsistence crises were politically expedient not only because they could look well to aid donors, but also because they were (believed to be) vital to regime survival due to what famine meant for political legitimacy. The reorientation of public policy reflected this new priority:

> [Zia] was for a strong government that would be able to deliver the goods—a government that would be acceptable to the majority of the people, the Islamic world, the international aid agencies, and, perhaps, the military.
>
> (Chowdhury et al. 1996, 25)

[21] Zia 'spouts the rhetoric of the international development establishment but remains both a pragmatist about implementation and, in many ways, a rather conservative Bengali Muslim' (Franda 1981c, 368).

Under conditions of such extreme and widespread hunger, 'the food problem [is] indistinguishable from the totality of the development problem' (Osmani 1991, 307), and food security became a key focus of the Zia regime. Avoiding a repeat of the famine 'remained uppermost in the minds of donor programmers and government policymakers for the next 20 years'; what had been learned was that poor people faced famine when food prices rose: managing public stocks, including of food aid, was key, and rationing probably worsened, rather than helped, the situation (Atwood et al. 2000, 153). Over the next twenty years, food and agriculture policies gradually used procurement and pricing policies to move in the direction of increased production and stable prices, while simultaneously reducing the regressive subsidies through the rationing system, and targeting what remained to the vulnerable poor. All of this was supported by a system that was geared towards responding to shocks, through price monitoring, scalable food transfers and subsidies, and deregulating foodgrain trade.[22]

Zia's regime set the direction for this reorientation of food policy, with a characteristic blend of elite-pandering, donor-placating, and popular participation. Technocratic rather than political advice was taken, including from bureaucrats from the elite Civil Service of Pakistan (CSP) corps who were reinstated to run Ministries of Rural Development and Cooperatives and Agriculture (also Industry and Planning); they developed a 'clear and unambiguous development strategy for Bangladesh [which] discarded the socialistic pretensions of the Mujib regime' (Maniruzzaman 1988, 200). Zia threatened to remove the ration system, but in fact rationing was extended to the military and other 'essential priority' groups on his watch, and it was only when facing another food crisis and episode of inflation in 1978 that the PFDS was put firmly on the agenda for reform (Banerjee et al. 2014). While donors continued to press for the abolition of rationing, for government, the capacity to manage food consumption remained vital to public policy well into the 1980s (Chowdhury 1986).

Like the Awami League government, Zia ensured that agriculture policy continued to favour the crucial rural elite class, but there was now less effort to control prices and production, and fewer subsidies for farmers (Hossain 1996a). Local elites were kept satisfied with new programmes of rural credit and a vast programme of canal digging, as part of a World Food Programme-supported food-for-work programme. To this day, local elites reap rich rewards in the form of infrastructure from the free labour of food-insecure agricultural

[22] There are a number of good sources on these developments, many of them published in the aptly titled Ahmed et al. (2000). On the PFDS, see Chowdhury (1988); Chowdhury (1986); Adams Jr (1998); Atwood et al. (2000); Osmani (1991). On the politics of food policy, see Raihan (2013); Islam (2012). For a summary, see Hossain and Jahan (2014).

wage labourers. Zia lacked Mujib's charisma and populist appeal, but he earned popularity by showing up at these sites. An iconic image of Zia, much used by the BNP, has him in a peaked cap, trademark sunglasses, and *genji* or undershirt (the garment of a working man, although worn with jeans—not the usual attire of the peasant); the suggestion is that he has been at a worksite, possibly even doing manual labour, something Bengali upper-middle classes would consider degrading even for symbolic value (see also Franda 1981c). The famous images of Mujib, by contrast, always have him in full rhetorical flow, entrancing vast audiences with his oratory.

Less than two decades after the famine, Osmani argued that the notion that Bangladesh had successfully avoided famine since 1974 remained untested. Chronic hunger had become an even more serious problem, partly because of efforts to prevent famine. The country still lacked robust, redistributive modernizing agricultural policies and the only notable improvement was a stronger rural bias in the PFDS. When food crises threatened in 1979 and 1984 it was lucky enough to have reoriented the PFDS, and to have a healthy foreign exchange reserve and good aid relations to get it out of a tight spot (in 1987).[23] Osmani is correct: these three factors would not necessarily be sufficient to prevent famine in future, as was seen in 2008, where neither good aid relations, a pro-poor PFDS, nor a healthy bank balance, but market prices saved the day. What has changed since 1974 is a path rupture in food policies: a pragmatic approach to food (by extension, development) policy in which the domestic elites and international actors are kept on board, while also keeping an eye on how the masses are faring at the margins. That is, the technical details of institutional change matter, but less, overall, than the powerful political motivation to avoid famine.

6.6 Class and Group Relations/Post-Famine Political Sociology

Relations between those who rule during famine and those who starve rarely survive intact. Modern episodes of famine have encouraged some rulers to view populations in Malthusian terms, as subjects in experiments governed by 'natural laws' of demography or political economy, or conversely (and sometimes simultaneously) as reason to expand their sphere of biopolitical controls on populations and modes of reproduction (Ross 1998). Ireland not only lost most of its population to death or migration; it was also treated by its British rulers as a laboratory for the testing of Malthusian ideas. Experiments with medical and poor relief were made in this period, and more profound changes

[23] See also Crow (1984); E. Clay (1985); Ahmed et al. (2000); Atwood et al. (2000).

aimed to reconfigure agrarian relations towards a more capitalistic, surplus arrangement of landlords and labour (Nally 2008; Kinealy 2002). It was said that 'Ireland died of political economy' (Gráda 2000, 6), but the famine played ideological and functional roles in how it reshaped Irish society to be more receptive to capitalist agricultural growth (Nally 2008). The idea of famine as shocking society into accepting radical system change fits the 'disaster capitalism' setting of aid-dependent Bangladesh. Similarly, communist famines 'helped the regimes to enforce the collective order', enabling a rapid forcing-through of industrial and other policies (Wemheuer 2014, 248).

Famines typically alter perceptions of and relations between ruling classes and the population. Strict internal migration controls to keep peasants from flooding to the cities and draconian birth control policies were adopted after China's Great Leap Famine (Wemheuer 2014). Reforms to Chinese agriculture—and other aspects of state policy and economy (Jisheng 2012)—were approached with caution, and efforts to control or eradicate peasant modes of production were replaced with investments in modernizing technology. In the USSR, state policy strongly emphasized mass living standards after the famine, and foodgrain imports to stabilize and strengthen food security became more important from Khrushchev onwards (Wemheuer 2014). Bangladeshi public policy was reoriented towards rural, agricultural, and food security concerns after the famine, and successive regimes have reversed, or at least taken the edge off, urban bias in public policies on food security, social protection, and agriculture.[24]

6.6.1 *Reconstructing the Broken Moral Economy: The Origins of Non-State Social Action*

The famine violated any lingering notions that benevolent patronage would protect the poor and vulnerable in times of crisis. The old moral economy was no longer functional, if it ever had been, because for the majority of the rural poor, the relations of production on which it rested and which it helped reproduce were gone.[25] The famine hit rural landless folk who usually depended on seasonal labour markets. The landless were rural proletarians: at the best of times they had employers, not the kind of patrons on whom they might depend for loans or grain in crisis times.[26] As had happened in 1943,

[24] The point is developed in 'Out of the Shadow of Famine' (Ahmed et al. 2000).

[25] See Alamgir (1980) on the extent of gifts to famine victims. The BIDS survey found that people in famine areas were more likely to get charitable assistance from local sources, but the amounts were reported to be very small. Razzaque notes that during the famine, mortality rates increased by 28 per cent even among the richer classes, based on analysis using the Matlab DHSS data (Razzaque 1989).

[26] By the 1970s, land frontiers had probably been reached across much of East Bengal, barring the hill regions. In the absence of agricultural intensification, in the presence of high population

the famine reinforced trends towards landlessness (Alamgir 1980) (BRAC 1992, 6). When the land goes, so do all possibilities of independence from the patron (although see Indra and Buchignani 1997). All of this is a far cry from the relatively flat social structure assumed by the Comilla model of rural development that had previously dominated thinking about the organization of peasant life (Abdullah 1974; Wood 1994). Into the breach left by this broken moral economy, at a time of authoritarian rule and political bankruptcy, came a new set of energies and organizations, initially financed substantially by non-state or charitable funds in aid donor countries and by domestic sources, including from the government, and only somewhat later by official aid.

The best-known activities of these organizations are rural credit or microfinance groups. In recent years, the Bangladesh microfinance industry has come under fire for promoting rural indebtedness and charging high interest rates (among other practices),[27] but microfinance was once regarded as an alternative to exploitation by traditional moneylenders, in a context where control over rural credit is associated with patronage, land, and social and political power (see Bose 1986).

After the famine, rural social relations started to be recast as a site of exploitation and oppression, far from the idyllic *Sonar Bangla* of the Bengali cultural imagination. This meant a rewriting of the moral economy, or the rules of crisis protection, and was a matter of great significance even if rural harmony was more imaginary and symbolic than lived (Hossain 2005).[28]

growth rates and periodic natural disasters, and with relatively slow urban growth until the 1980s, rural landlessness had very likely been on the rise for generations by the time of the famine. Already by 1960, an estimated fifth of the rural population had no cultivable land of their own (Van Schendel 2009). Alienation from the land in East Bengal, or, more accurately, reliance on agricultural wage labour by rural people, was noted on a significant scale from at least the 1920s, and possibly earlier, increasingly dramatically in the 1940s; credit relations and the famine played an important part in dispossession and land control (Bose 1986). A 1978 land survey found that 29 per cent of rural people owned no arable land, and half of those no land at all (cited in Cain 1983). On the impacts of demographic and ecological change, and the 1943 famine, on moral economic institutions, see Greenough (1983); Greenough (1982).

[27] There is such an extensive body of critical literature on microcredit now that it is difficult to know where to start. A close-grained recent account that pulls no punches and benefits from many years of ethnographic field research is Karim (2011).

[28] Bengali literature had motifs of dispossession and destitution throughout the twentieth century, narrating the decline in Bengali peasant living standards from the late nineteenth century on. By the 1970s, Bengali literary fiction is exploring themes of peasant political autonomy, most famously in the writing of Mahasweta Devi (see Beck and Bose 1995). In cinema, Bengali auteurs Satyajit Ray and Mrinal Sen both made films about the 1943 famine in the 1970s, while Ritwik Ghatak dramatized rural poverty and displacement, often against a backdrop of the powerful rivers that are more actor than context in the lives of the rural poor. The wave of closely observed village or peasant studies of the 1970s and 1980s owes to a similar impulse. These studies contradicted the myth of harmonious peasant communities, stressing divisions and documenting mechanisms of exploitation, sometimes detecting in this rural proletariat signs of class-consciousness, in keeping with the Marxist tendencies in social science at the time and the realities of militant peasant struggles across Asia. See also Jahangir

By the late 1970s, the diagnosis was that current institutional arrangements fail to protect against the crises endemic to the environment. This is the biographical context in which the two major development initiatives on which some of Bangladesh's positive external reputation depends got their start. In his Nelson Mandela Annual Lecture, Professor Yunus of the Grameen Bank relates the following:

> Bangladesh has a massive poverty. When it became an independent country it was devastated by war. And bloodshed. And on top of it there was . . . massive poverty. And then came the famine in Bangladesh, in 1974. As a young teacher, teaching economics, telling the students that how wonderful that subject is, how elegant the theories are. And outside the classroom, the famine is raging. Then the frustrations come. What good these theories are, if its not working for people.
> (7th Nelson Mandela Annual Lecture Prof Muhammad Yunus 2012)

His biography gives a more graphic account:

> The year 1974 was the year which shook me to the core of my being. Bangladesh fell into the grips of a famine . . . They were everywhere. You couldn't be sure who was alive and who was dead. They all looked alike: men, women, children. You couldn't guess their age. Old people looked like children, and children looked like old people. The government opened gruel kitchens to bring people to specified places in town. But every new gruel kitchen turned out to have much less capacity than was needed . . .
>
> One could not miss these *starving* people even if one wanted to. They were everywhere, lying very quiet.
>
> They did not chant any slogans. They did not demand anything from us. They did not condemn us for having delicious food in our homes while they lay down quietly on our doorsteps.
>
> There are many ways for people to die, but somehow dying of starvation is the most unacceptable of all. What a terrible way to die. It happens in slow motion. Second by second, the distance between life and death becomes smaller and smaller . . . I started to feel useless in the face of so many starving people pouring into Dhaka. Social organizations set up feeding centres in various parts of the city. Neighbourhoods made special efforts to find food for the hungry. But how many can one feed every day? Famine was spreading before our eyes in all its ugliness. (Yunus and Jolis 1999, 3–5)

These events caused him to question the value of economic theory, and to consider what practical action he could take. Yunus' accounts of how the thinking behind the Grameen Bank evolved emphasize the iterative process of his learning: he took his lessons directly from the people he sought to

(1978); Thorp (1978); Arens and van Beurden (1977); Hartmann and Boyce (1983); Wood (1994). Adnan (1990) summarizes the key themes and debates of this body of literature.

serve ('I decided I would become a student all over again, and Jobra [the village in which he learned about rural usury] would be my university' (ibid., 5)) and saw the urgency of personal action of some kind and the need to make it last, not to create dependencies that would leave these people more vulnerable.

Biographical sketches of F. H. Abed, founder of BRAC, similarly cite the 1974 famine as a key event, but in his case it was the 1970 cyclone that put him on the path to founding BRAC. Like Yunus, Abed notes the need to learn, to diagnose a problem before he can act on it. He goes on to emphasize that BRAC early on set up a research unit to study the problems it sought to address; famine was one of the topics it studied:

> In 1975 we set up this research department... And we did a series of monographs on who gets what and why, how resource flows through Bangladeshi villages, and how it is captured by groups who are powerful, and never gets into the hands of the poor... What happens during famine? Relationships break down. And there was a very interesting monograph written on what people feel and think about famine... All the men go away. When the men leave, women have to look after the malnourished children. The men leave because there's nothing to do in that area to earn money. They leave for the towns. (Harvard Business School 2014, 16)

The famine is a turning point for Abed, because he learned that they needed to work directly with women. Social norms or cultural tradition could not be allowed to get in the way, because unless they reached the women, they would not reach the people who needed their help the most. In a conversation I had with Abed in 2006, he recounted his surprise at the numbers of women who turned up for a food-for-work pilot project BRAC was developing with UNICEF. This was in late 1974, after the official end of the famine. Marty Chen, one of BRAC's earliest employees, has documented the episode. She noted that instead of the 100 women expected to come, 840 showed up, defying all norms about *purdah* and manual labour for women. This counter-cultural pattern recurred in 1975 and 1976 and into the late 1970s, until, Chen notes, researchers and practitioners were able to convince public policymakers (including then-President Zia Rahman) that women should be able to work on the schemes alongside men as a matter of public policy (Chen 1995). That poor rural women could and would come out to work made it clear that the famine had induced institutional innovation in gender relations—more practically, that poor rural women really, desperately needed the opportunity to work, in a context where the old forms of protection failed.[29]

[29] See Kynch (1998) on how famine induces change in gender relations.

6.6.2 *Biopolitics and Sovereignty*

Edkins argues that modern famine should be viewed as akin to mass murder, and that famine should be viewed as the 'commitment' of acts of mass starvation (2006). If famine is state failure, neither ultimately due to natural disaster or Malthusian effects, this implies that the state must at least have the capacity—if not the will—to act. But as Khondker notes, 1974 was 'more of a sin of omission' (1985, 137), evidence the new state lacked basic capacities to reconcile demands on its capacity with the balance of political power. As the Bhola cyclone showed, the failure to protect the population against the risk of annihilation by ecological disaster or external economic shock was a sufficient mandate for political liberation. Pakistan had lacked the means and the motivation to protect its East-wing citizens from the disasters they faced, and that was an important reason why Pakistan could not rule.

And so the 1974 famine was not just another disaster; it had to be the final one. It signalled that the Bangladesh state was not properly sovereign; it lacked the control over the life and death of its population, or the 'biopower' that is characteristic of the modern state (Rabinow and Rose 2006). At its lowest point, the Awami League regime 'committed' starvation when in early 1975 it expelled 200,000 slum-dwellers from Dhaka, herding around 50,000 into a camp in Demra, outside the city. There, conditions were harsh, meals meagre at most, and health services notional. 'Either give us food or shoot us', one inmate told a *Guardian* journalist (Leslie 1975), succinctly summarizing the biopolitical dilemma facing the state that lacked the power even to encamp its population. To emerge as a sovereign state within the modern global system, the people of the Bengal delta had to better their chances of bare survival in a hostile setting.

We are used to thinking of a state in the Weberian sense as a monopolist of the means of violence over a territory; but what about when the forces that kill are the elements or faceless international markets? A state that faces not military invasion but tidal bores and commodity price shocks is not sovereign unless it can manage, at the least protection against mass annihilation from invaders, whatever form they may take. Foucault specifically cites famine as an example of how human life 'escapes' governance and administration, arguing that a society only reaches its '"threshold of modernity"... when the life of the species is wagered on its own political strategies' (Foucault 1978, 143). A state that cannot decide who lives and dies cannot be sovereign, nor can it be integrated within the modern world order (also Nally 2011).

To expand its sphere of biopower, the Bangladesh state had to abandon hopes of independence from western powers and seek aid, in which it succeeded to the extent that Bangladesh's development policies moved in the donor-desired direction. The international community, or at least the Western powers, had also taken lessons from the famine. But Bangladesh was not alone in struggling with food crisis in late 1974; as the World Food Conference in November that year showed, Bangladesh was one of several Third World countries struggling to feed its population after the OPEC oil price crisis of 1973 (Gerlach 2015). The Bangladesh famine confirmed what was already believed in Washington: that in a context of global commodity crises like those in 1972–4, even the US might struggle to supply all the foodgrains needed; humanitarian concerns could compete with business interests in the allocation of scarce grains, and unalleviated hunger could potentially lead to revolution or mass migration (CIA 1974). Other lessons included that food aid could be used to discipline recalcitrant governments, and that even pro-Western hungry nations did not need to be lavished with aid. So even though the US was more inclined to aid Bangladesh after Mujib was gone, the Bangladeshis were still going to have to work for it.[30]

The short-term effects of the famine tied Bangladesh more tightly by the bonds of aid, but in the longer term, the famine expanded its sphere of sovereign action over its own population. As we will see in Chapters 7 and 8, transforming vulnerable bodies into resilient Bangladeshis capable of self-protection has been central to the human development project since the mid-seventies. Even if the main political parties represented distinctively different elite interests (they did not), they all shared an interest in growing the capacity for 'more or less rationalized attempts to intervene upon the vital characteristics of human existence' (Rabinow and Rose 2006, 2); in other words, an interest in building biopower. The subsistence crisis contract was a matter of sovereign power, or of biopower: the capacity to keep the population alive by changing how they live and reproduce, quite distinct from the politics of party, regime or aid. International aid proved to be very supportive of this project of transforming Bangladeshis, as we will see in Chapter 7.

[30] Hours after Mujib's assassination, an exchange between then-Secretary of State Kissinger and Assistant Secretary of State Arthur Atherton gives a flavour of the US mood. Kissinger describes the coup as 'absolutely inevitable' and notes too his view that Bangladesh could just as easily have tilted pro-China as pro-US, signalling his concerns about the revolutionary potential on this eastern edge of South Asia. Atherton sees this as an opportunity to increase aid to Bangladesh but Kissinger sees no need to rush in—while some recognition of the new regime's new tilt is in order, even a pro-US Bangladesh could not expect generous aid terms in a time of global food stress (United States Department of State 1975).

7

Making Bangladeshis

7.1 Governing the Population

> Self-assured commentators who saw Bangladesh as a 'basket case' not many years ago could not have expected that the country would jump out of the basket and start sprinting ahead even as expressions of sympathy and pity were pouring in... It is important to understand how a country that was extremely poor a few decades ago, and is still very poor, can make such remarkable accomplishments particularly in the field of health, but also in social transformation in general. (Sen 2013, 1966)

The powerful impulse to protect people against subsistence crises set the stage for people to become more resilient, by raising smaller, healthier, better educated families equipped to take advantage of the opportunities afforded by an open economy. New and extended services included family planning and basic health services delivered by frontline 'paraprofessionals', often women from the communities themselves; a massive expansion of the primary school system; and a series of public health campaigns that successfully changed mass behaviour, tackling in particular the main childhood killer diseases. To do this, the state needed to know its population, and the origins of the state's strong statistical effort are to be found in the turbulent early years, when the foundations for development planning were being laid. Given its limited capacities and the need to achieve these changes with aid, space for and partnerships with the growing number of NGOs became critical to delivering these services. These were all mass services, from which no Bangladeshi was excluded—or exempted. This was not about 'target groups', but about governing the population in its entirety, to become capable of reproducing itself in the numbers and quality necessary to compete in the global economy into which Bangladesh was now to integrate. Almost immediately, after a visible blip around the early to mid-1970s, life expectancy started to rise. Bangladeshis now expect to live among the longest lives in the region (see Figure 7.1).

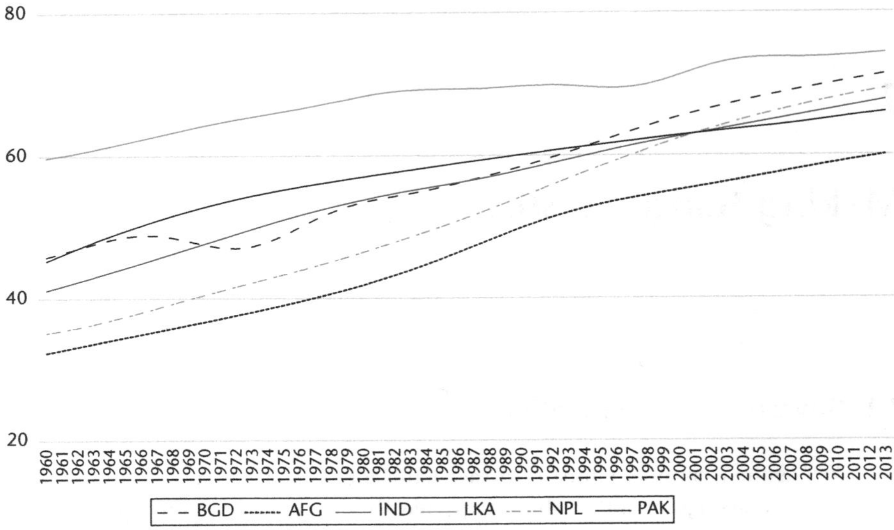

Figure 7.1. Life expectancy in South Asia (years), 1966–2013
Source: World Development Indicators. Accessed 31 December 2015. http://databank.worldbank.org/data/reports.aspx?source=world-development-indicators.

7.2 The Political Economy of Large Populations

It is well known that a fear of exponential population growth drove much of the expansion of public services in the early years, but the overwhelming push on population institutionalized an enduring instrumentalism in the design and delivery of social policies and programmes. Improvements in health and education mattered, at least at first, mainly to the extent that they contributed to population control. The strong focus on population control was not limited to Western donors, but they, in particular the US, pushed forcefully on this issue, without regard to human—and, in particular, women's—rights (Akhter 1992; Hartmann 1987). The intellectual heritage of donor thinking about population control derived from pop-demography and right-wing treatises on the world food supply, as we saw previously (Paddock and Paddock 1968; Hardin 1974; see also Singer 1972); at the height of the world commodity crisis in 1973–4 there is little doubt that the idea of a population crisis (or 'Bomb', according to Paul Ehrlich) enabled a view that a 'state of exception' prevailed in hungry, populous countries, in which the law of human rights could justly be suspended for the greater good. Among other effects, these ideas gave theoretical respectability to the use of food aid for policy purposes, often specifically on population policy but also, as we saw in Bangladesh, on a country's economic and political directions. The food commodity crisis was believed to be contributing directly to the production of revolutionary hordes (CIA 1974). Armed, hungry, post-war Bangladesh, with its 6.7 babies per mother, could provide an unwelcome test of the thesis. As a policy solution to the food crisis everywhere, and in particular in one of the most densely populated countries in the world, population control was a priority goal (see also Rothschild 1976; Gerlach 2015). The Bangladeshi elite in power during the military decade and a half were largely in line with this thinking, perhaps particularly after the refugee and food crises.

Despite the coercive means with which much social policy was introduced, the aspirations of the national elite and the needs of the rural landless were often aligned towards the ends of basic social provisioning: healthier, more productive, and secure lives. The elite has itself recently arisen from the *mofussil* middle and landowning class, and continues to relate closely to rural life and relations. This proximity made it possible to identify the difference between their own (rational, modern) behaviour and the superstitions of the masses as in the latter's lack of awareness, or *chetona*, in turn a function of an absence of basic education. Without schooling, educated people believed, the masses would continue to be fatalistic, superstitious regarding life and death, resistant to modernity, impervious to good social policies like fertility control. People had to be made 'aware' or 'conscious' of their problems and the options available before any lasting development could be had. Mass basic education was the means (Hossain 2010a). This recognition that people needed to be 'primed' for development through social policy became a significant part of the 'will to improve' here (Li 2007). The larger agenda was an emerging elite consensus on development that drew elements from the 'Asian Tiger' success stories such as the need for economic openness, a shift to export manufacturing industry, and investment in human capital. These were ideologically acceptable broad policy parameters for donors; East and Southeast Asian success offered a suitable (and suitably non-Western) model for Bangladeshi elites. In my interviews with the national elite I recall that Japan was often a touchstone, notable in particular for similarities of ecology, ethnic homogeneity, and population density.[1]

The advantages of a large but slower-growing population now capable of reproducing itself to a reasonable standard continue to accrue to the economic elites of Bangladesh in the twenty-first century. This means that there is little political urgency with regard to further rises in the quality of the population or its skills (or human development) that might permit the labour-rich economy of Bangladesh to compete on a higher growth pathway. The population is still viewed as a potential resource, but the economy and the economic elite in

[1] I discuss both these points about fatalism and the need for 'awareness' among the masses, and the introduction of the 'tiger' development models, in Hossain (2005), chapters 3 and 4.

particular reap good returns with the current low levels of investment. The political imperative to provide basic services to the masses is consistently stronger than any to raise the standards of those services. This can be seen in the contrast between the lower priority given to what children learn in class compared to the political energies expended getting them into the classroom, as well as in the contrast between highly effective protection against food shocks and the neglect of nutrition and chronic hunger. A population capable of reproducing itself in a more controlled way, preferably to a standard that is improving, is, politically at least, sufficient for now.

7.3 Smarter Mothers, Valued Daughters

The transformation of Bangladeshi society that came to be noticeable in the new millennium can be judged against the change in the discourse: from worries about the quantity of the population and its rapid growth, development and donor discourse shifted attention to matters of quality—health and education indicators, signs that people were getting better off. Kabeer wrote of the 'quantity–quality' shift regarding children that accompanies demographic transition, showing how people's view of family relations and the value of children changes with the transition from high fertility–high mortality to fewer, more planned, highly valued children (Kabeer 2000). In Bangladesh this shift characterizes not only how families and relations changed, but also how the state started to view the population: as not just a burden to be controlled, but a potential resource meriting investment and support.

Bangladeshis are now far better able to care for themselves, investing in their smaller, healthier families, educating them in the hope of a good job and brighter future (see Table 7.1). Reproductive strategies that emphasize quality over quantity fit the way Bangladeshi society is changing. The population is sharply more urban than was the case at independence, from just over 8 per cent in the mid-1970s to almost one-quarter (24 per cent) of the population now in urban areas and almost half (46 per cent) in Dhaka (BBS 2015; 2011).

Table 7.1. Changing life chances

	THEN	NOW
Life expectancy at birth, total (years)	47 (1971)	71 (2013)
Contraceptive prevalence (% of women ages 15–49)	8 (1976)	62 (2013)
Births attended by skilled health staff (% of total)	10 (1994)	34 (2013)
Immunization, measles (% of children ages 12–23 months)	1 (1982)	89 (2014)
Improved water source (% of population with access)	68 (1990)	87 (2015)
Improved sanitation facilities (% of population with access)	34 (1990)	61 (2015)

Source: World Development Indicators, accessed 2 January 2016.

More than seventeen million women were economically active in 2010—an official labour force participation rate of 36 per cent—although more gender-sensitive measures yield a female participation rate almost double that, at 67 per cent (Mahmud and Tasneem 2011). Paycheck or no, domestic work still needs to be done, and Bangladeshi girls and women aged 15 and over clock up an average 4.8 hours of unpaid domestic labour per day, more if they do not work outside the home and considerably more than men (Huq 2015). This unpaid reproductive and productive labour by women and girls is of a large magnitude, comprising almost one-third of national income by some measures.[2] Women may have to combine more paid with unpaid work, but the drudgery of domestic labour may be somewhat reduced by the availability of water, sanitation, and health services that help prevent the illnesses of childhood and maternity (Table 7.1). In Bangladesh, as elsewhere, public services make a vast difference to the life chances of women.

The social transformation is far from complete, however. Half of all Bangladeshi women are said to be married before the legal age, in a widespread resistance to the law that shows what happens when the logic of the state runs up against the logic of society. Girls marry (or are married off) young, probably because of the dowry premium on female youth, the risk to sexual purity/reputation from modern life (and the continued importance of women's sexual purity), and the domestic labour of young wives. These factors combine in pressure on both givers and takers of brides to complete the transaction early in their lives.[3] Although the risk of dying in pregnancy or childbirth, as newborns, or as infants is far less now (and among the lowest in the region), the chronic problem of 'hidden hunger' in infancy and pregnancy relates to the early marriage phenomenon. Many young couples have children soon after marriage, so that many Bangladeshi babies are born to undernourished adolescents who married early, had limited schooling, and lack the means or knowhow to nourish themselves or their infants beyond basic calorie sufficiency (Hussain, Talukder, and Ahmed 2015). The new nutrition agenda seeks healthier, more mature mothers to give birth to bigger, stronger babies and then feed them the desired diversity of diet in sanitary surroundings. But the underlying fact of young women's disadvantage and lack of power remains, even among the wealthiest, so that, unlike the old problem of hunger, the problem of malnutrition is stubbornly persistent, and cuts across classes.

[2] A recent time-use pilot study by the BBS signalled an interest in addressing the burden of care, but it is not yet clear if this will become part of regular statistical collection (BBS 2013b; Huq 2015).

[3] Although recent evidence suggests the extent of early marriage might be an artefact of lying about age for dowry market purposes, and that most women may in fact be married at the legal age (Streatfield et al. 2015). If so, we have the peculiar situation in which the society *pretends* to be breaking the law en masse when it is in fact not, in order to get a better rate on dowry.

Women's rising economic participation is changing this, and will continue to do so. This is why other areas of gender relations have become more equitable in the smart new Bangladeshi family. Unlike in India or China, smaller-sized families have not meant stronger son preference or a more masculine sex ratio in Bangladesh. Girls may still need to be married off young, but society's views on the value of children have changed. The 'quantity–quality trade-off' at a time of more schooling for girls and paid work for women has been a growing validation of girls as earners. As one mother in her twenties reflected to Kabeer and colleagues,

> No, I don't want any more children. With the little income that my husband earns, if I cannot bring up my one daughter properly, then there is no point in having more children. It's not simply a question of deciding to have more children, it is also a question of bringing them up. (Kabeer et al. 2013, 16–17)

It is also a question of marrying them off. But in the smaller-sized family, daughters are valued as parental carers. Sons may leave home or daughters-in-law may not care, but the public norm has become a more visible recognition that daughters do much of the caring for older parents. This is in part the legacy of decades of public information campaigning around the desirability of smaller families, often featuring positive images of daughters (see Sultana 2015). The Bangladeshi family has become a smarter social unit—more prosperous, better oriented to the needs of the world and of its own reproduction. The changing perception of mothers and of daughters reflects and partly drives this change.

7.4 Accounting for Change

It is fitting that the concentration of major institutions of development—the Planning Commission; the World Bank/IMF; the United Nations; the Local Government Engineering Division; the Bangladesh Institute of Development Studies; and the Bangladesh Bureau of Statistics, just north of Sangsad (Parliament), the seat of national sovereignty—is bounded by Statistics Road. The Bangladeshi state takes the collection of statistics very seriously indeed, perhaps a reflection of the inherent unknowability of its vast human population. Governments count the things that matter to them, and the Bangladeshi state measures and tracks the state of its population ever more closely.[4] The Bangladesh Bureau of Statistics (BBS) is an authoritative and technically able

[4] Bangladesh scored 77 on the World Bank's 2015 'Statistical Capacity Index', somewhat above the South Asian average (71) and considerably above the IDA average, in the low 60s (http://datatopics.worldbank.org/statisticalcapacity/SCIdashboard.aspx; accessed 14 January 2016).

body with strong support from aid agencies, in particular the World Bank. It produces regular reports on social and economic characteristics using accepted techniques, its reports are universally cited, and its data are widely used. In many respects, the BBS is a model of public service: it has a clear mandate, which it is adequately financed to deliver; capacity in statistical data collection and use is good; there is both official and civil society demand for numbers, and scrutiny from Bangladesh's thinktanks and policy experts over its quality.

BBS was established in August 1974, at precisely the time the famine unfolded, and as the new state was planning its future. The new organization merged three large entities and a year later got its own Statistics Division under the Ministry of Planning, with high-level leadership. Before BBS, the state lacked much purchase on the daily realities of its large population, and had little influence over how it reproduced. Without credible statistics, the state recurrently failed to offer a credible account whether of the Bhola cyclone, wartime mortality, floods, or famine; the 'crying wolf' accusation made both during Bhola and during the 1974 floods was only possible because the state lacked the data to refute it. The early 1970s state was able neither to plan for nor to monitor its own performance. For some decades now Bangladesh has had a full complement of regular, authoritative, demographic, food security, and poverty statistics collected and disseminated, often with the support of aid agencies. The contrast between the state's weak accounting of its population in its disastrous past and its present reliance on official figures in its policy, planning, and service provision is striking, indicative in particular of the change in how the state relates to the people.

BBS is the central agency tasked with collecting official data, and its mandate is deep and wide. Several Bangladeshi ministries have working websites, but the BBS site possesses functionality that suggests a brisk traffic in official data and reports. Bangladesh Bureau of Statistics website gives a sense of the sweep of their authority to extract and use information, from the census, the counting of everyone, through to sectoral surveys of agriculture, housing, women and children, the economy. Note that the website hosts a tally of the population beneath a clock, a suggestion the population is forever being counted. Good national statistics mean Bangladesh's progress can be measured and represented in the Human Development Index. Interactive data make it possible to watch the progress of a quarter-century in a satisfying matter of seconds, as graphs showing improvements in the life chances of Bangladeshis climb steadily in the right direction: progress that has been sustained over the past thirty or more years.[5]

[5] See, for instance, the inimitable Hans Rosling, health data guru and Ted Talks star, on the 'Bangladesh Miracle' (Rosling 2007).

In the crucial and politically sensitive area of food policy, too, data collection and dissemination are now institutionalized. The food situation is closely monitored on the basis of key indicators of reserve levels, harvest conditions, global and national prices, production, etc. Wholesale and retail prices are closely monitored across the country, and some seasons or price changes may trigger open market sales or vulnerable group feeding activities.[6] Data are transparent, periodic, and accessible, leaving little room for the markets to misinterpret or manipulate food supply conditions, as in 1974.

7.5 The Population Problem

At 1,222 persons per km^2, Bangladesh is the eighth most densely populated country, preceded only by small islands and urban trading posts and financial centres like Monaco, Hong Kong, and Bahrain; none of these are agrarian societies (which require land and tend to produce low-value products in bulk), and none rank in the top ten largest countries by population.[7] The allegedly comic right-wing writer P. J. O'Rourke noted that at independence 'Bangladesh had only two international distinctions—being the world's largest poor country and the world's poorest large one' (2007, 34); donors certainly saw it that way, but the question of how to deal with a population whose needs were vast, severe, and urgent was uncharted territory, lending itself to urgent measures. From the point of view of those doing the developing, poverty could not be addressed if the numbers of the poor grew so far. But soon enough, population growth was under control (see Figure 7.2), starting to decline in 1979, and mostly continuing to do so since.

Debates about how this rapid decline in population growth came about are particularly telling about the epistemologies and ethics of the Aid Lab. But both sides of that debate agree that population was a clear political priority for donors and the government. Discussion of the urgent measures needed to put an emergency brake on population growth started immediately after the famine. The very first point of discussion in the very first meeting between the US Ambassador and the man who now ran Bangladesh was reported back to Washington as a conversation about population control:

> General Zia and I were able to have several minutes of private conversation at a dinner Saturday night. Uppermost on his mind, evidently, was a desire for us to understand that they had registered our concern that a really effective attack on Bangladesh's population problem was long over due...

[6] See www.fpmu.bd.gov (accessed 2 January 2016).

[7] World Development Indicators, http://databank.worldbank.org/data/home.aspx (accessed 31 December 2015).

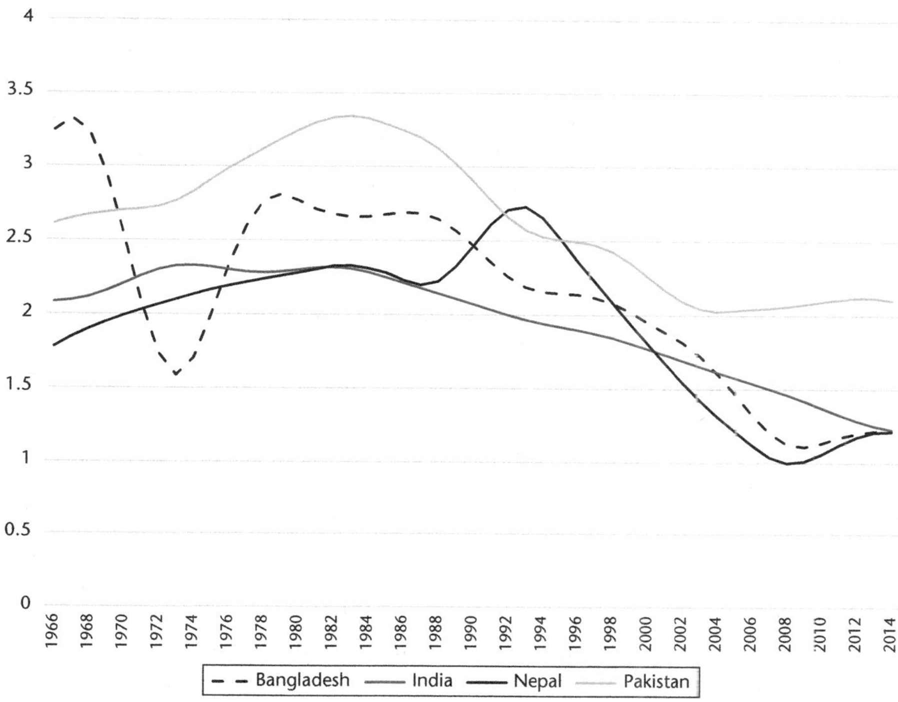

Figure 7.2. Population growth rates in South Asia (%)

Source: World Development Indicators. Accessed 2 January 2016. http://databank.worldbank.org/data/reports.aspx?source=world-development-indicators.

> Zia opened our conversation by referring to the points Senator McGovern had made to him last week about Bangladesh's urgent population problem and said he wanted us to know that they understood this was their top priority...
>
> I said I was pleased to hear this as both here and in Washington during my recent consultation I had been hearing more and more expressions of concern about what had been considered, quite frankly, an unsatisfactory record. Questions were being raised about the purpose of the enormous amounts of aid we are putting into Bangladesh if there was so little to show in the way of checking population growth. (US Ambassador to Bangladesh Boster, US State Department Telegram, January 19, 1976; US Department of State Office of the Historian 1976)

With the state now prioritizing population control, personal behaviours that were proscribed by religion were sanctioned by the highest levels of state, and religious institutions and leaders were successfully conscripted in the struggle. Mujib was said to have been reluctant to push against religious sentiment, sensitive as he was to the charge of being un-Islamic. But Zia had covered his Muslim bases by declaring Islam the state religion, and with strong backing, or pushing, from the donors, was willing to make fertility control a priority

(Franda 1981c). It also seems likely that the religious leadership were as aware as the aid donors and the national and local elite of the mismatch between resources and population, and put up little resistance. A series of highly successful advertising campaigns was sufficiently powerful and/or attuned to mass feeling to defuse any serious resistance, and to increase popular acceptance of contraception (see Sultana 2015). The first Five Year Plan (1975–80) put population control on an equal footing with food security, combining fertility reduction schemes with maternal and child health and public communications efforts to create a broader family planning programme, which, with astute handling of the religious leadership, faced little opposition (Lewis 2011). It was a policy that would continue into the Ershad period, and, with less urgency as women had ever fewer babies, into the democratic era.[8]

Academic debates over fertility decline illustrate the instrumental treatment (by some influential actors) of Bangladeshi women as objects of public policy. In one of the early constituent arguments for the 'Bangladesh paradox' idea, researchers at the World Bank sought to explain the surprising fact of rapid progress in fertility control. Live births dropped from seven to below five by 1994 and continued falling to 2.3 births per woman, while contraceptive use went from 3 to 40 per cent in the twenty-odd years after independence. Theory did not predict such a rapid decline: as the largest of the twenty poorest nations at the time, 'Bangladeshi society remains predominantly conservative, traditional, and agrarian' (Cleland 1994, 1). This was important because, as the largest recipient of foreign aid and of aid to population control specifically, Bangladesh presented 'the most challenging test of what can be achieved when strong government commitment confronts complex population problems with sustained resolve'; the implications were to be mined for their lessons for other countries. The authors paint a rich and detailed picture of the recent crises and social, economic, and political changes that could potentially explain the fertility decline, speculating that 'the disruptions and misery of the early 1970s' may have been a critical juncture. But if so, it was as a political more than a societal trigger: 'The specter of a Malthusian deterioration certainly appears to have stiffened political resolve to address the population problem. The genesis of the current family planning program can be traced back to 1975' (Cleland et al. 1994, 69).

The authors persist in a view of the essential resilience of the patriarchal model in which fecund wives receive protection in a situation of acute human insecurity. Based substantially on quasi-experimental evidence a) of latent

[8] Just as the first discussion between Zia and the US Ambassador zeroed in on population, Ershad used his first discussions with the US Ambassador of that period to assure her that within the development field, 'very high on his priority list [were] accelerated efforts in the field of family planning' (ADST 1986, 97).

demand for contraception, b) that offsetting the costs of fertility control helped, and c) that 'doorstep' services reached women in seclusion, Cleland and colleagues argue that 'program effects', the delivery of family planning services in a context of 'unmet need', drove the fertility decline (1994).

That high-level political and bureaucratic commitment, external resources, and an innovative strategy bringing village healthworkers to women played a major role is likely. But Cleland and colleagues dismiss their own analysis of social and economic change in favour of a truncated conclusion about the genius of programming. This is an early example of 'magic bullet' solutions tested on Bangladeshi soil, in which simple explanations enable outsiders to make sense of the complexities of what has gone right in an unpromising setting. In these accounts, the nature of the social and political consensus on economic growth and human development—a settlement over which generations of the population of East Bengal struggled—is disregarded, or reduced at most to shadowy 'political will'. The emphasis on the organizational details of bureaucratic–managerial projects reflects the bureaucratic–managerial nature of the aid agencies that specialize in such analytical products.

Other close observers countered the 'programme effects' thesis, identifying more evidence of change in Bangladeshi gender relations than Cleland and colleagues treated as admissible. Caldwell and colleagues concluded that whether or not other determinants of fertility decline could be decisively pinpointed, Bangladesh was most certainly not the 'controlled experiment testing the program's effect the researchers have been seeking' (1999, 81). Kabeer re-examined the question from a historical, culturally and class-differentiated standpoint, finding that fertility decline most likely pre-dated the crisis period of the 1970s, as the relative material benefits of children had declined for landless families (2001b). As Chapter 4 argued, the crises of the 1970s crystallized and made visible, but did not cause, the breakdown in the patriarchal bargain. At the same time, variations in rates of fertility decline across cultural and economic contexts, despite the same family planning programme being in place, meant that 'ideas and economics' had to be factors, each coming to the fore in different ways and at different moments (Kabeer 2001b). The programme mattered, but it was the receptiveness of the setting in which it intervened that let it work—or not. Women's agency may have been constrained, but instead of subjects in a maternal health laboratory experiment, they were decision-making actors in a fast-changing world. The programmes were well-designed interventions, but less the drivers of social and economic change than the passengers in a vehicle that was already going that way.[9]

[9] It should also be kept in mind that Bangladesh was one of several countries which saw relatively rapid fertility rate declines starting in this period, and that in global perspective, its

7.6 Tackling the Baby-Killers

It is in the startling achievements in public health that the Bangladesh paradox is at its most contrary: how did such a legendarily poorly equipped, badly governed, understaffed, over-crowded health system defy 'the expert view that improvement of population health is a straightforward function of reducing poverty and increasing resources for health' (Adams et al. 2013, 2109), confounding 'any simple association between health system effectiveness and human development outcomes' (Ahmed et al. 2013, 1747)? In themes that will by now be familiar, the answer lies in: a close focus on reaching women and the rural poor; a pragmatic mix of public and private provision and aid-supported partnerships; and experimentation and learning.[10]

A shining success has been reduced infant and child mortality rates, achieved to a significant degree by tackling the main childhood diseases through high immunization coverage and improving diarrhoeal disease management. Infant and child mortality were closely implicated in high fertility and sensitive indicators of human wellbeing in the mid-1970s. An early assessment of the situation noted that not only could almost half of infant and child deaths be easily prevented through basic vaccines and better diarrhoea management, but '[m]ost of the technologies required are already developed, available at low cost, and readily applicable'. The challenge was political, financial, and organizational: the need to 'generate the political commitment, mobilize the necessary resources, and organize the health care providers and local communities to deliver the services' (Chen et al. 1980, 32).

Bangladesh has done well on saving children from preventable deaths, but as Figure 7.3 shows, it has not done noticeably better on this (and other related indicators) than its regional comparators. What does make it stand out is its 'positive deviance': its gains have come at relatively low cost, low GDP, and high poverty levels (Chowdhury et al. 2013; Koehlmoos et al. 2011). This reflects the fact that Bangladesh suffers from a chronic shortage of health professionals, with only 0.58 per 1,000 people—well below the World Health Organization's cut-off point for a 'serious shortage of human resources for health', which is 2.28 (El Arifeen et al. 2013, 2014). The success is partly explained by the involvement of community-based health workers, often women, on a national scale in delivering services and communicating public health messages, including fertility control. A range of models for deploying

'achievements' in this respect are not all that remarkable. It is mainly when viewed from the perspective of the Malthusian preoccupations of aid donors of the early 1970s that Bangladesh's transition appears so dramatic. Many thanks to Andrew Fischer for pointing this out.

[10] For this section, I have mainly drawn on the 2013 special issue of *The Lancet* which analyses Bangladesh's health achievements and challenges. See Chowdhury et al. (2013) for an overview.

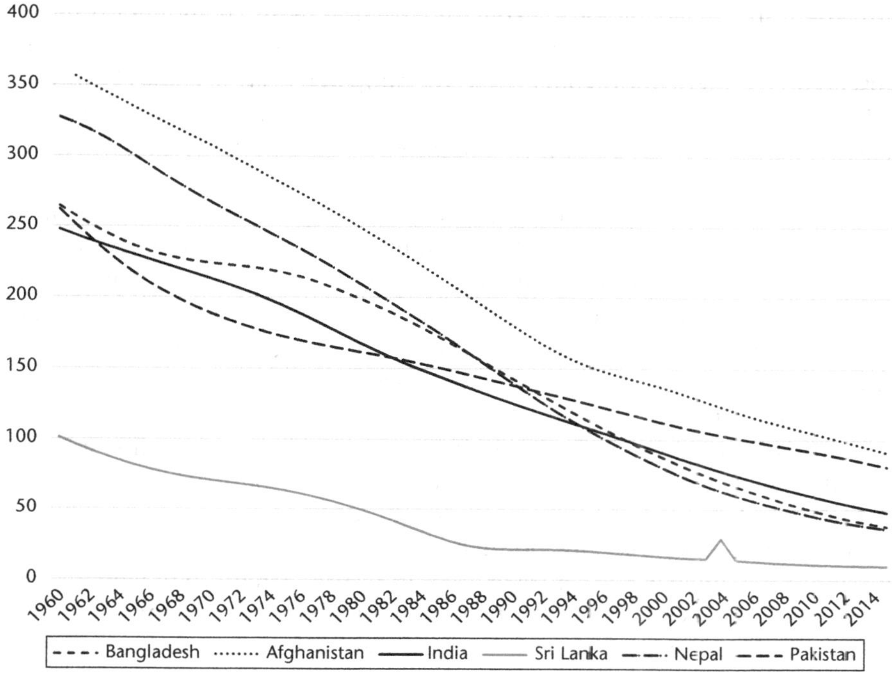

Figure 7.3. Under-5 mortality rate in South Asia (probability of dying per 1,000 live births under 5 years)

Source: World Development Indicators. Accessed 3 January 2016. http://databank.worldbank.org/data/reports.aspx?source=world-development-indicators.

these workers have been trialled with varying success by state and non-state providers. Although they deliver few care services, community health workers play a significant role in health promotion and prevention by virtue of being able to reach and communicate with rural women in particular. Of the around 200,000 community healthworkers, a quarter are government and the rest NGO workers, at least half of whom are employed by BRAC (El Arifeen et al. 2013). To some extent, then, the success of the Bangladesh model enables those so inclined to point out that public health advances need not depend on expanding public health bureaucracies: the private (albeit substantially non-profit) sector can do some of the heavy lifting.

It seems to be true that effective government–NGO partnerships and a generally pluralist approach to provision has helped in this 'whatever works' context. Amartya Sen notes that the devotion to ideological purity over private or public provision common in other health systems has been absent here, replaced by a pragmatic approach to getting all hands on deck in what was, in the 1970s at least, an emergency situation (Sen 2013). The government of Bangladesh has created space for independent NGO action but also partnered with them in a range of ways, explicitly and otherwise, including on major public health efforts such as the successful tuberculosis treatment (Directly Observed Treatment Short course—DOTS) campaign (May et al. 2011), as well as in the Expanded Programme on Immunization (EPI) since 1980—widely termed 'a near miracle' because of the pace at which coverage was achieved (Huq 1991)—and more recently on water and sanitation. It certainly had miraculous effects: between 1987 and 1997 alone, an estimated 1.2 million child deaths were prevented by immunization. This pluralism brings problems—a weakly governed health system with apparently little incentive to increase the numbers of doctors and nurses, or to spread them beyond urban centres, among others (Ahmed et al. 2013). These will pose significant challenges to the next generation of health provision (Adams et al. 2013). But for this first generation of substantially preventive and promotive public health programmes, pluralism enabled an under-resourced and informal system to benefit from the advantages of different providers—outreach, cost, public authority, scale, monitoring, innovation, and so on.

Their reproductive roles, including nourishment and caring for infants and the sick, put women at the centre of gains in health. Attention to women and gender inequality closely guided the design and delivery of many successful programmes, and women health workers were a key part of the strategy. Assumptions about what women could and could not do were thrown out, no doubt reflecting the recognition that times had changed and so had gender relations (see also Chen 1983). Early on, the NGO BRAC took an explicit learning approach to its initiatives, testing models out before scaling them up (not only in the health sector) (Korten 1980; Smillie 2009). In the process it learned about what parts of gender relations could—and could not—change to accommodate an approach to infant and child health that depended directly on mothers' knowledge and capacity to act. The public backing of the government for programmes like the EPI lent it public authority, in a context in which the population have relatively high levels of trust in their state. At the same time, NGOs were able to build a network that spread across villages and into homes, working directly with rural women who had rarely been in contact with outsiders or officials before.

The successes have also been marked by the rapid uptake of innovations—several, such as oral rehydration therapy (ORT) for the treatment of diarrhoea, home-grown in the aid lab itself, designed specifically for the conditions of rural Bangladesh. The NGO BRAC pioneered this, but at different times with the involvement of the government and the ICDDR,B (or Cholera Hospital, as it was once called). The development and adoption of the saline solution (an easily prepared and orally administered mix of salt, molasses, and water) is believed to have saved millions of young lives over the decades, as diarrhoea was the single greatest killer of children by the 1980s. The ORT programme was particularly striking for its combination of lab-like conditions and private sector incentives. The approach was carefully designed, with different options costed and tested, and a process of learning built into the programme. A careful system of monitoring was developed and healthworkers were 'incentivized' to ensure they taught mothers correctly through small performance-based payments based on retention of the knowledge of how to prepare the solution (Chowdhury 2001; Chowdhury and Cash 1996).

One achievement in health that cannot go unmentioned is the Essential Drugs Policy, passed in 1982, which restricted the activities of transnational pharmaceutical companies to encourage production of essential drugs and help grow the local pharmaceutical industry. This is a remarkable tale of a battle between Big Pharma and a military dictator-backed group of medical professionals and activists in which, for once, the little guy won (Chowdhury 1995; Chowdhury 1996). The Bangladeshi pharmaceuticals industry now exports drugs to 107 countries and produces 97 per cent of locally used drugs (*Dhaka Tribune* 2015), and the policy continues to be credited with having brought good-quality medicines in reach of the masses.

7.7 Taking Off: The Hope of Education

> Rafiqul is the son of a betel farmer. He had always been interested in science, even as a small child. One day, he read an article in Prothom Alo [newspaper] about an essay competition organized by NASA, for children from poor families. The prize was to be a trip to space! To everyone's amazement, Rafiqul's essay won first prize. He became very famous and he was even interviewed on the TV. His primary and secondary schools became famous as well. He also got a golden A+ in his SSC exam. Unfortunately, he could not claim his prize, as he was refused an American visa. But the schools he attended remain well known, and have become very popular in the area. (Recounted by Kushtia schoolchildren to Mamunur Rashid; in Hossain and Tavakoli 2008, 33)

Rafiqul's story may or may not be true, but it meant enough for the children from the southwestern village to tell it to visiting researchers. I remember and retell this story because it strikes me as a child's-eye view of the adult world's enthusiasm for education. With hard work and innate ability, not even the sky is the limit! It may not be quite enough to gain legal entry to the US, but (local) fame and fortune await those who succeed at school. The view it encapsulates is an essential optimism about the prospects of education, in which society is seen as basically meritocratic, so that a modest background is no barrier to advancement for people with luck and hard work in their favour.

I wrote in Chapter 3 ('The Elites, the Masses and Their Donors') that political culture here contains a strong meritocratic streak, a blend, perhaps, of Islamic egalitarianism (among men) contrasted against Hindu caste hierarchies, a protracted political history of evicting foreign economic elites, and a more recent experience of rapid social mobility via education among the upper middle classes. To be a Bangladeshi should mean that with hard work, innate ability will make success possible. Faith in education as the means to both national and individual progress appears to unite the elites and the masses.

There are distinct perceptions of the purposes of education. The first is the development of what educationalists call 'non-cognitive skills', a variant of the Bangladeshi elite's 'awareness' (in Bangla, *chetona*). This denotes a capacity for rational thought, a familiarity with the modern world or an ability to engage with it.[11] For bureaucratic elites, basic education is essential to be able to cope with the disciplines of the state—registration of vital life events, the literacy required to absorb most state communications, the behaviours and speech required of formal organizations. There is little point investing in schemes and policies to protect people against crises and poverty if they remain mired in fatalism and unable to help themselves. You may be able to vote with a thumbprint, but full citizenship presumes literacy. And there is more: young people with whom I have spoken about the value of school have said that education offers the prospect of a 'beautiful' life, suggesting an openness to the possibilities of the world and of intellectual fulfilment. Of course, as enrolment rates have risen over the decades (see Figure 7.4), going to school has increasingly become just what one does to remain part of society, to avoid being left behind (see in particular Hossain 2010a).

Second, there is the materialistic dimension of education, the fact that it increases people's economic productivity. With good credentials, the individual stands a chance of a good job. With higher average skills, the nation stands a chance of competing, turning its burdensome human population into a valuable human resource:

> Our problem is this issue of poverty—we have these economic problems, this is true, but manpower, that we have. For example Japan, they have manpower. But they can properly utilise this resource of manpower, and develop this in a highly technical way, which is why they are now one of the leading countries in the world. If we were able to train up our manpower in that way, give them

[11] A set of ideas with an intellectual heritage in the Bengal Renaissance, the nineteenth and early twentieth-century social and cultural reform movement among the Bengali elite which sought to 'awaken' Indians from religious superstition in the struggle against empire. This draws on my own research into basic education in Bangladesh (Hossain 2010a; Tariquzzaman and Hossain 2009; Hossain and Tavakoli 2008; Hossain et al. 2002; N. Kabeer and Hossain 2004; FMRP 2007; Hossain 2006).

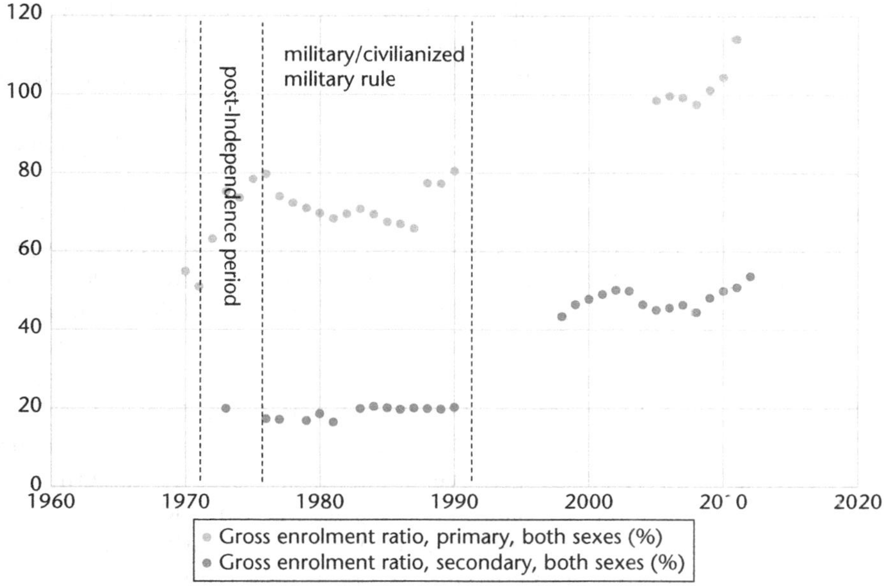

Figure 7.4. Education enrolments

Source: World Development Indicators. Accessed 6 January 2016. http://databank.worldbank.org/data/reports.aspx?source=world-development-indicators.

> employment opportunities in that way, then manpower itself is a big asset. This is something that foreigners don't understand...
>
> (Senior civil servant interviewed in 1998; in Hossain 2005, 58)

My research in the late 1990s identified a clear vision among the national elite about the role of education in transforming the population into an asset, a vision in which Japan featured prominently:

> There is a lot to count our blessings for. As a Japanese friend once told me, 'you are better off than we are...You have a population problem, we had a population problem, and we are exposed to the elements, no less than you are, and we have more severe winters. We need heating, warm clothes, which you can do without most of the year. And then you have natural gas, we don't even have that. We fought two world wars, and got the atom bomb into the bargain in the last one. These went on for years, and Bangladesh only fought a war for nine months. The destruction there was unprecedented.' This is a way of speaking: the point is what is it that made Japan do what it did, in terms of engineering economic wonders? Land management, human management, human resource management.
>
> (Intellectual and journalist interviewed in 1998, in Hossain 2005, 58)

A third purpose of mass education is the transmission of national identity, a more explicitly partisan political goal. The two main parties have used the curriculum to transmit values of secularism or faith, and to instil their own accounts of liberation history. This too had its positive effects, as it probably created competitive pressures that drove the rapid expansion of the primary education system in the 1990s, as each incoming government sought to stamp their own visions and versions of nationhood on an incoming school cohort (Hossain et al. 2002).

The trajectory of educational enrolments displays marked political patterns. First, from the spike in the early 1970s, we can read off the high hopes for education that marked the immediate post-independence period. The new Awami League government nationalized 26,000 erstwhile community schools and brought them and their staff under the ambit of the state, while the new Constitution declared education a right; enrolment rates soared, although the system had few trained teachers or classrooms to cope with the influx. An education commission declared the value of education to be 'mass-oriented, universal', progressive, modern, and secular, targeting in particular the *madrassahs* or Islamic schools for reform. Aid donors were ambivalent about mass education programming in the early years, seeing these as nation-building activities and as potentially contributing to the revolutionary tendencies of the masses, rather than as relevant to economic development (Hossain et al. 2002).

After the assassination of Sheikh Mujib in 1975, General Zia's Islamicizing tendencies were reflected in education policies, but education remained a relatively low priority until General Ershad took power in 1982. What Zia was to food security and population, Ershad was to mass education. Recognizing the popularity of education, Ershad sought to legitimate his civilianized military rule by expanding school provision. Primary and to a lesser extent secondary enrolment started to rise in the early 1980s, as public spending on basic education rose, and a new Directorate of Primary Education was established to manage the expansion. A new emphasis was put on getting girls into school, and technocratic committees drew up plans to establish compulsory primary education (Unterhalter, Ross, and Alam 2003). By the time the Jomtien Conference in 1990 kickstarted the global push for educational expansion, Bangladesh already had a Fifth Five Year Plan (1990–5) to establish universal primary education and was well positioned to expand its system (Hossain et al. 2002).

Democracy has been particularly important for the expansion of basic education, in Bangladesh as in other developing countries with open economies governed by competitive polities (Ansell 2008; Stasavage 2005; Avelino, Brown, and Hunter 2005; Hecock 2006). It was in the democratic period since 1991 that mass education really took off. Under the BNP's Khaleda Zia (1991–6), trends away from nationalization and towards Islamicization continued, and budgets for *madrassahs* increased. The policy issues that stand out during this regime are pro-poor efforts to increase access through the pioneering food-for-education scheme, an early conditional transfer scheme started in 1993 (Ahmed and del Ninno 2002). Data are sketchy for the period from 1991, but enrolment rates of girls started to rise sharply at this time, as did recruitment of teachers (particularly women). The employment of women as teachers has been so significant, with two-thirds of all government primary school teachers now women, that it has been credited with helping close the gender wage gap at the upper end of the wage spectrum (Al-Samarrai 2006). The feminization of education has contributed to the changing face not only of the public sector but also of opportunities for educated middle-class women. As we will see in Chapter 8, it has also been important in driving women's formal sector employment, in the manufacturing industry and services.

Under the Awami League's Sheikh Hasina (1996–2001), the policy of secularizing education was revived. The Education Commission set up during this period echoed the 1974 Qudrat-e-Khuda Commission in proposing modernization of *madrassah* education. The 1999 National Plan of Action and 2000 'Education for All' policy sought to universalize primary schooling. While Awami League governments have not reduced budgets for *madrassahs*, they generally took a more active approach to tackling some of their management and governance issues.

The Seventh Five Year Plan (2016–20) marks a shift in the emphasis on the size of the system towards a focus on quality and a new recognition that education is the basis of the skills through which the labour force can compete on a global scale. For the first time, there is not merely a focus on getting children into school to acquire rudimentary learning and non-cognitive skills, but a fuller focus on educational attainments. A close eye is increasingly being kept on schooling outcomes, as distinct from a historic focus on the inputs of classroom, teacher, textbook, and student number (GED 2015b).

Not all Bangladeshis have had equal access to schooling, however. The extent to which different regimes have attempted to make schooling more inclusive, and for which groups, reflects on their visions of nationhood and national identity. Both main parties have seen the rural poor as key excluded groups, reflecting their numerical importance and historical exclusion from modern education. Both parties have also been content to allow *madrassahs* to flourish, with state-supported Islamic education comprising a significant part of public spending on schooling. This reflects the enduring importance of Islam, perhaps particularly in the education of girls. It has been argued that this 'holy alliance' of tolerance for religious schooling alongside the push for gender equity which has featured across different political regimes has helped Bangladesh overcome social barriers to girls' schooling (Asadullah and Chaudhury 2009).

Bangladesh has been rightly famous for its non-formal primary education models, in particular the BRAC and Gono Shahajjo Shangstha (GSS) approaches.

Special curriculum and pedagogical approaches were combined with targeting mechanisms to ensure the poorest children, and girls in particular, could attend and succeed in those schools. The BRAC schools were single-class units in which well-trained volunteer teachers compressed the official five-year curriculum into fewer (first three, later four) years, then fed the graduates back into the state system. To date some five million children have graduated from these schools, two-thirds of them girls from very poor and disadvantaged families, and the majority have entered the state system (BRAC 2016).

Both the BNP and the Awami League have experimented with food or cash initiatives to attract disadvantaged groups—chiefly girls and poor children—to school. A pioneering food-for-education scheme, one of the early variants of the conditional transfer programmes that included Brazil's *Bolsa Familia* and Mexico's *Progresa* schemes, was established with the rump of the old Public Food Distribution System in 1993; this was then monetized in the late 1990s, to become the almost entirely government-funded Primary Education Stipend programme. A secondary school stipend for girls established under the BNP government was expanded by its Awami League successors to reach boys from poor backgrounds. A current push is on to make cash stipends and school meals available to all primary school students (GED 2015b). While there are good reasons to believe several of these schemes endure more out of political popularity than because of evidence of positive impact on learning (see Baulch 2011), they both send strong signals to the public about the value of education for all children, in particular girls and poor children, and they channel resources to low-income families, typically via mothers and girls.

Minority ethnic groups and non-Muslims are not served by the large *madrassah* system, nor have children in the more remote locations such as the Chittagong Hill Tracts or the tea plantations in the East been well served by the expansion of basic education. The urban poor are also typically unserved by state schools, which are not established in slums to avoid establishing permanent settlements in sites deemed illegal. From the 1990s, these groups were left largely to the efforts of NGOs and donor programmes; under the Awami League government that took office in 2009, there have been new efforts at more inclusive education, through 'mother tongue' learning policies and programmes to include children with disabilities within the mainstream system.

Bangladesh's successes in getting poor girls into school have been widely discussed (Hossain 2007b; Kabeer and Hossain 2004; Chowdhury et al. 2002; 2003). But while more girls have gone to school from all classes, boys from the poorest groups have lagged. This partly reflects the strength of economic growth and the persistent strong demand for the labour of young boys; cultural proscriptions on young girls and women working outside the home and the continuing premium on their sexual purity has meant the same has not happened to girls. The comparative failure to reach poor boys may also reflect the strong emphasis on gender equality in aid programming, which mainly translates into programmes to promote girls' education without attention to matters of class. In my view, the 'boys left behind' reflect the same patterns of human development found elsewhere: progress is made where the policies of the state go 'with the grain' of societal desires and needs. There has to date been relatively little desire to abolish child labour (particularly boys' paid labour) within Bangladeshi society, substantially because of a sympathetic attitude towards poor parents. The state pushes only gently and with limited effect on enduring social practices that run counter to public policy (Hossain 2006; Tariquzzaman and Hossain 2009).

We turn next to what Bangladeshis have done with their new control over their lives and capacities, with a focus on employment in the readymade garments (RMG) industry, international migration, and the micro-financed informal sector.

Part 4
The Bengal Tiger

8

Aerotropolitans and Cinderellas

Bangladeshis in the Global Economy

Imperialism, trade, and migration placed people from the Bengal Delta on the frontline of a recognizably capitalist world economy hundreds of years before twentieth-century Bangladeshis started migrating abroad for work, manufacturing exports, or transacting financial services en masse (Lewis 2011).[1] By the eighteenth century, 'Golden Bengal' was a major source of the lucre circulating in the City of London; the British state financed its Indian adventure through taxes on peasants under the Permanent Settlement, and financial markets were fuelled by the profits of European investments in lucrative indigo, opium, tea, silk, and jute (Van Schendel 2009). Exposed to the vicissitudes of global markets under East India Company rule, East Bengal's peasants turned to rural elite moneylenders for protection (Van Schendel 2009; Bose 1986). So while rural exploitation in the money markets and through economic migration and the global export trade are nothing new, in the twentieth century the population of Bangladesh came to participate directly in global production networks, albeit at the bottom of global value chains, where they have been incorporated on terms that are often individually empowering yet collectively adverse (Phillips 2016; Phillips 2011).

Human resources came to generate wealth for elites and incomes for its population in manufacturing exports, chiefly of readymade garments; labour migration, in particular to the Gulf states; and the heavily garlanded and equally criticized microfinance industry, which channels (mainly) aid funds to circulate in the rural erstwhile subsistence economy. This chapter explores

[1] People in the Bay of Bengal could speak Portuguese in the seventeenth century, presumably having learned through trade (Van Schendel 2009). Sake Dean Mahomed, an early travel writer from India, opened the first Indian restaurant in eighteenth-century London (Narain 2009); Bengali Muslim sailors were arriving in Dundee with Scotland's jute imports as early as the mid-nineteenth century (Ansari 2004; see also Gardner 1995 on histories of travel in Bangladesh).

the scale and impact of these major 'growth sectors' on the national economy, and perspectives on their influence in transforming an agrarian society into one shaped by globally connected wage workers and entrepreneurs. It also surveys the experimental and incremental nature of the policies and programmes through which they were introduced, or which gave them space to grow. Aid played a major role in financing, learning from, and cheerleading for microfinance, but was less important, at least in any direct sense, with regard to RMG and 'manpower' exports. Donor engagement encouraged broadly pro-global market shifts, and human development and poverty reduction policies that specifically supported goals of market integration.

The three sectors interact in real lives, with microcredit paying for upfront costs of international migration and garments workers migrating abroad for factory work; together, these represent momentous changes in livelihoods since the 1970s. A combination of factors was essential: openness to free markets and the global economy; foreign and economic policies satisfactory to Western aid donors and their political leaderships and acceptable to the Middle East; and human and social development policies that allowed people to 'accumulate' human capital in the form of basic health and education. Moving into labour-intensive garments and migration was a step away from the crises of subsistence and survival of the 1970s, and generated enormous wealth from the 1980s and in particular the 1990s. Yet in its more mature post-global financial crisis phase, it is clear that Bangladesh and Bangladeshis at the heart of global production networks are highly exposed to shocks in the global political economy, whether spiky rice prices, export order cuts, industrial accidents, or racist immigration policies.

8.1 The Growth and Growth of the Readymade Garments (RMG) Industry

It is hard to overstate the significance of this sector. Export industry dominates economic growth, and Bangladesh stands out among less developed countries in the high share of manufacturing in its base (Kathuria and Malouche 2015). RMG dominates: of the USD 30 billion earned in exports in 2014–15, more than 80 per cent was from woven and knitted garments, a proportion that has risen since the 2008 global financial crisis (Bangladesh Bank 2015; MoF 2015b; see Table 8.1). Frozen and processed foods, engineering and chemical products, leather goods, ceramics, and pharmaceuticals are growing fast, but the export concentration on RMG exports has grown (Sattar and Ahmed 2012).[2]

[2] Examining Bangladesh's performance in and recovery from the global economic recession, some scholars argue fears of overly high export concentration levels are overstated, and that

Table 8.1. RMG as % of total exports, 2006–15

	2006	2007	2008	2009	2010	2012	2013	2014	2015
Total exports (US$, millions)	10,526	12,178	14,111	15,565	16,205	22,924	24,288	27,018	30,177
Annual % change	21.6	15.7	15.9	10.3	4.1	41.5	5.9	11.2	11.7
Garments as % total exports	75.1	75.6	75.8	79.3	77.1	78.1	78.6	79.6	81.2

Source: Kathuria and Malouche (2015, 3).

More than half of industrial employment is in RMG alone: by 2012, 2.8 million of the 5 million workers employed in officially classified industrial sectors were garments workers (BBS 2013a). Trades union activity remains strictly, if unofficially and not always effectively, controlled, despite recent changes in the law (ILO 2014b). Minimum wages are set by the government.

8.1.1 *Brand Bangladesh*

Instead of the outsider's cheery account of social transformation through export industry (Sachs 2005), this book could have opened with the gruesome image of Rana Plaza, the cheaply built factory complex that collapsed, killing more than 1,130 workers and maiming and injuring 4,500 more, in 2013. That disaster was a parable of globalization, caused as much by the weight of poorly constructed masonry as by the pressures in a system that profits from implausibly low labour costs to produce disposable 'fast fashion'—cheap mainly because its social and environmental costs go unpaid (Siegle and Burke 2014). In a meaningful sense, Bangladeshi garment factories collapsed because low inputs costs have been key to competitiveness to date, and worker safety has been a low priority (and resistance remains to improving matters, despite massive efforts). This in turn reflects the fact that workers are effectively prevented from organizing and, as of 2011, Bangladeshis were the lowest paid export workers in Asia, with real monthly wages averaging USD 91 compared to 126 in Cambodia, 170 in India, 255 in Vietnam and a princely 325 in China.[3] Please note these are real wage rates based on PPP (purchasing power parity) indexes (see Moazzem and Raz 2014 for details). Note too that this was *after* the minimum wage rises for which workers had fought in 2008–11, when costs of living rose exponentially with the global food crisis

Bangladesh's exports and the markets to which it sells are sufficiently diverse (Taslim and Haque 2011).

[3] Calculated in terms of PPP or purchasing power parity, the commonly used means of comparing poverty lines, wages, and costs of living across the world. The analysis was by the Workers' Rights Consortium, reported in Moazzem and Raz (2014).

(Hossain and Jahan 2014). Anu Muhammad notes that the wage was 'still a malnutrition wage, and it is still the lowest wage for garment workers in the world' (2011, 24).

There is no argument that the low wages of its workers substantially explain the success of the RMG sector to date. Labour is a major part of the cost of garments manufacture, and RMG is a classic 'starter' industry for developing countries (Saxena and Salze-Lozac'h 2010), particularly ones with large poor rural populations of 'nimble fingers' and presumed docility (Elson and Pearson 1981; Benería and Sen 1981; Beneria et al. 2000). In the early years, workers were recruited from owners' rural home districts, signalling protection of vulnerable women workers and establishing continuities between old rural patronage and new paternalisms in global export production (Kabeer 2002). At a global level, low wages created the conditions for the Multi-Fiber Arrangement (MFA), through which developed countries attempted to protect their own low-waged workers from competition from those in developing countries. The MFA inadvertently helped foster the manufacturing sector in labour-surplus countries like Bangladesh, although without incentives to improve productivity or build backward linkages to expand the scope of the industry: market share was guaranteed and, in Bangladesh, profits assured thanks to low-cost labour, easy credit on which to import supplies, and scope for on-selling of quotas themselves. By the time the MFA was phased out under World Trade Organization rules in 2005, fears that the Bangladesh industry would be unable to survive full-on competition with China had subsided. The sector had diversified, raised quality to some extent, and improved production times (Saxena and Salze-Lozac'h 2010). With labour costs—and associated workers' rights—still the most minimal among major manufacturers, the Bangladesh industry has continued to thrive in the twenty-first century. It actually experienced a 'Walmart effect' during the global recession, when European and American consumers bought more of its cheap goods (Taslim and Haque 2011).[4]

In the wake of Rana Plaza, the sector faced strong pressure to raise labour and ethical standards while also improving quality, raising productivity, and staying competitive. The balancing act needed was summarized in a World Bank trade diagnostic study: 'opportunities for growth in the apparel manufacturing sector lie in enhancing productivity within existing production value chains without adversely impacting social welfare in the sector' (Kathuria and Malouche 2015, 91). Productivity is low and lead times long. Orders take an average of eighty-eight days in Bangladesh from order to

[4] There are a number of good detailed sources of the RMG industry at different stages of its development. See Bhattacharya and Rahman (1999); Khatun et al. (2007); Kabeer (2002); Mahmud and Kabeer (2003); Rahman et al. (2009).

delivery, compared to 40–60 in China and 50–70 in India. This is partly due to the need to import cotton, delays at Chittagong Port, and problems with energy, but also to lower worker productivity in Bangladesh, where workers make 13–27 polo shirts in the time Chinese workers make 18–35, and produce more waste and rejects. So despite lower wages, the overall cost of the shirt is USD 3.46 in Bangladesh, USD 3.93 in China, and only USD 3.03 in Ethiopia (Kathuria and Malouche 2015, 92).

8.1.2 *The Changing Political Economy of the RMG Sector*

Although its importance now makes its growth seem inevitable, the sector's relatively early start (Bhattacharya and Borgatti 2012) and rapid expansion warrant a political economy explanation. Rather than the inevitable result of Bangladesh's comparative advantage in cheap, unregulated labour and free-market policies, Khan observes that the sector got its start because of specific conditions in the foundations of the political settlement: a) powerful political pressure to liberalize, including from the new proto-capitalists with hot cash; b) global trade rules, in this instance the MFA, as we saw previously; c) the 'accidental' transfer of technology that started with the 1979 Daewoo-Desh Garments venture; and d) strong but informal elite political protection, from the highest levels (Khan 2008).

For Khan, the critical factor is the emergence of a new vernacular capitalist class in the post-Independence period. This part of Bengal had never had important modern manufacturing or an industrial elite class (Kochanek 1994; Sobhan and Sen 1988). Despite the energetic presence of the left throughout the formative years of the nationalist struggle from the 1960s on, the balance of power that emerged in the mid-1970s depended on the state creating and protecting space for business investment. A new Bengali Muslim business class had emerged almost overnight, benefiting from good connections in the newly independent state to engage in a rapid process of primitive accumulation, including from sales of public assets, grabbing 'enemy property', and smuggling (Khan 2008). By the mid-1980s, the trade regime began to be liberalized under pressure from the small old industrial elite and the emerging new class of 'at least hundreds of individuals who could if called upon raise $100,000 or more of capital in the form of land, liquid capital or collateralized bank loans for investment' (Khan 2008, 88).

A 'lucky accident' in 1979 sped matters up, establishing a partnership where, under the leadership of the ex-civil servant Nurul Quader Khan, Desh Garments provided capital and reassuring political protection, while the Korean firm Daewoo transferred the technology and trained staff (many of whom later went on to establish their own firms) (Khan 2008, 89). Then-president Ziaur Rahman personally backed the initiative, and his and his successor Ershad's personal support for RMG entrepreneurs pushed through import credit and bonded warehouse facilities that overcame some of the tougher barriers to entry or growth (Ahmed et al. 2014). The National Industrial Policy in 1982 set up incentives and support for foreign direct investment, including through export processing zones (EPZs) (Kabeer and Mahmud 2004; Kochanek 1994). The 1990s saw more incentives, encouraging the growth of locally owned firms (Bhattacharya and Rahman 1999).

No important interests opposed this growth, and the sector did not even face real opposition to the dependence on female labour when the state took on a more Islamic appearance in the 1980s (although see Shehabuddin 2008). The Khan analysis (2008; also 2011) is of a piece with his wider thesis on the origins and the nature of the political settlement that underpinned Bangladesh's sustained economic growth. It reminds us of the foundational areas of consensus and shared interest within the elite, cohering around the need for openness to the global market and to labour-intensive exports. Political protection 'heavily nurtured' garments entrepreneurs, ensuring policies that eased trade processes as well as insulation against unpredictable and unstable forms of corruption (Ahmed et al. 2014, 266). The business classes have had an on–off agreement to protect the sector from the *hartal* (strike) politics that devastate just-in-time production schedules (Hassan 2013).

8.1.3 *The Question of Empowerment*

RMG employment has wrought broad change in women's lives and gender relations in Bangladesh. A recent analysis found the industry had played a 'key role in the remarkable progress Bangladesh has made in improving women's lives over the past 40 years' (Heath and Mobarak 2015, 13). The transition to women's factory work can be contentious and conflictual, and change does not come overnight. But factory work offered women the 'power to choose', bringing with it new internal strength and stronger bargaining power at home (Kabeer 2002). Factory work was a step up, or a step away, from the domination of the patriarch at home, the meagre returns of rural enterprise, or the 'choice' of barely paid and oppressive domestic service.[5]

Garments (and other income-earning) work is contributing to emerging norms of conjugal equity and complementarity (Schuler et al. 2013), and, depending on the kind of work, to empowerment in spheres from the household to public and civic domains (Kabeer et al. 2011). It has dramatically feminized

[5] Kabeer and Mahmud (2004) found that RMG sector workers were generally from slightly less poor backgrounds than other wage workers (including live-out maids); Karim (2014) similarly notes that, despite its hardships, rural women preferred factory work to domestic services, which is notorious for physical, mental, and sexual abuse; see also Blanchet (1996).

the public space, giving visibility and significance to women and their labour (Hossain 2012). Millions of individual women have been financially better off, and shared social and public institutions have become somewhat more equitable; women are increasingly viewed and treated as worker-citizens, at least by the state. RMG employment clearly played a role in that, not least because the political and business elite could see the benefits in an argument that alchemized low-waged factory labour into socially transformative women's empowerment. Garments workers were the 'new golden girls' of the nation, labour leader Nazma Akhter stated, drawing a direct line to *Sonar Bangla* cultural ideals about national prosperity. Siddiqi notes that:

> [T]he Bangladesh government... tried to capitalize on its image as a Muslim but moderate country, the second largest Muslim democracy, and a trailblazer in the emancipation of Muslim women's rights. The emerging rhetoric invoked the image of oppressed Muslim women coming out of seclusion and into the liberated world of wage labour. Officials based requests for US [trade] concessions on warnings of threats to women workers' new-found empowerment (thereby resonating with both the neo-liberal and anti-terror agendas). (Siddiqi 2009, 165)

The factory may have represented an escape from family patriarchs, but never a total escape from patriarchal control (Kibria 1995; 1998). The factory was itself a site of domination: women remained under powerful and still gendered modes of control in 'a highly policed, mechanised domesticity' (Siddiqi 2000, L14). Women were expected to be docile and grateful for paid employment, and less likely to organize for labour rights. But factory work is exhausting, a relentless grind that requires immense stamina; few women can last more than a few years (Mahmud and Kabeer 2003; Kabeer and Mahmud 2004). The work is welcome, even if the conditions can be dangerously poor. On being arrested for protesting about lack of compensation for the Rana Plaza disaster, Kalpana Akter of the Bangladesh Center for Worker Solidarity was at pains to stress her support for the industry: '"These jobs are important," she said. "My very clear message: 'We want these jobs, but we want these jobs with dignity.' There is no point asking for a boycott."' (Greenhouse 2015).

Exposure to the volatilities and pressures in the global economy since 2007 has shown that this group has no effective protection of their jobs, their conditions of labour, safety at work, or (because pay is not inflation-indexed) their real earnings. Workers are effectively blocked from building the kinds of organizations that would collectively articulate and defend those and other interests. Credible sources charge the state with joining employers in union-busting, and in recent years labour leaders have been harassed, imprisoned, tortured, and even killed (Muhammad 2011; Ganguly 2015). Collective empowerment to address the conditions of labour through trades unions remains a distant prospect.

8.1.4 *The Politics of Flexible Labour*

Analyses of the experiences of factories date back to the 1990s, when factories and women workers were novel. Since then several cohorts of women and girls have spent time working in a garments factory and it is just one of the work options available (although still the single biggest sector). Factory work has almost certainly lost its shine. Current generations of RMG workers came of age in an era when the downsides of globalization were inescapable: rock-bottom wages failed to meet skyrocketing basic costs of living; workers subsisted on potatoes, sleeping in shifts because slum rentals are so small that all renters cannot lie down at once.[6] They are at the mercy of their low level in the global value chain, and neither employers, nor garment buyers, nor the fast fashion-wearing Western consumer have an interest in raising wages. Employer resistance to organized labour has survived even the intense global and domestic pressure on the sector after Rana Plaza (Ganguly 2015; Brown 2015) and the loss of Generalized System of Preferences (GSP) trade privileges with the US, despite a concerted effort at corporatism involving business, government, labour, and civil society (CPD 2014); also (ILO 2014b).

Workers were never 'heavily nurtured' like the factory owners, but nor was the state always actively aligned against them (Ahmed et al. 2014). So what claims can and does organized labour effectively make in globalizing times? A conclusive test of the idea that the Bangladesh state is grounded in responsibility to protect against subsistence crisis would be how it has responded to the globalized volatilities facing its essential industrial workforce. The two main parties, the Awami League and the BNP, broadly shared ideological principles and policy practice since the 1990s, aligning the elite consensus along pro-owner lines. That there is no important partisan difference on the issue of worker rights is clear from the responses to industrial action in the past decade. Starting in 2005, major clashes over workers' rights abuses—unpaid wages and benefits, sackings and factory closures, use of violence against workers—were staged in and around Dhaka and the industrial heartland of Ashulia (IGS 2006). Real wages declined in light of high inflation, in particular in the basic costs of living, rent and food being primary concerns. Food price spikes were matched by peaks in violent episodes in factories, and struggles over wages took on a moral economy cast, as workers loudly proclaimed that they could not eat on their wages (Hossain and Jahan 2014). None of this attracted significant party political attention, let alone competition.

But there are shades of party political difference regarding the incorporation of labour that date back to the independence struggle. The Awami League has

[6] This is what I observed and was told by garments workers in Chittagong and Ashulia, just outside Dhaka, in 2013. See Hossain and Jahan (2014) on the grievances of garments workers during the global food, fuel, and financial crises of 2008–11.

historically been aligned with mass and popular movements, in contrast to the BNP's affinity to business, industry and the military; it has been the Awami League government from 2009 that has presided over raising minimum wage levels, however imperfectly, and moved its highly politicized criminal justice system to act after the global spectacle of Rana Plaza, signalling the end of impunity for industrial crimes. In the present period of rule since 2009, the Awami League is emerging as the more corporatist of the two parties, and gives clear indications of taking account of both owners' and workers' interests, as well as a view to the strategic nation importance of the sector as a whole.

8.2 Getting Out, Getting On: International Labour Migration Remittances

The other heavy hitter in the national accounts is remittances from international labour migration. Bangladesh ranked eighth in the world in total remittance earnings at USD 14 billion in 2012 (BBS 2014); was among the top ten countries for emigration, with 7.6 million migrants in 2013; and is among two of the world's busiest immigration corridors, one with India and the other with Saudi Arabia (World Bank 2016). Remittances from international labour migration have grown particularly fast since the 2000s (see Figure 8.1), and the latest figures suggest almost ten million Bangladeshis, mostly men in their twenties and thirties, were abroad as temporary workers (MoF 2015b). But growth has been uneven in the 2000s, increasing by 32 per cent in 2008 and declining by 1.6 per cent in 2015 (Kathuria and Malouche 2015). In the most recent year, around half of all remittances were from the oil-rich economies of Saudi Arabia, the United Arab Emirates, and Kuwait; most of the rest was from the US, Malaysia, and the UK, although migration to both Singapore and Oman rose fast in recent years (MoF 2015b). A small but fast-growing group of migrant workers are women—from 0.54 per cent of migrants in 2002 to 13 per cent only a decade later; around one-quarter of a million Bangladeshi women have officially migrated for work since the 1990s, although taking into account unregistered migration, the true figure is likely to be double that (ILO 2014a).

Remittances are hugely significant for the national economy. The macroeconomic impact of overseas remittances in Bangladesh remittances includes improving the balance of payments, raising national income, finance for productive investment, higher consumption, and counter-cyclical effects (the evidence is summarized in Hatemi-J and Uddin 2014, 376; see also Siddiqui 2005). Bangladesh's respectable first ever financial markets ratings in 2010—BB from Standard & Poor and Ba3 from Moody's—were credited to the 'high share of remittance flows in GDP and their high growth rate'

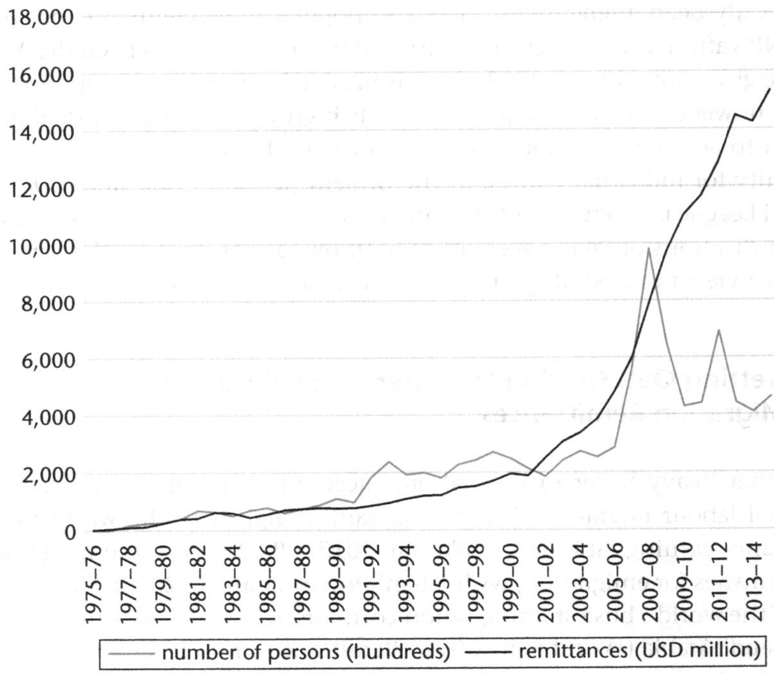

Figure 8.1. Labour migrants and remittances, 1973–2014
Source: Bangladesh Bank 2016, Table XX.

(Mohapatra and Ratha 2010, 308). The 'manpower export' industry has also prompted financial service development, with Bangladesh pioneering mobile money and banking technologies, to speed up and ensure safe international remittances (Mohapatra and Ratha 2010). In 2011, a bank was set up specifically to support would-be migrants with the costs of migrating; these average between BDT 200,000 and BDT 300,000 (USD 2,600 to 3,800 as of April 2016; xe.com) to get to the Middle East, and can take two or three years for a migrant worker to repay (Rahman and Hossain 2012).

Remittances are of equal importance for the sending-household economy, but the extent of unofficial migration means official figures cannot capture their true impact (Rahman and Hossain 2012). The recent BBS survey tells a clear story about the poverty impacts of official migration. In 2013, most migrants were from disadvantaged backgrounds: fully 85 per cent of the heads of remittance-receiving households and 70 per cent of the migrants themselves had less than secondary education. For 78 per cent of receiving households, remittances were their primary source of income. The majority send money home to parents (45 per cent) and spouses (39 per cent), and although remittances are generally spent on everyday consumption, 88 per cent invested in property, building a house or buying an apartment (BBS 2014). But while remittances all but self-evidently reduce household poverty, the relationship works the other way too, so that reduced poverty also leads to higher earnings from labour migration and 'remittances and poverty reduction are causally reinforcing each other in Bangladesh' (Hatemi-J and Uddin 2014, 380). Remittances are a measure of migration success, however, and not all succeed: many migrants are cheated or fail to repay the debt incurred, or otherwise see few benefits from the experience (Kibria 2008).

8.2.1 *The History and Political Economy of Labour Migration*

Bangladesh would be a very different place, and far poorer, without the high-volume international migration of unskilled young men to the Middle East. Labour migration was not new to people in East Bengal, but they had not to date been active in its more organized forms. Efforts to abolish indentured labour started in 1910 and were legislated on under the Emigration Act of 1922. In the 1920s, British Indian officials negotiated over the conditions of Indian migrants in east and South Africa, Mauritius, Ceylon, and Malaya (Shirras 1931), just as the present-day Bangladesh government lobbies migrant-receiving countries to protect Bangladeshi workers. Emigration concerns related in particular to the exploitation of unskilled workers sponsored by private agents, and the 1922 Act sought to license 'Passage Brokers', the sea-based equivalents of the present-day recruiting agents. Men from Chittagong and Nohakhali on the coast had been mobile for centuries (for instance, Chan 2005; see also Siddiqui 2003). However, documented emigrants from East Bengal appear to have been relatively few, particularly compared to the flow of southern Indians departing in the early twentieth century (World Bank 1981).

Within India, labour migration was a common survival strategy after the famine- and recession-studded late nineteenth and early twentieth centuries (Davis 2001). There were 1.7 million migrants from other parts of India in Bengal alone at the beginning of the twentieth century (de Haan 1997). Bengalis themselves moved elsewhere in Southeast Asia, sometimes seasonally. The historical period leading up to Bangladesh's independence, partition in the 1940s, and the refugee crisis after the liberation war of independence had displaced millions of people, so that this was a population accustomed to moving and being among (or subject to) outsiders—a collective experience that marked social and political identities as Bengali Muslims, Bengalees, or Bangladeshis (Feldman 1999; Feldman 2003).

Apart from with Britain, where Sylhetis moved from the 1950s, there were no established legal migration routes. The migration corridor with the Middle East opened up in the early 1960s, when small numbers of men moved to

Saudi and Qatar for work on an unofficial basis, sometimes taking advantage of Muslims' rights to visit the holy sites of Islam to stay and work. This was easy at first, but—unlike (West) Pakistanis and Indians—few in then-East Pakistan knew about job opportunities in the Middle East. Bengalis were soon found by employers to be 'hard-working, disciplined and more productive', as well as cheaper than other workers. Some successful migrants encouraged employers to recruit more workers from Bengal, making the arrangements through their existing networks at home, setting the scene for labour migration en masse to the Middle East (World Bank 1981).

Mass labour migration to whichever country would take workers seemed almost inevitable in this context: 'The unemployment situation was gradually deteriorating, consequently the flow of labour migration to the Middle East started almost automatically' (World Bank 1981, 2). It is possible that fears of a substantial unemployed youth population reflected a potential political threat, in a context in which student politics had been particularly influential. Another push towards new migration may have come from the political crisis over illegal migration to Assam and other parts of India in the 1970s (see Franda 1981c).

In the early 1970s, the 'manpower export' business was a corrupt and risky prospect for workers, much like the old indentured gangs, except instead of ships, men were now moved by air. In 1976, the government started to establish policies to promote manpower export but also to regulate labour recruitment, but due to 'flexible conditions, recruiting agents grew like mushrooms and middlemen continued to exploit the prospective migrants in as many ways as they could' (World Bank 1981, 8). After independence, Bangladesh set up an independent body to handle manpower export matters, the Bureau of Manpower Export and Training, and from 2002 a dedicated Ministry of Expatriates' Welfare and Overseas Employment was tasked with overseeing recruitment, regulation, and return. The 2006 Bangladesh Overseas Employment Policy aimed to promote labour migration and protect workers while abroad, requiring migrant workers to have valid contracts and work visas, arranged by private recruitment agencies under official licence. A Wage Earners' Welfare Fund created in 1990 and funded through levies on employers and workers provides a range of assistance to workers and their families, and is managed by a board comprising government agencies and the recruiters' association BAIRA (the Bangladeshi Association of International Recruiting Agencies).[7]

The government of Bangladesh now takes a position on global migration matters, and in December 2016 chaired the ninth meeting of the Global

[7] See Siddiqui (2005); also http://sitreport.unescapsdd.org/labour-migration/governance-labour-migration (accessed 30 July 2016).

Forum on Migration and Development (GFMD) in Dhaka. Announcing the event, the government declared that:

> Migration is a sensitive, political, development and social issue and Bangladesh wants to push for its new governance structure in the GFMD, which is a global platform on discussion... [The Foreign Secretary] said attitude and perception towards migration need to be changed, otherwise the problems related to it would never solve. (*Dhaka Tribune* 2016)

In an astute move, Bangladesh proposed connecting improved global governance of migration to the Sustainable Development Goals, showing again how successfully the country's policymakers have turned the aid lab into their own machine.

8.2.2 *Aerotropolitans*

Other than the national accounts, the most outwardly visible signs of this flourishing industry are the workers as they move from the world of home to the world of the global production network. If you travel internationally, and in particular if you fly the Middle East–South Asia routes, you will have encountered these aerotropolitans. Bangladeshis are also making a living in North America, across western and southern Europe, legally and otherwise in South and Southeast Asia, and even in Africa, notably through the recruitment of Bangladeshi garment factory workers to work in Mauritius. They travel not for pleasure, to make business deals, or to sell commodities, but because their numerous bodies make them a kind of commodity in themselves (Phillips 2016).[8]

These workers are aerotropolitans because their work fundamentally depends on their rapid and cheap transport through international hubs at the core of global trade and commerce. Airports, where the effects of globalization are at their most intense, are often spaces of luxury and pleasure for middle-class travellers. But those travelling to sell their labour are denizens of the global economy and have few rights or privileges, in transit or at the receiving end. Should they be deemed to have misbehaved by protesting some abuse or other, their right to work can easily be withdrawn by a change in receiving-country policy. It may even be domestic politics and policies of which labour-receiving countries disapprove; the hanging of Jamaat-i-Islami politicians convicted of

[8] Drawing on the idea that the aerotropolis, or airport-city, will increasingly be the centre of economic activity in successful, integrated economies (Kasarda and Lindsay 2011). Although Kasarda and Lindsay do not say much about the population that services the aerotropolis, the idea that global transport hubs are increasingly characteristic of fast-growing world cities fits well with the observable facts of economic growth in labour-rich countries like Bangladesh. Getting out has become more possible, and it has become more important for getting on. But people are moved much like commodities within the aerotropolis, and the aerotropolitan—the international migrant worker—is a denizen, a body without rights.

war crimes in 1971 was a factor in the declining share of Bangladeshi workers in Saudi in recent years (*The Economist* 2013), and new Bangladeshi migration only restarted in 2015 (*International Business Times* 2015). Abuses of Bangladeshi workers abroad continue to make headlines. A recent report documenting working conditions on a United Arab Emirates facility set to house developments by the Louvre, the Guggenheim, and New York University reported a range of serious and regular abuses of workers' rights: unpaid wages, police action including summary deportation if they protested, employers holding passports and cancelling visas of protestors. Some workers were jammed into small, insanitary living spaces (McGeehan 2015).

Unlike workers who stay on Bangladeshi soil, the aerotropolitans stay or move between home and work for several years. They accumulate profoundly life-changing experience and knowledge, not just remittances. Some of those experiences have influenced religious practice and identity (Kibria 2008). Kibria found experiences of migration to the Middle East to be 'marked by sharp consciousness of its Muslim context' (Kibria 2008, 525). An outward-facing, worldly model of religion should in theory attract these global persons:

> A more orthodox approach to Islam, one that is not apparently tied to the vagaries of specific local culture, may be especially compelling to the migrant who is facing the culturally inflected diversity of Muslim practice. There is a desire under these conditions to adhere only to the core tenets of Islam and to strip Islam of extraneous cultural influences, including ideologies of nationalism. With these strategies, migrants also affirm the *ummah*—the idea that the bonds of Muslims, based on their adherence to the core tenets of Islam, are far more important than differences of culture and nationality. In general, the notion of the *ummah* may resonate in especially meaningful ways for those who have crossed national borders and are so faced with the complex realities and meanings of national membership. (Kibria 2008, 520)

But if an orthodox globalized Islam offers the promise of egalitarianism and solidarity beyond national borders, in reality Bengalis who go to the Middle East as migrant labourers are stigmatized and looked down upon. Most learn painful truths about their position in class and global hierarchies, developing a 'globalized national consciousness, defined by a critical awareness of the relative poverty and low status of Bangladesh as a nation in the global order' (Kibria 2008, 532). Some become critical of the democratic regimes at home, the hypocrisy and irreligiosity in the societies they serve, and are disappointed by the lack of solidarity and community among Muslims (Kibria 2008, 527–9).

The mass migration experience may not encourage extremism, but it 'poses a challenge to secular values':

> Islam in Bangladesh—which has traditionally been spiritual, tolerant and syncretistic in nature as idealized in the folk songs of the philosopher-poet, Lalan Shah—

> is now faced with challenges from the radical strains of Islam often grown in the context of globalization that produces shifting identities and a condition of generalized hopelessness and alienation. (Khondker 2010, 200)

It is among these rising waves of global radical Islam that young men return to Bangladesh, bringing their embittering but enlightening experiences of the heartlands of religious culture, oppression by fellow Muslims, and precarious toil at the bottom of the global value chain (Phillips 2016, 7).

8.3 Microcredit and the Market Frontier

If RMG and labour migration pushed the Bengal frontier (Eaton 1993) out into the global economy, microcredit pushed it deeper down into the domestic economies of subsistence and survival. This famous model for addressing poverty by lending money to poor women started small, with a professor of economics trying to figure out how best to apply his economics training to help a poor woman—the legendary Sufiya Begum (Yunus 2008)—grow her tiny enterprise at a time of post-war devastation and famine. The idea worked (or appeared to), kept working, and spread at a rapid rate in Bangladesh and then beyond. It now boasts a 'movement for financial inclusion' founded by a Nobel Peace Prize-winner and backed by world leaders and celebrities. As of 2013, microfinance worldwide tallied 211 million clients, almost half living in extreme poverty. It is a long way from Sufiya and her beautiful small baskets (Microcredit Summit Campaign 2015). But this best known of all development interventions has been controversial for charging high interest rates and indebting poor women (Karim 2011), and faces a major intellectual backlash against its claims to reduce poverty and empower women (in particular Duvendack et al. 2011; Vaessen et al. 2014; but see also Khandker and Samad 2014 for a robust defence).

It is as hard to assess the significance of microfinance in Bangladesh as to establish its real-world impacts. Yet the technology has undeniably earned the country acclaim and spawned a thousand flattering imitators. Bangladesh is the acknowledged home of the technology, as marked by the 2006 Nobel Peace Prize for Professor Yunus and the Grameen Bank he founded. The Nobel Prize sits atop a long and distinguished list of accolades and awards; Professor Yunus has even achieved the ultimate token of worldwide recognition by appearing as a cartoon character on the classic American television show, *The Simpsons*, alongside such luminaries as Stephen Hawking and Tony Blair.[9] BRAC is the other behemoth microcredit provider; now an international NGO working in

[9] http://www.bbc.com/news/world-south-asia-10771300 (accessed 8 April 2016).

seven countries, it also provides other services to reduce poverty and empower women numbering in the tens of millions. BRAC's founder, Sir Fazle Hasan Abed KCMG, needs two paragraphs in his biography to list his honours and awards, and is among Fortune Magazine's 'World's 50 Greatest Leaders'.[10] Both Yunus and Abed have immense stature on the international development stage, and have mixed with the likes of the Clintons and the late Nelson Mandela, among others. Microfinance (if we include also the savings, insurance, and other financial services that accompany credit schemes) is now a global phenomenon of immense scale and power, but its development and successful sharing with the world mark it as a distinctly Bangladeshi technology.

It is relatively easy to see why capitalizing rural women to empower and pull themselves out of poverty was an attractive proposition: it fit the needs of policymakers fighting deep, wide poverty with a small, tight fiscal envelope, aid donors seeking to demonstrate value for money, financial markets seeking a toehold at the 'base of the pyramid', and feminists promoting women's autonomy and agency. Women themselves came forward to borrow money in their tens of millions, so the technology was clearly accepted for some reason—if not always the theory that it would grant women control of household income (Goetz and Gupta 1996). For a decade or more, microfinance was seen as the most promising approach to mass poverty reduction in the world. And that in turn had much to do with its excellent fit with the conditions and discourses of poverty in Bangladesh. Microcredit alerted the world to the possibilities of experimentation with poverty reduction, and it is arguably one of the country's most significant 'exports'.

So what were the effects of microcredit in Bangladesh? What was the significance of a technology that by 2015 reached an estimated thirty million borrowers, or half of all households in Bangladesh (Khandker and Samad 2014)? What did they do with all that credit, and how did its significance and value change over time? In the early years, at least, microcredit played an important role in smoothing consumption, buying people time and giving them access to cash, under conditions when the average rural landless family faced the likelihood of frequent small and sporadic major shocks, unprotected by state or society. There is no way of proving this point conclusively, but these small loans helped people protect against individual and common crises, priming them to adapt and diversify, and to make use of the opportunities for more productive agricultural, off-farm, and non-farm livelihoods. It also, of course, pushed them into debt, many of them unmanageably so, and created immense stress among those tasked with keeping up repayments. In general, microcredit brought a

[10] For Yunus, see https://en.wikipedia.org/wiki/Muhammad_Yunus (accessed 5 April 2016). For Abed, see http://www.brac.net/chairperson (accessed 5 April 2016).

population into regular market relations, when their relationships to the market had previously been more episodic and on more exploitative terms. Whether or not you consider that to have been a negative development depends very much on whether or not you think rural Bangladeshis have benefited from economic growth and development. The microfinance crisis of the mid-2000s and the way in which the Bangladesh sector has recovered from it suggests, however, an important lesson about the limitations of microfinance for poverty reduction: that ultimately poverty reduction requires some transfers of resources and therefore of power to people who have little. There are no quick, easy, and costless solutions to poverty, and it is unlikely to be eradicated through reliance on the workings of financial markets.

8.3.1 *The Origins and Evolution of Microcredit and Other Non-State Action*

An understanding of the origins and evolution of microcredit is inseparable from an understanding of the origins and evolution of the non-governmental organizations and/or 'social enterprises' (as the larger entities now prefer) in Bangladesh. Both Yunus and Abed attribute their original motivations for founding what eventually grew into vast organizations to the foundational disasters in Bangladesh's history; other NGO leaders make similar observations.[11] The relatively generous aid flows to anti-poverty action at this time fuelled and to some extent directed their rapid growth. This situates the start of organized non-state action firmly within what I have called the subsistence crisis contract between the elites, the masses, and their donors.

Many post-colonial or democratic transitional settings feature well-intentioned middle class and elite activists that do not go on to found vast non-state organizations that reach across and beyond the borders of the country. So what in the institutional setting of newly independent Bangladesh made it possible to give birth to and grow such unusually large and powerful organizations? Lewis locates the answer in a unique combination of social organization, political history, and external dependence on aid:

> Local traditions of voluntary action were deepened and transformed by the experience of resistance, war and natural disasters [coupled with a new] familiarity with the international 'aid industry' [which] facilitated their access to funds and outside ideas. Continuing mass poverty during the 1970s and 1980s generated widespread disillusionment with government-based rural development work... Relief and development NGOs were, therefore, established by various sections of the middle classes—by sincere members of the reformist elite, former student radicals

[11] Chen and Rutherford (2013) make the same point, albeit more succinctly.

> alienated or restricted by formal politics and members of the new emerging middle class seeking to build socially useful careers in social work or in the professionalizing worlds of development. (Lewis 2011, 113–14)

Most established NGOs had their origins in the left-leaning idealism common to the post-war reconstruction period (Devine 1999; Hashemi 1995; Kramsjo and Wood 1992), but with leftist party politics aggressively suppressed from the 1970s, NGOs provided the 'non-party political space' in which progressive or pro-poor elites could operate (Kothari 1984; see my argument in Hossain 2005). White noted that:

> It is likely that at least some of the NGO leaders would in different political conditions have gone into politics. With successive regimes dominated by the military, the NGO world offered a relatively open space in which people with a progressive vision could operate, and see concrete results which the formal politics of the time did not offer. (1999, 321)

An NGO leader told me he had returned to Bangladesh from being educated abroad with the aim of joining an underground (leftist) political party, only to find that

> there weren't any. I found out about the NGOs then, I thought this will give me an opportunity to stay in the rural areas. Safer than an underground political party. I stayed for nine months. Then at some point, I thought I would need some money to do what I wanted to do, I got some foreign money. I worked with the villagers, set it all up, wrote the constitution. Now we are one of the fastest-growing NGOs. (Hossain 2005, 113–14)

Early approaches by these non-state actors were informed by critical views on agrarian structure and institutions, which identified grossly skewed land ownership and powerful ideological institutions (norms of benevolent patronage, *samaj* or moral community) as the basis and means of rural exploitation (notably BRAC 1986; see also Lewis 2011). Microcredit also had its historical precursors, in this instance cooperative credit schemes introduced under British rule, 'the beginning of the region's century-long experimentation with credit as an instrument of social policy' (Mader 2013, 47). The Agricultural Loan Act of 1885 established soft loans for peasants affected by natural disasters; exploitative credit relations were legislated on during Fazlul Huq's stint as Chief Minister of Bengal in the 1940s (Rutherford 1995). In the 1960s, rural development experiments under Akhtar Hameed Khan's Comilla model worked with cooperatives of landless peasants, presaging the group-based lending model. Strategies were devised to challenge local elite strongholds on rural communities, or to sidestep them by building organizations of the landless poor.

The leftist and socially progressive origins of (most) NGOs contrast with the view that non-state action in general and microcredit are vehicles for integrating the poor within neoliberal development policy. But in Bangladesh, at least in the early decades of independence, pro-market and progressive were by no means a contradiction in terms. NGOs have been accused by the left of perpetuating poverty as 'agents of international capital' (Hashemi and Hassan 1999, 130), yet many within the NGO movement still identify with the left, and there remain strong links and continuities. Important exceptions to the neoliberal drift include Nijera Kori ('We Do It [For] Ourselves'), which have had a significant impact on people living with poverty and vulnerability, as well as offering an alternative model to the private delivery of public services and the financialization of poverty (Kabeer and Sulaiman 2015; Kabeer et al. 2012).

Most non-state action on poverty moved away from leftist organizing principles and tactics to service provision and helping its members integrate into markets from the 1980s onwards, reflecting the wider embrace of experiments in the market as the solution to Bangladesh's development problems. In a setting where the state had not historically played an important role in mass or rural welfare, in which mass impoverishment left the majority on the brink of survival, and in which there was little national wealth to redistribute, a market- and growth-oriented strategy arguably made sense, even for leftists and social progressives (Hossain 2005). The shift to the market also uncoupled the rural poor from their dependence on landed patrons, giving them new patrons in the form of NGOs, 'freeing' them to sell their labour and their products beyond the old constraints of a moral economy that no longer afforded them protection or support, if it ever did (Lewis 2011; see also McGregor 1989). Even the far left took an accommodating view of the anti-poverty technology, as Atiur Rahman found in his study of the impacts of Grameen Bank on the rural power structure. A Communist Party activist told him: '[w]e cannot stage a revolution with dead men. [Grameen Bank] is at least keeping them alive' (Rahman 1987, 53). Indeed, microcredit claims staunchly pro-poor origins, with its social mission powerfully framed by resistance to the ruinous usury of the traditional moneylenders (Osmani and Mahmud 2015; Rutherford 1995, 25).

Bangladesh's important NGOs have been organizations of the elite and the well-connected educated middle class; their eliteness has been important in their success, and helps to explain the part they have played in delivering on the subsistence crisis contract. These progressive NGO leaders were well placed to recruit other elites to their cause through the tightly knit personal networks and contacts of the upper classes. Professor Yunus notes that the 'handful of people' who ran the country included many old connections. In his case he was able to access the government funds he needed to expand his project into a bank through personal acquaintance with a former senior civil servant, later (and again, at the time of writing) Finance Minister Muhith, who

> took my proposal directly to the president. I had never met the president. As a military dictator he had no political legitimacy, and maybe he saw in Grameen a chance to score some political points by creating a bank for the poor. Whatever his thinking was, it worked in our favour. Muhith knew exactly how and when to present the proposal to him, and he must have given him the right sales pitch, for the president gave it his blessing. (Yunus and Jolis 1999, 170)

The elite origins of (at least the more established) NGOs have helped them establish themselves as acceptable anti-poverty actors, as well as carving out what has largely been, to date, a non-party political space for progressive or pro-poor elites. NGOs enfolded significant frontline actors into the wider social contract between the elites, the masses, and the donors.

The national elite were also fully behind microcredit, as an apparently sustainable anti-poverty technology that worked and improved the international image of the country. When I interviewed members of the elite in the late 1990s, many viewed the country's image as 'a basket case' to be a serious and material problem, but also thought that image had improved, largely because of the work of NGOs, and that microcredit had been particularly successful. A top-ranking civil servant thought that 'by giving the marginal people, particularly the women, some economic independence by lending small amounts of money', Grameen Bank and other organizations had improved the lot of many people, and given them more autonomy and confidence. An editor spoke of 'an immense reservoir of entrepreneurial skill at the grassroots level' and of 'capitalism at its most democratic best' (Hossain 2005, 110). In the late 1990s, there was much talk of the Nobel Prize for Yunus (eventually awarded in 2006), and the Prime Minister Sheikh Hasina herself graced the 1997 Micro-credit Summit in Washington DC. But while the eliteness of these organizations has assured them clout, it also means they are organizations that represent the masses, not mass organizations. BRAC makes virtually no pretences to public participation in the governance or design of its programmes. Even Grameen Bank, which advertised the fact that its women borrowers were shareholders, issued no dividends for almost a quarter-century (Karim 2011). Matters are very different in Nijera Kori and other organizations, but these are by no means the norm.

8.3.2 *The Rise, Fall, and Recovery of Microcredit*

The rapid expansion of non-state action in the 1990s was largely driven by the success of credit schemes that enjoyed wide popular uptake, appeared to be tackling poverty, and promised financial sustainability; the increasing focus on credit moved non-state action away from its more radical, organizing agenda and onto a market-oriented pathway marked by the delivery of services. In Bangladesh, a race for expansion among the four big MFIs between 2002 and 2007 meant that 'growth targets over-rode good judgment' (Chen and Rutherford 2013, 11).

As we have seen, the events surrounding liberation drew elite attention to the severe and widespread problem of rural landlessness and poverty, in particular that of women. Muhammad Yunus was among those who focused his efforts on doing something for his country, starting with tiny experiments from which he learned, theorized, and gained the confidence to seek financing. From the USD 27 Professor Yunus lent to families in the 1970s, the sector eventually grew to reach an estimated 36 million borrowers, almost a quarter of the entire population, at its peak in 2009.[12] More than half of all Bangladeshi households have been involved with microfinance at some point, and almost half still are at present (Raihan et al. 2015). In 2000, 90 per cent of villages had at least one NGO branch present (Gauri and Galef 2005), at least 90 per cent of which were providing credit. The availability of aid, a dense population, good communications, and a 'simple' regulatory framework helped the rapid spread of the anti-poverty technology, in particular encouraging the development of the 'franchise model' of local cost-centre branches (Zaman 2004; see also Jain and Moore 2003). Most organizations also have other education, health, or social protection schemes that depend to some extent on the viability of their microfinance programmes, in particular for the bulky costs of establishing offices and staffing infrastructure. 'Pure' MFIs, such as the Association for Social Advancement (ASA), are some of the biggest actors in Bangladesh and the world.

This vast scale grew out of a process of experimentation with different modes of loan delivery, client, personnel and fund management. As Yunus put it, '[a]n empiricist, I was willing to learn by my mistakes and those of others' (Yunus and Jolis 1999, 65). Sir F. H. Abed similarly describes his many experiments and what was learned from the failures in the early days of BRAC (see Korten 1980). The sector is nothing if not dynamic, and it responds closely to signals from the ground. We can see this in how certain of the more celebrated elements of the original microcredit models have been formally dropped from the theory after having being dropped in practice many years earlier. As anyone who has spent significant amounts of time with rural women in Bangladesh will know, the peer collateral, group lending, and 'conscientizing' activities that supposedly went with the distribution of loans and gathering of savings were quietly shelved many years before, as

[12] Microcredit statistics across the industry from before the 2000s are hard to come by. The 36 million figure is from the Credit and Development Forum (CDF), the microfinance industry association: http://www.cdfbd.org/new/ (accessed 11 April 2016). Mixmarket.org figures record 14 million borrowers in Bangladesh as of 2014, from their smaller sample MFIs.

loan officials and borrowers got down to brass tacks, focusing on the giving and taking of cash. Such ideas as peer collateral were arguably always mere frippery. As Lamia Karim has pointed out, the technology worked chiefly because of the disciplines it applied to poor rural women: it was less out of empowerment than out of lack of power, and in particular due to the culturally specific manipulation of women's shame and family honour, that loans were repaid so promptly (2011).

The story of ASA (which reads as 'Hope' in Bangla) exemplifies the transformation of the NGOs into MFIs, and is its most extreme and its most complete instance of the change. The founder of ASA, Shafiqual Haque Chowdhury, was born into a rich peasant family, and early on became a follower of the 'Red Maulana' Bhashani, alert to the exploitation and precariousness of peasant life (see Chapter 2). From his first job in what became the Bangladesh Academy for Rural Development (which hosted Akhtar Hameed Khan's Comilla experiments), Shafique learned all about the business and politics of rural credit (Rutherford 1995). When Shafique and a group of his comrades set up ASA in 1978 it was to be a radical alternative to the staid developmentalism into which BRAC was already settling, 'something in between an NGO and a people's movement' (Rutherford 2009, 53). But ASA found the struggle to mobilize against landlords and moneylenders fruitless, particularly when the people they sought to organize faced the most basic subsistence crises and frequently had none other than the local patron to turn to for protection. By the mid-1980s, ASA was accommodating itself to working as a conventional service delivery NGO, recognizing 'there was no alternative to credit'; by 1991 it had become a microfinance provider, even jettisoning the 'development education' with which it initially dressed up its loan schemes (Rutherford 2009). By the 2000s, ASA was exporting its methodology abroad, and setting up offices in China, Viet Nam, and Nigeria. The NGO's biographer concludes, in what could neatly summarize the state of play in the sector as a whole:

> Just as its core product, the small general-purpose loan, is running up against its limits in its home territory, ASA is gearing up to get it going in the vast space of China, India, Nigeria, and elsewhere. If the assessment of the core product presented in this book is right—a useful service that may not always transform poor people's lives but rarely fails to help them—ASA's internationalization is something to celebrate. (Rutherford 2009, 213–14)

By the 1990s, a micro-industry in the study of the impacts of microcredit had sprung up. Classic studies by Mark Pitt and Shahidur Khandker of the World Bank showed that credit raised household welfare, particularly if given to women, and had some impacts on women's power in the households (Pitt and Khandker 1998). Along a range of dimensions, impact evaluations of

BRAC, Grameen, and the government's Bangladesh Rural Development Board (BRDB) programme found that participation benefited the poor, particularly women and children, in particular if women were the main participants (Pitt and Khandker 1996). However, their results proved sensitive to assumptions and setting, and a careful inspection of their study concluded that 'benefits from risk reduction may be as important (or more important) than direct impacts on average levels of consumption' (Morduch 1999, 1606).

On the issue of women's empowerment, too, there was early contention. Studies challenged the idea that women were being empowered by these loans on the grounds that most relinquished control to their husbands or other family men (most notably, Goetz and Gupta 1996), stimulating a rich seam of debate about the meanings and indicators of women's empowerment (see in particular Kabeer 1999). Naila Kabeer argued persuasively that studies that showed 'negative' impacts on women's empowerment typically did so from an external standpoint that was not always relevant to women's lived realities: 'empowerment contains an irreducibly subjective element' which, when taken into account, indicated a more positive impact on women's power within households (as perceived by themselves) (Kabeer 2001a, 79).

The much-replicated anti-poverty technology hit its high point internationally in 2006, when Professor Yunus and the Grameen Bank he founded won the Nobel Peace Prize. Since then, microcredit's star has fallen far and fast, and its reputation for both financial regularity and a poverty mission has been irreparably damaged, going 'from hero to zero' over a mere decade (Ghosh 2013, 1203). The devastating Andhra Pradesh microfinance crisis of 2010 was particularly damning (Taylor 2011; Mader 2013). Jayati Ghosh describes the spiral of indebtedness in a context of agrarian crisis, absent state intervention, as a kind of Ponzi-scheme in that setting (2013). The 2000s had seen growing interest in 'impact investing' by private investors (Reille and Forster 2008), but it tailed off immediately after the global financial crisis period, since when public funding for microfinance has grown faster than private (Dashi et al. 2013). While the big four MFIs (Grameen Bank, BRAC, ASA, and Buro Bangladesh, providing between half and three-quarters of all lending) relied on commercial funding to expand from the 1990s onwards, they have not sold equity to outsiders, and so 'retained a nimbleness that helped them to adapt quickly and avoid a crisis' (Chen and Rutherford 2013, 7).

Although this matter has as yet received little attention, it is clear that growing reliance on credit for everyday livelihood activities and consumption exposed people in new ways to global volatilities (Constantinou and Ashta 2011; Daher and Le Saout 2015; Duflos and Gahwiler n.d.), leaving those worst equipped to cope with food price spikes and credit crunches at the sharp end of the shock. Arguably, microcredit was most useful to people facing spikes in the prices of food, on which the poor could easily spend 60 per cent of their income, but it helped create a spiral of indebtedness. It has even been argued (although never shown) that microfinance may actually retard rural economic development by starving more productive small and medium enterprises of finance to feed 'unproductive' micro-schemes (Bateman and Chang 2012).

'No evidence of impact' is of course not the same as evidence of no impact. But given that this is a multi-billion dollar sector, it is surprising that the evidence does not stand up to contemporary standards of impact assessment rigour, and significant that those same standards have been applied to challenge some of the more cherished myths about the positive-sum possibilities of global poverty reduction through credit. And the main champions of the view that microcredit contributes to poverty reduction, particularly for women, have by no means given up the argument. A panel study post-dating the critical systematic reviews and replication studies examined the impacts of microcredit over two decades and argued that the results 'unequivocally' find significant positive effects on household welfare, including higher per capita consumption, income, non-land assets, net worth, children's education (boys' and girls'), and reduced poverty, the latter in particular if the loans go to women (Khandker and Samad 2014). They also find, however, that the implications of lending have changed over time, that credit had a greater impact in the past, and that many communities show signs of declining returns, partly because microcredit chiefly financed activities in low-skill and low-technology trading activities, with which local markets are now saturated (Khandker and Samad 2014).

Other recent analysis has concluded that microcredit probably accounts for between 9 and 12 per cent of national GDP and (by a low estimate) between 13 and 17 per cent of rural GDP in 2012 (Raihan et al. 2015). The impacts on rural labour markets are also estimated to be significant, at an additional fifty-three employment days per year—an increase of 19 per cent compared to people who do not take credit (Osmani 2015). Microcredit and rural credit in general has been causally connected to the relatively rapid reduction in extreme rural poverty in Bangladesh in the 2000s, in particular through the rise in leased land for cultivation by landless peasants (Sen and Ali 2015).

In its homeland of Bangladesh itself, all has not been quiet on the microcredit front. After an ill-judged foray into national non-party politics during the army-backed caretaker regime of 2007–8, and criticism over his fund management tactics, Yunus became embroiled in national politics. Proshika, another of the big MFIs, has been greatly weakened, having run similarly afoul of the financial and political rules. Problems of indebtedness started to become obvious to anyone who troubled to look (Karim 2011). And yet, despite the loss of its reputation as a fundamentally sound tool for tackling poverty, it is by no means the end of the story for microfinance in Bangladesh.

The market may be 'saturated', yet it weathered the global microfinancial crisis (Chen and Rutherford 2013). MFIs have diversified and innovated further, now addressing both concerns about the 'missing middle' of small and medium enterprise (SME) finance and the exclusion of the extreme poor from poverty reduction strategies that depend on people's capacity to service debt. As of 2016, the Institute for Microfinance (InM) has been renamed the Institute for Inclusive Finance Development, billing itself as a 'centre of excellence in research, training, education and knowledge management',[13] and boasting an impressive array of evidence on the dimensions and impacts of the technology in Bangladesh.

The shift towards discussing the technology as a tool for 'financial inclusion' has been a worldwide phenomenon. The Microcredit Summit Campaign has now set the target of helping to lift 100 million families out of extreme poverty as its contribution to meeting the Sustainable Development Goals (SDGs), a task it approaches as a matter of global 'financial inclusion' of the more than half of adults in the poorest 40 per cent of the world's population who have no access to financial services.

Experimentalism and learning-by-doing continue to characterize the sector, which has evolved further (at least in Bangladesh) after the global financial crisis of the 2000s (Chen and Rutherford 2013). The sector grew particularly aggressively between 2002 and 2007, but the reverberations of the 2008 global financial (and food) crisis on microfinance saw borrower numbers plateau and loan sizes increase. Big players like BRAC and Grameen have diversified, moving up the value chain, lending more to small and medium business, entering banking proper, creating new financial services such as remittance payment systems and insurance and mobile money. The poverty mission is being tackled with more generous programmes of support to the 'extreme poor', including those affected by climate change. These 'ultra-poor' approaches have now themselves been exported to other countries, but this time are being tested with the apparent rigour of randomized control trials (RCTs) (Hashemi and De Montesquiou 2011), the experimental approach to the measurement of impact at present considered the gold standard for international development policy research.

8.3.3 *Microcredit and the Subsistence Crisis Contract*

By way of concluding this lengthy discussion of microcredit, I will note that much of the evidence supports the view that small loans were often used to smooth consumption. This is frequently taken as a negative finding, because it suggests that they therefore played no role in poverty reduction. But as

[13] http://inm.org.bd/about-inm/ (accessed 11 April 2016).

earlier chapters have shown, the early decades of Bangladesh were a time of great trauma and risk; it is probable and perhaps even likely that microcredit helped provide people with the buffer they needed to replenish their depleted human, social, and physical resources, before or while turning to the matter of material advancement. But while microcredit reduced the vulnerabilities of a population that was already depleted by its *longue durée* experience of impoverishment, and its more recent crises of subsistence and survival, it did so by tying people into wage labour to make the regular repayments, and exposing them to the downside of debt. In Bangladesh at present, microcredit remains all but omnipresent, thoroughly part of the social, economic, and indeed political landscape. But its recent growth has been upward, with the financial sustainability and economic growth agenda served by larger loans and more integration into formal systems. The poverty mission has also come to renewed attention, with schemes better tailored to the needs of the ultra-poor; this includes not debt but subsidized support, including for consumption. It is hoped and expected that the ultra-poor will 'graduate' into microfinance when they have moved sufficiently far out of poverty to make good use of small loans. Whatever the impacts of microfinance in other settings, in Bangladesh at least, it seems that the technology emerged at the right moment and served an important purpose—even if it was not that which the theory assumed.

While it contained a large subsidy element, credit probably helped a great deal in preventing people from sinking further: its main intervention was on vulnerability. As has been established in Chapters 2 to 5, the population in the 1970s and 1980s had seen their resources depleted by the onslaught of disasters, wars, and famines of the period. The evidence seems to support the view that what microcredit did was to protect a minimal level of consumption, to get as close to a reasonable level of social reproduction as was possible for people without assets in an under-developed labour-rich rural economy. Credit bought time in moments of crisis, space for some longer-term livelihood adaptation, countering the worst effects of bad short-term coping mechanisms. The micro-entrepreneur, the Cinderella figure in this story, turns out to be women engaging in a wider range of essentially domestic activities, some small investments, but chiefly expenditure-saving and consumption work. These were mainly subsistence activities. But it is the idea that a population this undernourished and weakened could have been expected to focus on more than the task of keeping going that is misplaced here. It is surely in this vital domain at the very core of social reproduction or care, in the consumption-smoothing of the economics language, that credit mattered most.

Evidently there are no magical market solutions to poverty. The poor cannot pay so much of the privatized costs of their basic social protection. Subsidy is essential: some redistribution of resources—and of power—remains essential to make any inroads on poverty.

8.4 Bangladeshis in the Global Economy

A key conclusion from this brief survey of developments in the microcredit, international labour migration, and garments sectors is that the empowerment they bring is the individual power of the cash-earning consumer, the strength of people with the capacity to pay because of what they earn. But individual empowerment has rarely, to date, aggregated to institutionalized forms of collective power. Garments workers continue to struggle for basic rights to organize; the absence of genuine industry-wide trades unions means that the many and frequent worker abuses push them to risk their lives and livelihoods through last-resort mobilization, often involving violence. Migrant workers have little to no protection or rights in the countries in which they work, in particular the Middle East, and the government is regularly criticized by civil society groups for its failure for protecting its workers' rights. And microfinance users remain clients and have little to no role in the governance of the institutions that so strongly shape their lives; of the vast literature on the impacts of microfinance in Bangladesh, few, if any, studies mention that poor rural women are governed by these organizations, and have no effective means of holding them to account. There are major downsides to this inventiveness, and courageous expansion: these new economic sectors have emerged without safety nets, informal or official, to protect these brave new entrants from the inevitable risks of economic activity. When markets dip, crash, or fail, those who have been stitching T-shirts, servicing the international rich, or borrowing from financial markets are exposed to the downturn. It is increasingly plain that a new social contract is needed to protect against these risks.

9

Post-Malthusian Futures

Towards a New Social Contract

9.1 Nationalizing the Aid Lab

> In 2015, as the 6th FYP [Five Year Plan] draws to a close, Bangladesh has accelerated the pace of socioeconomic transformation—in many instances surpassing its targets—even in the backdrop of a global recession during this period. In that respect, Bangladesh is a 'development outlier' to its credit. The 7th FYP has been formulated with full recognition that the 'outlier' phenomenon is not merely a blip on the development path but rather a sustainable occurrence chartering a new development trajectory. Lauded as a 'Development Surprise' by prominent international media, Bangladesh has emerged as a shining example for countries throughout the world as it continues to defy traditional, linear development models and innovate a novel, alternative pathway for socioeconomic progress. (Government of the People's Republic of Bangladesh,
>
> Seventh Five Year Plan, 2016–2020; GED 2015b, xxx–xxxi)

Once the world's laboratory for experiments with human life and society, Bangladesh has reclaimed its own development project, retooling it as an engine for generating a particular model of high-value development, one in which the progress of people outstrips the advance of economies. It has cast off its 'basket case' label, and has now started on its career through middle-income status. It is by any stretch an impressive achievement in a short space of time with a great many challenges to overcome. There remains much to be done, and the second generation of challenges may be more complex than the first—it is easier to build schools and enjoin children to attend them, for instance, than it is to ensure that they learn something useful once there. But the foundations are in place. Protection against disaster makes human development at least possible. And the population that once grew so rapidly in size now raises its expectations at a similar pace, transforming the state–society relations on which its unexpected development success to date has rested.

Among the emerging and new challenges are those of raising the skills and productivity of Bangladesh's population. Further growth and development entail moving up the global value chain, and fast. It is clear that this requires both substantial additional investments in human development, and a political governance system capable of overcoming the old weaknesses of corruption and inefficiency so those investments can bear fruit. Bangladesh must gear itself up to equip its people for a far higher standard of education, health, and social protection, one fit for the middle-income country it has become. But this depends on the political economy being right: business and industrial elites need to recognize and act upon their material interests in a smarter, stronger, well-nourished population. It is in their direct economic interests that, for example, the masses have access to safe water and sanitation; their teachers and doctors are in attendance; workers have safe passage to work, fair and enforceable contracts at home and abroad, decent shelter, and good food. And when labour and commodity markets and political democracy fail to ensure such good things are affordably and fairly available, workers must have the organizational means with which to argue for such reasonable claims. The sweatshop era is not gone, but after Rana Plaza, it is no longer an assured means of making a profit. The business elites and the labouring classes have a mutual interest in higher standards of human development, but while a smarter, more globally oriented generation of business leaders increasingly recognizes the imperatives of the quality of the population, this has not yet found its political expression or policy space.

While Bangladesh looks to the future, it is crucial to reflect on the lessons of the past. This book has argued that a people-oriented approach to development was set on its pathway by the human, economic, and political fallout of the 1974 famine. That approach jettisoned a broadly leftist–statist ideology inherited from the liberation struggle in favour of a pragmatic 'try anything' market-driven model, in which the method was constantly judged against the results. Often with their partners—aid agencies, NGOs, civil society, the business community, and even the rump of the old left—successive governments of all political stripes put in place or created space for policies and programmes that were sometimes mould-breaking and frequently untested, retaining and protecting what seemed to work, and abandoning the rest. It was often, but not always, consistent with a neoliberal ideology favouring free markets. The state always intervened or allowed intervention to make food markets functional for hungry people, make credit available to those without insurance or capital, advance the interests of labour-intensive industries, and subsidize family costs of school attendance. An active, politicized population kept watch, legitimating what worked, sanctioning (if only in the withdrawal of their consent) the failures. In this formula, the country broke with patriarchal tradition by drawing women's issues out of the private domain and into the public; the public sphere became feminized in key respects, and gender issues became core problems for public policy. In its attention to 'the woman issue' in particular, Bangladesh was a pioneer.

The higher-order aim of these policies was always clear and always the same: to protect the masses against the kinds of crises of subsistence and survival that had scarred their pre-Liberation history, and to which they were prone because of their ecological, economic, and social characteristics. To do that it was essential to transform those economic and social characteristics, and manage the ecological risks. It meant transforming the Bangladeshi population into people capable of rearing and socializing healthy and capable children, and enabling them to enter into the world economy as the sole available means of absorbing the growing millions of 'surplus' labour.

This achievement is politicized in the Seventh Five Year Plan, an achievement framed by an Awami League government as the realization of the nation's founding father Bangabandhu Sheikh Mujib's dream of a '"Shonar Bangla" (Golden Bengal) where the common citizens of the country live in prosperity and have equitable access to quality education, healthcare, rule of law and employment opportunities'. Those alert to the divisive party politics of the country will read in this politicization an attempt to capture the gains of development as a partisan triumph. Certainly the achievements of the Awami League government since 2009 merit their own analysis; that has not been provided here, concerned as this book has been with unearthing the political history of this development success. But those achievements, too, are latter-day extensions of a core project whose foundations were in place from the mid-1970s. National development was always a nationalist project, and protection of the population, not least from the tidal bores and torrents which many of those on its ecological frontline faced, always the raison d'être for the state of Bangladesh. It is fitting to situate this success as the achievement of the goals of the national liberation struggle—albeit not of a single party, however central to that struggle that party may have been. It should be clear from the thrust of the argument that the apparently different nationalisms of the polarized political parties share far more than divides them, at least with respect to the development project. Elite consensus has been central to Bangladesh's unexpected development success.

In the dominant World Bank rendering of 'the Bangladesh paradox', the success owes substantially to the early embrace of market forces as the driver of development, with the supporting action of non-state actors. This is only true to a limited extent, and it conceals more than it reveals. The turn to the market depended fundamentally on politics. It needed the achievement of a political settlement founded upon an effective elite consensus about the vital challenges of subsistence and survival. It meant that—whatever else the elite got up to and however else they sought to accumulate capital and prestige and rewards—they backed an agreement with the masses and their aid donors about the bedrock requirements of a functional state.

Several of the arguments in this book have been made in different ways and with different emphases by others. But the important contribution here is to trace the specific of this subsistence crisis contract to the aftermath of the third terrible disaster in the early history of the country: the famine that should never have happened, which demonstrated so acutely and painfully the risks of a state that lacked the power to keep its population alive. Although this is difficult to prove in any empirical sense, this event appears to have left an indelible scar on the national psyche, rarely mentioned except as a positive expression of the consistent and still-present priority to protect against such disasters. Recent conversations with senior government officials have re-affirmed this sense that lurking beneath the surface of governmental logic is an awareness of that terrible moment, with its terrible political and human consequences. Certainly it is from the political aftermath of that event—and the brutal murder of the nationalist hero and founding father of the country and his family to which it must be connected—that the violent, winner-takes-all politics takes its cue. Some of the wide lessons from this account are also of relevance to theorizing the effects of famine, an area of analysis only now beginning to generate attention.

9.2 On Aid

Debates about the worth and futility of foreign aid-sponsored development rage on, without much insight into the deep political structures that force aid dependence on countries positioned on the periphery of the world system, or how those external relations influence domestic political settlements (Hickey 2013; Yanguas 2016). Has aid been a boon or a burden for Bangladesh? The classic two-handed social science response would be to point out the ways in which aid supported progressive and solidaristic pathways to development, undercut by a reminder of the contract of domination into which the Bangladeshi elite and the Bangladeshi masses were drawn by the crises of the early 1970s, and the effective absence, at the time, of viable alternatives. But the argument can and should be turned on its head: aid has certainly been good for Bangladesh, but Bangladesh has been exceptionally valuable to the aid industry. Countless veteran aid officials, scholars, and activists have cut their teeth on Bangladesh. Many of these people are progressive-minded individuals, with egalitarian and solidaristic aims. Some have been part of organizations that sought to make the world fairer, a few that had more radical objectives, and the majority who simply saw desperate human need and wanted to help. That they are part of a larger world system in which progress and indeed survival for a marginal and fragile corner of the world implied incorporation on adverse terms may not detract from their individual motivations. The individuals, and most certainly the organizations and agencies, have benefited vastly from their Bangladesh development experience. And the project of economic and human development under globalizing capitalism has, above all, gained from its star example. If Bangladesh can do it, anywhere can. The successes of the erstwhile basket case continue to provide an important justification for the continuation of aid, even among those who think aid has generally failed.

In any case, the aid industry, and those of us who have made a career with its resources, owe explanations to those who have paid for these achievements, those who provided the foreign finance, but in particular those who were developed through its projects, to examine the motivations and interests that drove them, the means through which they were delivered, and their effects in the wider societal and national perspective. Many of the important motivations and interests were generous and benign, and the road to development has been paved with individually good intentions. But there have been uglier motivations, too, framed by frank abuses of power that it is in the interests of historical accountability to record properly. The crises of the mid-1970s in particular appear to have been engineered or permitted because of an intellectual Malthusianism that justified the political abuse of humanitarian aid. There has been no real accountability for these crimes against humanity, if that is indeed what they were. It is among the unfinished business in the history of this country that still warrants attention and justice.[1] But nor are such anti-humanitarian ideologies an anachronism. The wave of anti-migrant feeling in the industrialized countries against seaborne refugees from climate, conflict, authoritarianism, and poverty in the second decade of the twenty-first century is an echo of the profoundly unethical ideologies of the past that shaped the response to the Bangladesh famine. The present moment has demonstrated once again how powerfully such ideas influence the international politics of aid.

9.3 The Political Unsettlement

There are important gaps in this story, and the history of a national development project is by no means the history of a nation. It is correct to remember

[1] In particular, the roles of the US and other governments in withholding food aid during the 1974 famine remain imperfectly understood, and merit further attention.

how hard everyday conditions of life continue to be for many millions of Bangladeshis. Official figures state that almost twenty million people still suffer from basic calorie-deficit hunger, that is, do not get enough to eat, and several million children face severe acute malnutrition, that is, are *at risk of starving to death* in this famine-free success story. Many other such figures are available, but the visitor need not even leave the smart diplomatic zones to witness extreme poverty at first hand. Reports of the demise of Bangladesh's poverty have been greatly exaggerated, for all its vast achievements.

This book also excludes consideration of the 'accumulation by dispossession' through Bengali resettlement in the Chittagong Hill Tracts and on other lands of indigenous or *adivasi* populations, even though it is plain that this, too, has been core to the national development project. But these are matters upon which others, such as scholars Shapan Adnan and Amena Mohsin, are better placed to analyse and comment. Nor is the marginalization, persecution, and frequent brutalization of religious and other minorities such as Hindus, Christians, Buddhists, Ahmadiyas, and the so-called Bihari population discussed here, not because these are unimportant or insignificant either in scale or implication for social inclusion, but again, because justice cannot be done here to these important matters.

A key recent change has been in the political basis of the development project: domination by the Bengali Muslim majority is becoming associated with shifts in the balance of political power that seem likely to undermine the elite consensus, undercutting the competitive pressures that once existed to deliver development. The details are matters of fact: having governed for an unprecedented two successive terms (2009–13, 2014–present), the Awami League government has presided over impressive socioeconomic development gains and a significant consolidation of political power. From a competitive but clientelist pattern of national politics that dominated the quarter-century after the return to multiparty democracy in 1991, Bangladesh has been moving towards one dominated by a single party. This is reminiscent of the early years of nationhood, and among the chattering classes at least, references to BAKSALization[2] are common. Yet there are crucial differences to the mid-1970s: the country, population, and state is stronger and richer; its macro-economy is now managed with caution and skill; and it no longer relies on the variable goodwill of the international community to protect its people from disasters. This latter is true even though it is more, not less, vulnerable to the climatic and financial vicissitudes of the global system.

The main opposition remains the BNP, which, while significantly weakened, is not yet spent. Its heir-apparent Tarique Rahman (BNP leader Begum

[2] A centralization of social, political, and economic power within the dominant ruling party, featuring control of the media and political dissent.

Khaleda Zia's son) has been in effective exile abroad since his purportedly brutal treatment at the hands of the military- (and international community-) backed caretaker regime of 2007–8. The BNP's frontline activists have lost their clout, possibly partly because of their over-reliance on the *hartal* for their political repertoire. It is certainly true that the main power of the *hartal* strategy—to hold the society and the economy to political ransom through the passive demonstration of support for the strikers' demands—has been dissipated through overuse since 2013. No doubt this political maturity is itself an effect of development: in a society and an economy greatly dependent on globalized industries, on just-in-time delivery, on getting kids to school and workers to offices and factories, Bangladeshis can no longer afford to indulge politicians in their contentious political posturing. But the BNP has yet to devise alternative strategies for mobilizing or testing public opinion. It has no other way of doing politics.

The leadership of the BNP, and even more so that of its usual coalition ally, the Jamaat-i-Islami, has also been greatly weakened by convictions for crimes committed during the liberation struggle of 1971. Prominent opposition politicians have been convicted of war crimes under the effort to bring war criminals from 1971 to account through the so-called International War Crimes Tribunal. This has done much to decimate the leadership of the comparatively moderate Jamaat, a religious party that has been tactically positioned to form coalitions with both major parties at different times, but which itself never won even close to double-digit popular support in elections. Several top leaders have been convicted and hanged; others await trial. The international media has taken an apparently obtuse position on the war crimes trials, framing them as partisan efforts to stamp out political opposition without recognizing their legitimate aims. However, the popular mood seems strongly supportive of the moral guilt of those convicted in the war crimes trials, and generally unmoved by concerns about procedural correctness.[3]

Even though the legitimate aims of the war crimes tribunal are to achieve a long-overdue transitional justice, it is the case that centralizing and authoritarian tendencies run deep in the Awami League. This essentially petty bourgeois party brought to power on the back of charismatic leadership has repeatedly tried, with only partial success, to incorporate contenders and dissenters into its loosely pro-people platform. More recently, notably since civil society actors supported the extended caretaker-government regime, the Awami League leadership has taken a harder line against civil society and

[3] The Tribunal has its own website (http://www.ict-bd.org/ict1/indexdetails.php). Other sources include the East–West Center's project (https://bangladeshtrialobserver.org/) and David Bergman's blog (http://bangladeshwarcrimes.blogspot.co.uk/). See also Chopra (2015) on the closing of space for critical scrutiny of the process.

NGO activity, and indeed any political or social dissent. Most recently there have been efforts to clamp down on independent media (Sattar 2016). A law has also been drafted restricting discussion of the Liberation War and its surrounding history (Mohaiemen 2016; Bergman 2016).

Despite, or perhaps because of, the official effort to clamp down on political and social dissent, and very likely in part as a result of the closing of space for Islamist politics, the Awami League's second term since 2014 has been punctured by growing signs of Islamist mobilization. This has chiefly taken the form of murders of secularist writers and activists, members of religious minorities, human (including lesbian, gay, bisexual, and transgender) rights defenders, foreigners, and other groups at odds with extreme salafist ideology. In July 2016, a terrorist attack on a busy cafe popular with foreigners and wealthy locals in the well-heeled Gulshan area killed more than 20 people, mostly foreigners. These murders have been claimed by groups associating themselves with the terrorist movement Islamic State. Awami League government officials at first refused to accept the possibility of internationally connected terrorism on its soil, arguing instead that the criminals were associated with opposition parties who wish to defame Bangladesh and its government (Graham-Harrison and Hammadi 2016). Since the July attack it has taken a more active role in apprehending, sometimes killing, suspected terrorists.

Having earned a reputation for religious moderation and tolerance within the region, this radical Islamist turn has meant a new, unwelcome 'Bangladesh surprise'. Too little is known of these murderous groups to make sense of their motives and meanings. What might this political unsettlement mean for Bangladesh's development project? It is too soon to say, but not too soon to consider the possibilities. It is true that a strong party committed to development may avoid the pitfalls of short-termism associated with intense competitive electoral pressures. It may be possible for a powerful government of Bangladesh to bring about politically difficult decisions on, for instance, infrastructure, energy, and bureaucratic reform, that could unleash faster growth and higher-quality human development (see, for instance, Levy 2014).

Yet Bangladesh's political history suggests that competition and responsiveness, not autonomy and power, has driven its development successes to date. Even during its more authoritarian eras in the 1970s and 1980s, the Bangladeshi state was comparatively weak, always broadly responsive to the demands and concerns of a strong society (White 1999). The clampdown on free speech is a matter of particular concern in the complex conditions facing Bangladesh's future development: its pluralist service delivery model, capacity to respond to disasters, and international reputation all depend on the circulation of credible data and evidence, which in turn imply a degree of transparency, openness to criticism, and capacity to learn and innovate. The Bangladeshi state has never been strong enough to impose its will without the feedback and input of the far stronger society in which it is embedded. It continues to need to be able to respond to the messages from society, the economy, and the polity to succeed. Recall the significance of the absence of credible data in the failures to respond to the Bhola cyclone and the 1974 famine: a civil society and media fearful of criticizing the government may not publicize failures to address hunger or disaster. The government will experience weaker pressures to respond and the right triggers may not be activated for fear of crossing a line. Bangladesh thrives on its cacophony of debate and contention, and will be stifled without it.

* * *

Bangladesh learns from its own history in order to make sense of its future. But in the present historical moment of high globalization and the global crisis of climate change, the lessons of Bangladesh's social contract against subsistence crisis resonate more widely. At this moment in history, not long since the global financial crisis of 2008 and the global food crises of the same period, many people around the world have faced a 'perfect storm' of conditions resembling those facing the Bangladesh of the 1970s: people increasingly dependent on dysfunctional global markets for basic subsistence, wracked with sudden and slow-onset disasters of climate change. In short, many developing, and indeed developed, country populations face conditions structurally similar to those of the Bangladesh of the 1970s. As an early exemplar of life in an era of high globalization and accelerating climate change, Bangladesh demonstrates that the political foundations of human development, and the priority of a functioning state, must be protection against the crises of subsistence and survival. People cannot face the tsunamis (droughts, earthquakes, floods) without the state at their back; they cannot reproduce their families and their societies without the support of a state that depends on their success in doing so. At a bare minimum, there must be an unbreakable subsistence crisis contract. Aid can help bind that contract, but the Bangladesh experience suggests it needs to be rooted in national political struggles through which the masses hold elites accountable. From its vantage point in the historic heartlands of colonial domination and on the frontline of climate change, Bangladesh offers a glimpse of the future under advancing global capitalism. Such lessons are vital, not only for the former basket case, but for the rest of the world.

Glossary

Adivasi	literally, indigenous people; used to refer to diverse groups of people possibly numbering in the low millions, originating across the north and the southeastern regions of the country, concentrated in the hilly regions on the borders with India and Burma. These populations are sometimes referred to as 'tribal', and are culturally, religiously, and ethnically distinct from the Bengali Muslim majority
Ajlaf/atrap	ordinary or peasant and artisan classes
Ashraf	the respectable or elite classes of Muslim Bengal, mainly used in the 19th and early 20th century; in contrast to **ajlaf** or **atrap;** see also **Syed** and **Shaikh**
Bhadralok	the gentility or educated upper class; originally in reference to the educated Hindu elites of Calcutta during the Bengal Renaissance; now more widely used to mean educated middle-class people
birangona	war heroines; usually in reference to women who were raped by the Pakistani army during the Liberation War of 1971
Burqa (or burka)	a coat-like garment worn by some Muslim women, usually with a cape-like head-covering
chetona	awareness
gherao	siege
hartal	strike
hijab	head-covering warn by some Muslim women
izzat	honour, referring in particular to familial honour associated with perceptions of women's sexual purity
jihad	struggle against injustice
jonogon	common people, or the general public
jotedar	revenue-collectors for zamindars under the Political Settlement; medium-sized landowners
langarkhana	feeding camp
madrassah	Islamic school
maund	unit of grain measurement, equivalent to 37 kg

mofussil	rural areas
Mukti Bahini	The liberation army
muktijoddha	freedom fighters, specifically during the Liberation War of 1971
purdah	literally, curtain; used to denote the complex of seclusion and restrictions on women's and girls' mobility that are associated with the protection of their sexual purity or modesty; although associated with Muslim societies, Hindu women in India were also subjected to *purdah* although with differing rules and expressions
Rakkhi Bahini	Paramilitary force in operation in the early 1970s
Samaj	moral community, usually referring to village society
Shaikh	an honorific in Muslim Bengal, generally denoting a local religious leader with independent landholding; see also **Syed**
Sonar Bangla	Golden Bengal. A widely used expression of nationalistic ideals, expressed in the national anthem of Bangladesh, a song by the Nobel Laureate Rabindranath Tagore, 'Amar Sonar Bangla' ('My Golden Bengal')
Syed	An honorific denoting a family at the top of the socio-political and economic hierarchy, associated with land owning and possibly aristocratic status; see also **Shaikh**
tebhaga	literally, three parts; an agrarian movement that emerged in East Bengal after the 1943 famine, in which sharecroppers fought for a two-third share of the crop instead of the usual half
ummah	Islamic moral community
upazila	sub-district; these are geographical and administrative units of which there are at present 489
zamindar	landowner

Bibliography

Abdullah, Abu. 1974. 'Institution-Building in Agriculture—Implicit Social Theory in the First Five Year Plan.' Bangladesh Journal of Political Economy 1 (1): 183–92.

Abdullah, Abu, Mosharaff Hossain, and Richard Nations. 1976. 'Agrarian Structure and the IRDP Preliminary Considerations.' The Bangladesh Development Studies 4 (2): 209–66.

Abdullah, A. and Quazi Shahabuddin. 1997. 'Critical Issues in Agriculture: Policy Response and Unfinished Agenda.' pp. 28–76. In M. G. Quibria (ed.) The Bangladesh Economy in Transition, Delhi: Asian Development Bank/Oxford University Press.

Abdullah, Tahrunnessa A., and Sondra Zeidenstein. 1982. Village Women of Bangladesh: Prospects for Change: A Study Prepared for the International Labour Office within the Framework of the World Employment Programme. Oxford: Pergamon Press.

Adams, Alayne M., Tanvir Ahmed, Shams El Arifeen, Timothy G. Evans, Tanvir Huda, and Laura Reichenbach. 2013. 'Innovation for Universal Health Coverage in Bangladesh: A Call to Action.' The Lancet 382 (9910): 2104–11. doi:10.1016/S0140-6736(13)62150-9.

Adams Jr, Richard H. 1998. 'The Political Economy of the Food Subsidy System in Bangladesh.' The Journal of Development Studies 35 (1): 66–88.

Adnan, Shapan. 1990. Annotation of Village Studies in Bangladesh and West Bengal: A Review of Socio-Economic Trends over 1942–88. Kotbari Comilla: Bangladesh Academy of Rural Development.

Adnan, Shapan. 1993. 'Birds in a Cage: Institutional Change and Women's Position in Bangladesh.' pp. 285–315. In Nora Federici, Karen O. Mason, and Solvi Sogner (eds) Women's Position and Demographic Change. Oxford: Clarendon Press.

ADST. 1986. 'Ambassador Jane Abell Cane.' Association for Diplomatic Studies and Training. 1 The Association for Diplomatic Studies and Training Foreign Affairs Oral History Project Women Ambassadors Series. www.adst.org/OH%20TOCs/Coon,%20Jane%20Abell.toc.pdf.

Agamben, Giorgio. 2005. State of Exception. Chicago: University of Chicago Press.

Ahamed, E. 1978, 'Development Strategy in Bangladesh: Probable Political Consequences.' Asian Survey 18 (11): 1168–80.

Ahluwalia, Isher J., and Wahiduddin Mahmud. 2004. 'Economic Transformation and Social Development in Bangladesh.' Economic and Political Weekly 39 (36): 4009–11.

Ahmed, Aftab Uddin. 1983. 'The Mujib Regime in Bangladesh, 1972–75: An Analysis of Its Problems and Performance.' PhD thesis, University of London. http://ethos.bl.uk/OrderDetails.do?uin=uk.bl.ethos.339348.

Ahmed, Akhter U., and Carlo del Ninno. 2002. 'The Food for Education Program in Bangladesh.' Washington DC: International Food Policy Research Institute (IFPRI). https://ideas.repec.org/p/fpr/fcnddp/138.html.

Ahmed, Faisal Z., Anne Greenleaf, and Audrey Sacks. 2014. 'The Paradox of Export Growth in Areas of Weak Governance: The Case of the Ready Made Garment Sector in Bangladesh.' World Development 56 (April): 258–71. doi:10.1016/j.worlddev.2013.11.001.

Ahmed, Nabil. 2013. 'Entangled Earth.' Third Text 27 (1): 44–53. doi:10.1080/09528822.2013.753191.

Ahmed, Nesar, Edward H. Allison, and James F. Muir. 2010. 'Rice Fields to Prawn Farms: A Blue Revolution in Southwest Bangladesh?' Aquaculture International 18 (4): 555–74. doi:10.1007/s10499-009-9276-0.

Ahmed, Rafiuddin. 1996. The Bengal Muslims, 1871–1906: A Quest for Identity. New York: Oxford University Press.

Ahmed, Raisuddin, Steven Haggblade, and Tawfiq-e-Elahi Chowdhury (eds) 2000. Out of the Shadow of Famine: Evolving Food Markets and Food Policy in Bangladesh. Washington DC: International Food Policy Research Institute, Washington DC.

Ahmed, Syed Masud, Timothy G. Evans, Hilary Standing, and Simeen Mahmud. 2013. 'Harnessing Pluralism for Better Health in Bangladesh.' The Lancet 382 (9906): 1746–55. doi:10.1016/S0140-6736(13)62147-9.

Akhter, Farida. 1992. Depopulating Bangladesh: Essays on the Politics of Fertility. Dhaka: Narigrantha Prabartana.

Akmam, Wardatul. 2002. 'Atrocities against Humanity during the Liberation War in Bangladesh: A Case of Genocide.' Journal of Genocide Research 4 (4): 543–59. doi:10.1080/14623502200000463.

Al-Samarrai, S. 2006. 'Changes in Employment in Bangladesh, 2000–2005: The Impacts on Poverty and Gender Equity.' Mimeo. Background Paper for the 2007 Poverty Assessment by the World Bank. Dhaka.

Alam, A. M. Quamrul. 1993. 'The Nature of the Bangladesh State in the Post-1975 Period.' Contemporary South Asia 2 (3): 311–25.

Alam, E., and A. E. Collins. 2010. 'Cyclone Disaster Vulnerability and Response Experiences in Coastal Bangladesh.' Disasters 34 (4): 931–54.

Alam, Edris, and Dale Dominey-Howes. 2015. 'A New Catalogue of Tropical Cyclones of the Northern Bay of Bengal and the Distribution and Effects of Selected Landfalling Events in Bangladesh.' International Journal of Climatology 35 (6): 801–35. doi:10.1002/joc.4035.

Alam, Sultana, and Nilufar Matin. 1984. 'Limiting the Women's Issue in Bangladesh: The Western and Bangladesh Legacy.' Comparative Studies of South Asia, Africa and the Middle East 4 (2): 1–10.

Alamgir, Mohiuddin. 1980. Famine in South Asia: Political Economy of Mass Starvation. Cambridge, MA: Oelgeschlager, Gunn & Hain, Publishers, Inc.

Ali, Tariq Omar, and Naomi Hossain. 2006. 'Popular Expectations of Government in Bangladesh.' Chronic Poverty Research Centre Working Paper 13. http://papers.ssrn.com/sol3/papers.cfm?abstract_id=1757889.

Amundsen, Inge. 2012. 'Parliament of Bangladesh: Boycotts, Business, and Change for the Better.' CMI Brief 2. Chr. Michelsen Institute. www.cmi.no/publications/publication/?4423=parliament-of-bangladesh-boycotts-business.

Amundsen, Inge. 2014. '"Pay Up and Off You Go!" Buying Political Positions in Bangladesh.' pp. 140–7. In Tina Søreide and Aled Williams (eds) Corruption, Grabbing and Development: Real World Challenges. Cheltenham: Edward Elgar.

Anderson, Jack. 1972. 'Texts of Secret Documents on Top-Level U.S. Discussions of Indian-Pakistani War.' New York Times, 6 January.

Anderson, Robert S. 1976. 'Impressions of Bangladesh: The Rule of Arms and the Politics of Exhortation.' Pacific Affairs 49 (3): 443–75. doi:10.2307/2755498.

Ansari, Humayun. 2004. The Infidel Within: Muslims in Britain Since 1800. London: C. Hurst & Co. Publishers.

Ansell, Ben W. 2008. 'Traders, Teachers, and Tyrants: Democracy, Globalization, and Public Investment in Education.' International Organization 62 (02): 289–322. doi:10.1017/S0020818308080107.

An Unfashionable Tragedy. 1975. Documentary film aired on ATV in January 1975. Accessed 17 April 2016. http://johnpilger.com/videos/an-unfashionable-tragedy.

Arens, Jenneke, and Jos van Beurden. 1977. Jhagrapur: Poor Peasants and Women in a Village in Bangladesh. 2nd Edition. Birmingham: Third World Publications.

Argos, Maria, Tara Kalra, Paul J. Rathouz, Yu Chen, Brandon Pierce, Faruque Parvez, and Tariqul Islam. 2010. 'Arsenic Exposure from Drinking Water, and All-Cause and Chronic-Disease Mortalities in Bangladesh (HEALS): A Prospective Cohort Study.' The Lancet 376 (9737): 252–58. doi:10.1016/S0140-6736(10)60481-3.

Arnold, D. 1988. Famine: Social Crisis and Historical Change. Oxford: Blackwell.

Asadullah, Mohammad Niaz, and Nazmul Chaudhury. 2009. 'Holy Alliances: Public Subsidies, Islamic High Schools, and Female Schooling in Bangladesh.' Education Economics 17 (3): 377–94. doi:10.1080/09645290903142593.

Asadullah, M. Niaz, Antonio Savoia, and Wahiduddin Mahmud. 2014. 'Paths to Development: Is There a Bangladesh Surprise?' World Development 62 (October): 138–54. doi:10.1016/j.worlddev.2014.05.013.

Atwood, D. A., A. S. M. Jahangir, Herbie Smith, and Golam Kabir. 2000. 'Food Aid in Bangladesh: From Relief to Development.' pp. 148–65. In R. Ahmed et al. (eds) Out of the Shadow of Famine: Evolving Food Markets and Food Policy in Bangladesh. Washington DC: International Food Policy Research Institute.

Avelino, George, David S. Brown, and Wendy Hunter. 2005. 'The Effects of Capital Mobility, Trade Openness, and Democracy on Social Spending in Latin America, 1980–1999.' American Journal of Political Science 49 (3): 625–41. doi:10.1111/j.1540-5907.2005.00146.x.

Awami League. 2013. Bangabandhu Sheikh Mujibur Rahman at United Nations (25th September, 1974). Speech. Accessed 3 December 2014. www.youtube.com/watch?v=y_O5rfUvVxA&feature=youtube_gdata_player.

Bahar, Abid S. 2003. 'The Religious and Philosophical Basis of Bhasani's Political Leadership.' PhD thesis, Montreal, Canada: Concordia University.

Banerjee, O., T. Darbas, P. R. Brown, and C. H. Roth. 2014. 'Historical Divergence in Public Management of Foodgrain Systems in India and Bangladesh: Opportunities to Enhance Food Security.' Global Food Security, SI: GFS Conference 2013, 3 (3–4): 159–66. doi:10.1016/j.gfs.2014.06.002.

Bangladesh Bank. 2015. 'Quarterly Review on RMG: January–March 2015.' Dhaka: Bangladesh Bank, Research Department, External Economics Division. www.bb.org.bd/pub/monthly/agri_rural_financing/agri-mar2015.pdf.

Bari, Mohammad Rezaul. 2008. 'The Basket Case.' Forum 3 (3). March. Accessed 22 April 2014. http://archive.thedailystar.net/forum/2008/march/basket.htm.

Barman, Dalem Ch, M. Golam Rahman, Tasneem Siddiqui. 2002. State of Democracy in Bangladesh. International IDEA Country Study. Stockholm, Dhaka: International Institute for Democracy and Electoral Assistance/Department of Peace and Conflict Studies, University of Dhaka.

Barua, T. K. 1978. Political Elite in Bangladesh. Berne: Peter Lang.

Bass, Gary J. 2013. The Blood Telegram: Nixon, Kissinger, and a Forgotten Genocide. New York: Random House LLC.

Bateman, Milford, and Ha-Joon Chang. 2012. 'Microfinance and the Illusion of Development: From Hubris to Nemesis in Thirty Years.' World Economic Review 1: 13–36. http://papers.ssrn.com/sol3/papers.cfm?abstract_id=2385482.

Baulch, Bob. 2011. 'The Medium-Term Impact of the Primary Education Stipend in Rural Bangladesh.' Journal of Development Effectiveness 3 (2): 243–62. doi:10.1080/19439342.2011.570449.

Baxter, Craig. 1971. 'Pakistan Votes—1970.' Asian Survey 11 (3): 197–218. doi:10.2307/3024655.

Baxter, Craig. 1998. Bangladesh: From a Nation to a State. Boulder: Westview Press.

BBC. 1995. 'Human Laboratory Documentary Transcript.' BBC Television: Horizon. 5 November. Accessed 10 February 2015. www.oldthinkernews.com/2010/12/09/human-laboratory-documentary-transcript/.

BBC. 2013. 'Bangladesh to Execute 152 Soldiers for Mutiny Crimes.' Online news article. Accessed 15 April 2016. www.bbc.co.uk/news/world-asia-24817887.

BBS. 2011. 'Household Income and Expenditure Survey (HIES) 2010.' Dhaka: Bangladesh Bureau of Statistics, Statistics Division, Ministry of Planning.

BBS. 2013a. 'Survey of Manufacturing Industries 2012 (SMI 2012).' Dhaka: Bangladesh Bureau of Statistics, Statistics Division, Ministry of Planning, Government of the People's Republic of Bangladesh. http://bbs.gov.bd/WebTestApplication/userfiles/Image/LatestReports/SMI-%202012.pdf.

BBS. 2013b. 'Time Use Pilot Survey 2012.' Dhaka: Bangladesh Bureau of Statistics, Statistics Division, Ministry of Planning.

BBS. 2014. 'Report on Survey on the Use of Remittances (SUR) 2013.' Dhaka Bangladesh Bureau of Statistics, Statistics Division, Ministry of Planning, Government of the People's Republic of Bangladesh.

BBS. 2015. 'National Series: Population and Housing Census 2011: National Report Volume-01: Analytical Report 2011.' Dhaka: Bangladesh Bureau of Statistics, Statistics Division, Ministry of Planning.

Beck, Tony, and Tirthankar Bose. 1995. 'Dispossession, Degradation and Empowerment of Peasantry and the Poor in Bengali Fiction.' Economic and Political Weekly 30 (9): 441–8.

Becker, Jasper. 1996. Hungry Ghosts: Mao's Secret Famine. New York: Owl Books/Henry Holt & Co.

Beneria, L., M. S. Floro, C. Grown, and M. MacDonald. 2000. 'Introduction: Globalization and Gender.' Feminist Economics 6 (3): vii–xvii.

Benería, Lourdes, and Gita Sen. 1981. 'Accumulation, Reproduction, and "Women's Role in Economic Development": Boserup Revisited.' Signs 7 (2): 279–98. doi:10.2307/3173878.

Bergman, David. 2011. 'Sayedee Indictment—1971 Deaths.' Bangladesh War Crimes Tribunal. 11 November. http://bangladeshwarcrimes.blogspot.com/2011/11/sayedee-indictment-analysis-1971-death.html.

Bergman, David. 2016. 'The Politics of Bangladesh's Genocide Debate.' The New York Times, 5 April. Accessed 13 June 2016. www.nytimes.com/2016/04/06/opinion/the-politics-of-bangladeshs-genocide-debate.html.

Bertocci, Peter J. 1982. 'Bangladesh in the Early 1980s: Praetorian Politics in an Intermediate Regime.' Asian Survey 22 (10): 988–1008. doi:10.2307/2643756.

BGMEA. 2015. 'Two Years of Apparel Story.' The Apparel Story, August. www.bgmea.com.bd/media/newsletters/July-August-2015/July-August-2015.pdf.

Bhattacharya, Debapriya, and Lisa Borgatti. 2012. 'An Atypical Approach to Graduation from the LDC Category: The Case of Bangladesh.' South Asia Economic Journal 13 (1): 1–25. doi:10.1177/139156141101300101.

Bhattacharya, Debapriya, Towfiqul Islam Khan, Umme Salma, and Gazi Joki Uddin. 2013. 'Attaining the MDGs: How Successful Are the LDCs?' Dhaka: Centre for Policy Dialogue.

Bhattacharya, Debapriya, and Mustafizur Rahman. 1999. 'Female Employment under Export Propelled Industrialization: Prospects for Internalizing Global Opportunities in the Apparel Sector in Bangladesh.' UNRISD Occasional Paper 10. Geneva: United Nations Research Initiative on Social Development. http://kms1.isn.ethz.ch/serviceengine/Files/ISN/38716/ipublicationdocument_singledocument/7549d653-19d0-400b-8c45-5ad37b982c38/en/OP+010c.pdf.

BIGD. 2015. 'The State of Governance Bangladesh 2014-2015: Institutions, Outcomes, Accountability.' State of Governance Report Series. Dhaka: BRAC Institute of Governance and Development and BRAC University.

Blanchet, Thérèse. 1996. Lost Innocence, Stolen Childhoods. Dhaka: University Press Limited.

Bohstedt, John. 2010. The Politics of Provisions: Food Riots, Moral Economy, and Market Transition in England, c. 1550–1850. Farnham/Burlington: Ashgate.

Bose, Sugata. 1986. Agrarian Bengal: Economy, Social Structure and Politics. Cambridge: Cambridge University Press.

Bose, Sugata. 1990. 'Starvation amidst Plenty: The Making of Famine in Bengal, Honan and Tonkin, 1942–45.' Modern Asian Studies 24 (04): 699–727. doi:10.1017/S0026749X00010556.

Bose, Swadesh R. 1972. 'Foodgrain Availability and Possibilities of Famine in Bangla Desh'. Economic and Political Weekly 7 (5/7): 293–306.

Boucher, David, and Paul Kelly. 1994. 'The Social Contract and Its Critics: An Overview.' pp. 1–34. In David Boucher and Paul Kelly (eds) The Social Contract from Hobbes to Rawls. London: Routledge.

BRAC University, and Institute of Governance Studies. 2009. The State of Governance in Bangladesh, 2008: Confrontation, Competition, Accountability. Dhaka: Institute of Governance Studies, BRAC University.

BRAC. 1986. The Net: Power Structure in Ten Villages. 2nd ed. Rural Study Series 2. Dacca: Bangladesh Rural Advancement Committee.

BRAC. 1992. Peasant Perceptions: Famine, Credit Needs, Sanitation. 2nd ed. Rural Study Series 3. Dhaka: Bangladesh Rural Advancement Committee.

BRAC. 2016. BRAC Education Programme—Primary Schools. Online. Accessed 17 January 2016. http://education.brac.net/primary-schools.

Brown, Garrett. 2015. 'Bangladesh: Currently the Worst, but Possibly the Future's Best.' New Solutions: A Journal of Environmental and Occupational Health Policy 24 (4): 469–73. doi:10.2190/NS.24.4.b.

Buncombe, Andrew. 2010. 'How the West Poisoned Bangladesh.' The Independent. 20 March 2010. Accessed 9 February 2015. www.independent.co.uk/news/world/asia/how-the-west-poisoned-bangladesh-1924631.html.

Burchi, Francesco. 2011. 'Democracy, Institutions and Famines in Developing and Emerging Countries.' Canadian Journal of Development Studies/Revue Canadienne D'études Du Développement 32 (1): 17–31. doi:10.1080/02255189.2011.576136.

Cain, Mead. 1983. 'Landlessness in India and Bangladesh: A Critical Review of National Data Sources.' Economic Development and Cultural Change 32 (1): 149–67.

Cain, Mead, Syeda Rokeya Khanam, and Shamsun Nahar. 1979. 'Class, Patriarchy, and Women's Work in Bangladesh.' Population and Development Review 5 (3): 405. doi:10.2307/1972079.

Caldwell, John C., Barkat-e-Khuda, Bruce Caldwell, Indrani Pieris, and Pat Caldwell. 1999. 'The Bangladesh Fertility Decline: An Interpretation.' Population and Development Review 25 (1): 67–84. doi:10.1111/j.1728-4457.1999.00067.x.

Chan, Aye. 2005. 'The Development of a Muslim Enclave in Arakan (Rakhine) State of Burma (Myanmar).' SOAS Bulletin of Burma Research 3 (2): 396–420.

Chatterjee, Partha. 1993. The Nation and Its Fragments: Colonial and Postcolonial Histories. Vol. 11. Princeton: Princeton University Press.

Chatterjee, Partha. 2004. The Politics of the Governed: Reflections on Popular Politics in Most of the World. New York: Columbia University Press.

Chemi, Eric, and Joshua Green. 2014. 'The U.S. Has Higher Income Inequality Than Britain. And Bangladesh. And Ethiopia.' Bloomberg Business. Accessed 28 September 2015. www.bloomberg.com/bw/articles/2014-05-20/the-u-dot-s-dot-has-higher-income-inequality-than-britain-dot-and-bangladesh-dot-and-ethiopia.

Chen, Greg, and Stuart Rutherford. 2013. 'A Microcredit Crisis Averted: The Case of Bangladesh.' CGAP Focus Note no. 87. Washington, DC: Consultative Group to Assist the Poorest.

Chen, Lincoln C., and Jon E. Rohde. 1971. 'Famine and Civil War in East Pakistan'. The Lancet 298 (7724): 557–60.

Chen, Lincoln C., and Jon E. Rohde. 1973. 'Civil War in Bangladesh: Famine Averted?'. pp. 190–205. In Lincoln C. Chen (ed.) Disaster in Bangladesh: Health Crises in a Developing Nation. New York & London: Oxford University Press.

Chen, Lincoln C., Mizanur Rahman, and A. M. Sarder. 1980. 'Epidemiology and Causes of Death among Children in a Rural Area of Bangladesh.' International Journal of Epidemiology 9 (1): 25–34.

Chen, Martha. 1995. 'A Matter of Survival.' pp. 37–60. In Martha Nussbaum and Jonathon Glover (eds) Women, Culture and Development: A Study of Human Capabilities. Oxford: Clarendon Press.

Chen, Martha Alter. 1983. A Quiet Revolution: Women in Transition in Rural Bangladesh. Cambridge: Schenkman.

Chopra, Surabhi. 2015. 'The International Crimes Tribunal in Bangladesh: Silencing Fair Comment.' Journal of Genocide Research 17 (2): 211–20. doi:10.1080/14623528.2015.1027080.

Chowdhury, A. Mushtaque R., Abbas Bhuiya, Mahbub Elahi Chowdhury, Sabrina Rasheed, Zakir Hussain, and Lincoln C. Chen. 2013. 'The Bangladesh Paradox: Exceptional Health Achievement despite Economic Poverty.' The Lancet 382 (9906): 1734–45.

Chowdhury, A., Mushtaque R., Samir R. Nath, and Rasheda K. Choudhury. 2002. 'Enrolment at Primary Level: Gender Difference Disappears in Bangladesh.' International Journal of Educational Development 22 (2): 191–203.

Chowdhury, A., Mushtaque R., Samir R. Nath, and Rasheda K. Choudhury. 2003. 'Equity Gains in Bangladesh Primary Education.' International Review of Education 49 (6): 601–19. doi:10.1023/B:REVI.0000006929.59667.16.

Chowdhury, Abdul Muyeed. 2009. 'Abdul Muyeed Chowdhury.' Interview transcript. Innovations for Successful Societies, Princeton University. Accessed 29 September 2015. http://successfulsocieties.princeton.edu/interviews/abdul-muyeed-chowdhury.

Chowdhury, Afsan. 2001. Their War: A Documentary by Afsan Chowdhury on 1971. Accessed 12 April 2014. www.frequency.com/video/their-war-documentary-by-afsan-chowdhury/94603150.

Chowdhury, A. M. R., A. U. Bhuiya, A. Y. Choudhury, and R. Sen. 1993. 'The Bangladesh Cyclone of 1991: Why So Many People Died.' Disasters 17 (4): 291–304.

Chowdhury, A. M. Raza, and Richard A. Cash. 1996. A Simple Solution: Teaching Millions to Treat Diarrhoea at Home. Dhaka: University Press Limited.

Chowdhury, Mahfuzul H., Muhammad A. Hakim, and Habib Zafarullah. 1996. 'Politics and Government: The Search for Legitimacy.' pp. 18-40. In H. Zafarullah (ed.) The Zia Episode in Bangladesh Politics. Dhaka: University Press Limited.

Chowdhury, Mustafa. 2015. Picking Up the Pieces: 1971 War Babies' Odyssey from Bangladesh to Canada. Bloomington: Xlibris.

Chowdhury, Nuimuddin. 1986. 'Public Foodgrain Distribution System in Bangladesh in the Post-Liberation Period: A Historical Profile.' The Bangladesh Development Studies 14 (3): 67–95.

Chowdhury, Nuimuddin. 1988. 'Where The Poor Come Last: The Case of Modified Rationing in Bangladesh.' The Bangladesh Development Studies 16 (1): 27–54.

Chowdhury, Sadia. 2001. 'Educating for Health: Using Incentive-Based Salaries to Teach Oral Rehydration Therapy.' Private Sector and Infrastructure Network Note no. 235. Washington DC: World Bank. Accessed 13 January 2016. https://openknowledge.worldbank.org/handle/10986/11371.

Chowdhury, Tawfiq-e-Elahi and Steven Haggblade. 2000. 'Dynamics and Politics of Policy Change'. pp. 165–188. In Raisuddin Ahmed, Steven Haggblade, and Tawfiq-e-Elahi Chowdhury (eds) Coming Out of the Shadow of Famine: Evolving Food Markets and Food Policy in Bangladesh.

Chowdhury, Zafrullah. 1995. 'Bangladesh: A Tough Battle for a National Drug Policy.' In Making National Drugs Policies a Development Priority: A Strategy Paper and Six Country Stories. Development Dialogue 1995: 1. Uppsala, Sweden: The Dag Hammarskjöld Centre. http://apps.who.int/medicinedocs/documents/s19176en/s19176en.pdf.

Chowdhury, Zafrullah. 1996. The Politics of Essential Drugs: The Makings of a Successful Health Strategy: Lessons from Bangladesh. Dhaka: University Press Limited.

CIA. 1971. 'Prospects for Pakistan.' Special National Intelligence Estimates 32–71 131. Foreign Relations of the United States, 1969–1976. Washington DC: Central Intelligence Agency. Foreign Relations of the United States, 1969–1976. Accessed 19 May 2015. https://history.state.gov/historicaldocuments/frus1969-76ve07/d131.

CIA. 1972. 'Bangladesh.' Document 433. Foreign Relations of the United States, 1969–1976, Volume E-7, Documents on South Asia, 1969–1972—Historical Documents—Office of the Historian. Washington DC: Central Intelligence Agency. Foreign Relations of the United States, 1969–1976. Accessed 19 May 2015. https://history.state.gov/historicaldocuments/frus1969-76ve07/d433.

CIA. 1974. 'Potential Implications of Trends in World Population, Food Production, and Climate.' OPR-401. United States Central Intelligence Agency Directorate of Intelligence Office of Political Research. http://govtslaves.info/wp-content/uploads/2014/09/potentialtrends.pdf.

Clapham, Christopher. 1990. Transformation and Continuity in Revolutionary Ethiopia. Cambridge: Cambridge University Press.

Clay, Edward J. 1979. 'Food Aid and Food Policy in Bangladesh.' Food Policy 4 (2): 129–33.

Clay, Edward. 1985. 'The 1974 and 1984 Floods in Bangladesh: From Famine to Food Crisis Management.' Food Policy 10 (3): 202–6.

Cleland, J. G., ed. 1994. The Determinants of Reproductive Change in Bangladesh: Success in a Challenging Environment. World Bank Regional and Sectoral Studies. Washington DC: World Bank.

Cleland, John, James F. Phillips, Sajeda Amin, and Gholam Mostafa Kamal. 1994. The Determinants of Reproductive Change in Bangladesh: Success in a Challenging Environment. Washington DC: World Bank.

Constantinou, Dinos, and Arvind Ashta. 2011. 'Financial Crisis: Lessons from Microfinance.' Strategic Change 20 (5–6): 187–203. doi:10.1002/jsc.895.

Cooper, A. 1983. 'Sharecroppers and Landlords in Bengal, 1930–1950: The Dependency Web and Its Implications'. Journal of Peasant Studies 10 (2–3): 227–55.

Corbridge, Stuart, Glyn Williams, Manoj Srivastava, and René Véron. 2005. Seeing the State: Governance and Governmentality in India. Cambridge: Cambridge University Press.

CPD. 2014. 'Rana Plaza Tragedy and Beyond: An Update on Commitments and Delivery.' CPD Dialogue Report no. 10. Dhaka: Centre for Policy Dialogue.

Crook, Richard C., and James Manor. 1998. Democracy and Decentralisation in South Asia and West Africa: Participation, Accountability and Performance. Cambridge: Cambridge University Press.

Crow, Ben. 1984. 'Warnings of Famine in Bangladesh.' Economic and Political Weekly 19 (40): 1754–8.

Curlin, George T., Lincoln C. Chen, and Sayed Babur Hussain. 1976. 'Demographic Crisis: The Impact of the Bangladesh Civil War (1971) on Births and Deaths in a Rural Area of Bangladesh.' Population Studies 30 (1): 87–105. doi:10.2307/2173665.

Currey, Bruce. 1978. 'The Famine Syndrome: Its Definition for Relief and Rehabilitation in Bangladesh.' Ecology of Food and Nutrition 7 (2): 87–97. doi:10.1080/03670244.1978.9990517.

Currey, Bruce. 1992. 'Is Famine a Discrete Event?' Disasters 16 (2): 138–44.

Custers, Peter. 1987. Women in the Tebhaga Uprising. Calcutta: Naya Prokash.

Custers, Peter. 2010. 'Maulana Bhashani and the Transition to Secular Politics in East Bengal.' Indian Economic & Social History Review 47 (2): 231–59. doi:10.1177/001946461004700204.

Custers, Peter. 2011. 'Moulana Bhashani's Historical and Contemporary Significance.' Holiday (online version), 11 February edition. Comments page. Accessed 2 August 2016. www.weeklyholiday.net/Homepage/Archive/110211/com.html.

Cutler, Peter. 1985. 'Detecting Food Emergencies: Lessons from the 1979 Bangladesh Crisis.' Food Policy 10 (3): 207–24.

D'Costa, Bina. 2011. Nationbuilding, Gender, and War Crimes in South Asia. Routledge Contemporary South Asia Series. London and New York: Routledge.

D'Costa, Bina. 2014a. 'Victory's Silence.' The Daily Star, 12 April. Accessed 17 April 2016. www.thedailystar.net/victorys-silence-53364.

D'Costa, Bina. 2014b. 'Once Were Warriors: The Militarized State in Narrating the Past.' South Asian History and Culture 5 (4): 457–74. doi:10.1080/19472498.2014.936205.

D'Costa, Bina, and Sara Hossain. 2010. 'Redress for Sexual Violence Before the International Crimes Tribunal in Bangladesh: Lessons from History, and Hopes for the Future.' Criminal Law Forum 21 (2): 331–59. doi:10.1007/s10609-010-9120-2.

Daher, Lâma, and Erwan Le Saout. 2015. 'The Determinants of the Financial Performance of Microfinance Institutions: Impact of the Global Financial Crisis.' Strategic Change 24 (2): 131–48. doi:10.1002/jsc.2002.

Dasgupta, S. 1996. 'Making of an Alliance: Bourgeoisie and Army in Bangladesh.' Journal of Social Studies 71: 81–115.

Dashi, Edlira, Estelle Lahaye, and Ralitsa Rizvanolli. 2013. 'Trends in International Funding for Financial Inclusion.' CGAP Brief. Washington DC: Consultative Group to Assist the Poorest.

Dastagir, M. Rehan. 2015. 'Modeling Recent Climate Change Induced Extreme Events in Bangladesh: A Review.' Weather and Climate Extremes, SI: IGBP APN, 7: 49–60. doi:10.1016/j.wace.2014.10.003.

Davis, Mike. 2001. Late Victorian Holocausts: El Niño Famines and the Making of the Third World. London: Verso.

de Haan, Arjan. 1997. 'Unsettled Settlers: Migrant Workers and Industrial Capitalism in Calcutta.' Modern Asian Studies 31 (4): 919–49. doi:10.1017/S0026749X00017200.

de Waal, Alex. 1991. Evil Days: Thirty Years of War and Famine in Ethiopia. New York: Human Rights Watch.

de Waal, Alex. 1996. 'Social Contract and Deterring Famine: First Thoughts.' Disasters 20 (3): 194–205.

de Waal, Alex. 1997. Famine Crimes: Politics & the Disaster Relief Industry in Africa. African Rights & the International African Institute. Oxford: James Currey.

de Waal, Alex. 2000. 'Democratic Political Process and the Fight Against Famine.' IDS Working Paper 107. Brighton: Institute of Development Studies. http://opendocs.ids.ac.uk/opendocs/handle/123456789/3438.

Del Ninno, Carlo, Paul A. Dorosh, and Lisa C. Smith. 2003. 'Public Policy, Markets and Household Coping Strategies in Bangladesh: Avoiding a Food Security Crisis Following the 1998 Floods.' World Development 31 (7): 1221–38.

Devereux, Stephen. 1993. Theories of Famine. Hemel Hempstead: Harvester Wheatsheaf.

Devereux, Stephen. 2000. 'Famine in the Twentieth Century.' IDS Working Papers, IDS working paper, 105. Brighton: Institute of Development Studies.

Devereux, Stephen. 2001. 'Sen's Entitlement Approach: Critiques and Counter-Critiques.' Oxford Development Studies 29 (3): 245–63. doi:10.1080/13600810120088859.

Devereux, Stephen. 2006a. 'From "Old Famines" to "New Famines."' pp. 1–26. In Stephen Devereux (ed.) The New Famines: Why Famines Persist in an Era of Globalization. London: Routledge.

Devereux, Stephen. ed. 2006b. The New Famines: Why Famines Persist in an Era of Globalization. London: Routledge.

Devine, J. 2006. 'NGOs, Politics and Grassroots Mobilisation: Evidence from Bangladesh.' Journal of South Asian Development 1 (1): 77–99. doi:10.1177/097317410500100104.

Devine, Joseph. 1999. 'One Foot in Each Boot: The Macro Politics and Micro Sociology of NGOs in Bangladesh.' PhD thesis, University of Bath. http://ethos.bl.uk/OrderDetails.do?uin=uk.bl.ethos.301965.

Dhaka Tribune. 2015. 'Make Bangladesh a Powerhouse for Pharmaceutical Exports | Dhaka Tribune.' Editorial, 10 November. Accessed 13 January 2016. www.dhakatribune.com/editorial/2015/nov/10/make-bangladesh-powerhouse-pharmaceutical-exports.

Dhaka Tribune. 2016. 'Bangladesh Wants New Governance Structure in Migration | Dhaka Tribune.' Dhaka Tribune, 4 January. Accessed 4 April 2016. www.dhakatribune.com/bangladesh/2016/jan/04/bangladesh-wants-new-governance-structure-migration.

Di John, Jonathan, and James Putzel. 2009. 'Political Settlements: Issues Paper.' Emerging Issues Research Service of the Governance and Social Development Resource Centre (GSDRC). Accessed 16 February 2015. www.gsdrc.org/docs/open/eirs7.pdf.

Dikötter, Frank. 2010. Mao's Great Famine: The History of China's Most Devastating Catastrophe, 1958–1962. London: Bloomsbury Publishing.

Dirks, Robert, George J. Armelagos, Charles A. Bishop, Ivan A. Brady, Thierry Brun, Jean Copans, V. S. Doherty, et al. 1980. 'Social Responses During Severe Food Shortages and Famine [and Comments and Reply].' Current Anthropology 21 (1): 21–44.

Dowlah, Caf. 2006. 'The Politics and Economics of Food and Famine in Bangladesh in the Early 1970s—with Special Reference to Amartya Sen's Interpretation of the 1974 Famine.' International Journal of Social Welfare 15 (4): 344–56.

Duflos, Eric, and Barbara Gahwiler. n.d. 'Impacts and Implications of the Food Crisis on Microfinance: CGAP Survey of 45 Leading MFIs.' Mimeo. Washington DC: Consultative Group to Assist the Poorest.

Duvendack, M., Palmer-Jones, R., Copestake, J. G., Hooper, L., Loke, Y., and N. Rao. 2011. 'What is the Evidence of the Impact of Microfinance on the Well-being of Poor

People?' Working paper no. 1912. London: EPPI-Centre, Social Science Research Unit, Institute of Education, University of London.

Eaton, Richard. 2001. 'Who are the Bengal Muslims? Conversion and Islamization in Bengal.' pp. 26–51. In Rafiuddin Ahmed (ed.) Understanding the Bengal Muslims: Interpretative Essays. New Delhi: Oxford University Press.

Eaton, Richard Maxwell. 1993. The Rise of Islam and the Bengal Frontier, 1204–1760. Berkeley: University of California Press.

Economist Intelligence Unit. 1996. Bangladesh: Country Report. London: The Economist Intelligence Unit.

Edkins, Jenny. 2006. 'The Criminalization of Mass Starvations.' pp. 50–65. In Stephen Devereux (ed.) The New Famines: Why Famines Persist in an Era of Globalization. London: Routledge.

El Arifeen, Shams, Aliki Christou, Laura Reichenbach, Ferdous Arfina Osman, Kishwar Azad, Khaled Shamsul Islam, Faruque Ahmed, Henry B. Perry, and David H. Peters. 2013. 'Community-Based Approaches and Partnerships: Innovations in Health-Service Delivery in Bangladesh.' The Lancet 382 (9909): 2012–26. doi:10.1016/S0140-6736(13)62149-2.

Elson, Diane, and Ruth Pearson. 1981. '"Nimble Fingers Make Cheap Workers": An Analysis of Women's Employment in Third World Export Manufacturing.' Feminist Review 7 (1): 87–107.

ERD. 2014. 'Flow of External Resources into Bangladesh 2012–2013.' Dhaka: Economic Relations Division, Ministry of Finance, Government of the People's Republic of Bangladesh.

Faaland, Just, and John Richard Parkinson. 1976. Bangladesh: The Test Case of Development. London: C. Hurst.

Fahmida Khatun, Mustafizur Rahman, Debapriya Bhattacharya, Khondaker Golam Moazzem, and A. Shahrin. 2007. 'Gender and Trade Liberalization in Bangladesh: The Case of the Ready-Made Garments.' Greater Access to Trade Expansion (GATE) Project Report. United States Agency for International Development.

Fantom, Neil. 2016. 'The 2016 Edition of World Development Indicators is Out: Three Features You Won't Want to Miss'. Accessed 30 May 2016. Posted on The Data Blog, 15 April 2016. http://blogs.worldbank.org/opendata/2016-edition-world-development-indicators-out-three-features-you-won-t-want-miss.

Farndale, Nigel. 2013. 'Prince Moosa.' Nigel Farndale. 17 June. Accessed 25 September 2015. www.nigelfarndale.com/2013/06/prince-moosa/.

Feldman, Herbert. 1978. The End and the Beginning: Pakistan, 1969–1971. London: Oxford University Press.

Feldman, Shelley. 1999. 'Feminist Interruptions: The Silence of East Bengal in the Story of Partition.' Interventions 1 (2): 167–82. doi:10.1080/13698019900510291.

Feldman, Shelley. 2001. 'Exploring Theories of Patriarchy: A Perspective from Contemporary Bangladesh.' Signs 26 (4) 1097–127.

Feldman, Shelley. 2003. 'Bengali State and Nation Making: Partition and Displacement Revisited.' International Social Science Journal 55 (175): 111–21. doi:10.1111/1468-2451.5501011.

Feldman, Shelley, and Florence E. McCarthy. 1983a. 'Disaster Response in Bangladesh.' International Journal of Mass Emergencies and Disasters 1 (1): 105–24.

Feldman, Shelley, and Florence E. McCarthy. 1983b. 'Purdah and Changing Patterns of Social Control among Rural Women in Bangladesh.' Journal of Marriage and Family 45 (4): 949–59. doi:10.2307/351808.

FMRP. 2007. 'Governance, Management and Performance in Health and Education Facilities in Bangladesh: Findings from the Social Sector Performance Qualitative Study.' Dhaka: Financial Management Reform Programme, Ministry of Finance, Government of Bangladesh.

Foucault, Michel. 1978. The History of Sexuality. 1st American edition. New York: Pantheon Books.

Franda, Marcus. 1981a. 'Bangladesh after Zia: A Retrospect and Prospect.' Economic and Political Weekly 16 (34): 1387–94.

Franda, Marcus. 1981b. 'Food Policy and Politics in Bangladesh.' India Quarterly: A Journal of International Affairs 37 (2): 165–93.

Franda, Marcus. 1981c. 'Ziaur Rahman and Bangladeshi Nationalism.' Economic and Political Weekly 16 (10/12): 357–80.

Franda, M. 1982. Bangladesh: The First Decade. New Delhi/Madras: South Asian Publishers Pvt Ltd.

Frank Neil, L., and S. A. Husain. 1971. 'The Deadliest Tropical Cyclone in History?' Bulletin of the American Meteorological Society 52 (6): 438–44.

Fraser, Nancy. 1990. 'Rethinking the Public Sphere: A Contribution to the Critique of Actually Existing Democracy.' Social Text, no. 25/26: 56–80. doi:10.2307/466240.

Fraser, Nancy. 2012. 'Feminism, Capitalism, and the Cunning of History.' New Left Review 56: 97–117.

Ganguly, Meenakshi. 2015. 'Whoever Raises Their Head Suffers the Most': Workers' Rights in Bangladesh's Garment Factories. New York, NY: Human Rights Watch.

García-Moreno, Claudia, H. A. F. M. Jansen, Mary Ellsberg, Lori Heise, and Charlotte Watts. 2005. WHO Multi-Country Study on Women's Health and Domestic Violence against Women. Geneva: World Health Organization.

García-Moreno, Claudia, Henrica A. F. M. Jansen, Mary Ellsberg, Lori Heise, and Charlotte H. Watts. 2006. 'Prevalence of Intimate Partner Violence: Findings from the WHO Multi-Country Study on Women's Health and Domestic Violence.' The Lancet 368 (9543): 1260–9.

Gardner, Katy. 1995. Global Migrants, Local Lives: Travel and Transformation in Rural Bangladesh. Oxford: Clarendon Press.

Gauri, Varun, and Julia Galef. 2005. 'NGOs in Bangladesh: Activities, Resources, and Governance.' World Development 33 (12): 2045–65. doi:10.1016/j.worlddev.2005.05.009.

GED. 2015a. 'Millennium Development Goals: Bangladesh Progress Report 2015.' Dhaka: General Economics Division, Bangladesh Planning Commission, Government of the People's Republic of Bangladesh.

GED. 2015b. '7th Five Year Plan 2016–2020 Accelerating Growth, Empowering Citizens.' Five Year Plans, Government of Bangladesh. Dhaka: General Economics Division, Bangladesh Planning Commission Government of the People's Republic of Bangladesh.

GED/UNDP. 2005. 'Millennium Development Goals: Bangladesh Progress Report 2005.' Dhaka: General Economics Division, Bangladesh Planning Commission,

Government of the People's Republic of Bangladesh & the United Nations Country Team in Bangladesh.

Gerlach, Christian. 2010. Extremely Violent Societies: Mass Violence in the Twentieth-Century World. Cambridge: Cambridge University Press.

Gerlach, Christian. 2015. 'Famine Responses in the World Food Crisis 1972–5 and the World Food Conference of 1974.' European Review of History: Revue Européenne D'histoire, June, 1–11. doi:10.1080/13507486.2015.1048191.

Ghosh, Jayati. 2013. 'Microfinance and the challenge of financial inclusion for development.' Cambridge Journal of Economics 37 (6): 1203–1219.

Ghosh, Shyamali. 1990. The Awami League, 1949–1971. Dhaka: Academic Publishers.

GoB. 2012. Sixth Five Year Plan FY2011-FY2015 Accelerating Growth and Reducing Poverty Part-1: Strategic Directions and Policy Framework. Dhaka: General Economics Division, Bangladesh Planning Commission Government of the People's Republic of Bangladesh. www.unicef.org/bangladesh/Six-Five-Year-Plan-2012-Final.pdf.

GoB. 2015. Convention on the Elimination of All Forms of Discrimination Against Women (CEDAW): The Eighth Periodic Report of The Government of the People's Republic of Bangladesh. Dhaka: Government of the People's Republic of Bangladesh. http://mowca.portal.gov.bd/sites/default/files/files/mowca.portal.gov.bd/page/762c7e6e_69ce_4979_817c_f7dbc2b561ed/8th%20Periodic%20Report-%20CEDAW-2015.pdf.

Goetz, Anne Marie, and Rina Sen Gupta. 1996. 'Who Takes the Credit? Gender, Power, and Control over Loan Use in Rural Credit Programs in Bangladesh.' World Development 24 (1): 45–63. doi:10.1016/0305-750X(95)00124-U.

Graham-Harrison, Emma, and Saad Hammadi. 2016. 'Inside Bangladesh's Killing Fields: Bloggers and Outsiders Targeted by Fanatics.' The Guardian, 12 June. Accessed 13 June 2016. www.theguardian.com/world/2016/jun/11/bangladesh-murders-bloggers-foreigners-religion.

Greeley, Martin. 1983. 'Patriarchy and Poverty: A Bangladesh Case Study.' South Asia Research 3 (1): 35–55.

Greenhouse, Steven. 2015. 'Bangladesh Labor Leader Arrested during Rana Plaza Protest in New Jersey.' The Guardian, 15 March. Accessed 14 March 2015. www.theguardian.com/us-news/2015/mar/15/bangladesh-kalpona-akter-arrested-rana-plaza-new-jersey.

Greenough, Paul R. 1982. Prosperity and Misery in Modern Bengal: The Famine of 1943–1944. Oxford: Oxford University Press.

Greenough, Paul R. 1983. 'Indulgence and Abundance as Asian Peasant Values: A Bengali Case in Point.' The Journal of Asian Studies 42 (4): 831–50. doi:10.2307/2054767.

Greenough, William, and Richard Cash. 1973. 'Post-Civil War in Bangladesh: Health Problems and Programs.' pp. 241–54. In Lincoln C. Chen (ed.) Disaster in Bangladesh: Health Crises in a Developing Nation. New York and London: Oxford University Press.

Guhathakurta, Meghna. 1990. The Politics of British Aid Policy Formation towards Bangladesh: An Analytical Model. Dhaka: Centre for Social Studies

Guttmacher Institute. 2012. 'Menstrual Regulation and Induced Abortion in Bangladesh.' Accessed 17 November 2015. www.guttmacher.org/pubs/FB-Bangladesh-MR.html.

Hammadi, Saad. 2015. 'Third Atheist Blogger Killed in Bangladesh Knife Attack.' The Guardian, 5 December. Accessed 7 October 2015. www.theguardian.com/world/2015/may/12/third-atheist-blogger-killed-in-bangladesh-after-knife-attack.

Haque, C. E. 1997. 'Atmospheric Hazards Preparedness in Bangladesh: A Study of Warning, Adjustments and Recovery from the April 1991 Cyclone.' Natural Hazards 16 (2–3): 181–202.

Haque, C. E., and D. Blair. 1992. 'Vulnerability to Tropical Cyclones: Evidence from the April 1991 Cyclone in Coastal Bangladesh.' Disasters 16 (3): 217–29.

Hardin, Garrett. 1974. 'Commentary: Living on a Lifeboat.' BioScience 24 (10): 561–68. doi:10.2307/1296629.

Hartmann, Betsy. 1987. Reproductive Rights and Wrongs: The Global Politics of Population Control. New York: Harper and Row.

Hartmann, Betsy, and James K. Boyce. 1983. A Quiet Violence: View from a Bangladesh Village. London: Zed Books.

Harvard Business School. 2014. 'Interview with Fazle Abed, Interviewed by Tarun Khanna.' Cambridge, MA: Baker Library Historical Collections, Harvard Business School. www.hbs.edu/businesshistory/Documents/emerging-markets-transcripts/Abed_Fazle_Web%20Copy.pdf.

Hashemi, Syed. 1995. 'NGO Accountability in Bangladesh: Beneficiaries, Donors and the State.' pp. 123–31. In Michael Edwards and David Hulme (eds) Non-Governmental Organizations: Performance and Accountability: Beyond the Magic Bullet. London: Earthscan.

Hashemi, Syed and Mirza Hassan. 1999. 'Building NGO Legitimacy in Bangladesh: The Contested Domain.' pp. 124–31. In David Lewis (ed.) International Perspectives on Voluntary Action: Reshaping the Third Sector. London: Earthscan.

Hashemi, Syed, and Aude De Montesquiou. 2011. 'Reaching the Poorest: Lessons from the Graduation Model.' CGAP Focus Note 69. Washington DC: Consultative Group to Assist the Poorest. www.microlinks.org/sites/microlinks/files/gcontentadmin/files/reaching-the-poorest.pdf.

Hashmi, T. I. 1988. 'The Communalization of Class Struggle: East Bengal Peasantry, 1923–29'. The Indian Economic and Social History Review 25 (2): 171–204. Presented at the High Level Plenary on the Millennium Development Goals, New York, 20–22 September.

Hassan, Mirza. 2013. 'Political Settlement Dynamics in a Limited-Access Order: The Case of Bangladesh.' ESID Working Paper. Manchester: Effective States and Inclusive Development Research Centre. www.effective-states.org/wp-content/uploads/working_papers/final-pdfs/esid_wp_23_hassan.pdf.

Hatemi J. Abdulnasser, and Gazi Salah Uddin. 2014. 'On the Causal Nexus of Remittances and Poverty Reduction in Bangladesh.' Applied Economics 46 (4): 374–82. doi:10.1080/00036846.2013.844331.

Hayter, Teresa. 1971. Aid as Imperialism. London: Penguin.

Heath, Rachel. 2014. 'Women's Access to Labor Market Opportunities, Control of Household Resources, and Domestic Violence: Evidence from Bangladesh.' World Development 57 (May): 32–46. doi:10.1016/j.worlddev.2013.10.028.

Heath, Rachel, and A. M. Mobarak. 2015. 'Manufacturing Growth and the Lives of Bangladeshi Women.' Journal of Development Economics 115 (July): 1–15. doi:10.1016/j.jdeveco.2015.01.006.

Hecock, R. Douglas. 2006. 'Electoral Competition, Globalization, and Subnational Education Spending in Mexico, 1999–2004.' American Journal of Political Science 50 (4): 950–61. doi:10.1111/j.1540-5907.2006.00226.x.

Hickey, Sam. 2011. 'The Politics of Social Protection: What Do We Get from a "Social Contract" Approach?' Canadian Journal of Development Studies/Revue Canadienne D'études Du Développement 32 (4): 426–38. doi:10.1080/02255189.2011.647447.

Hickey, Sam. 2013. 'Thinking about the Politics of Inclusive Development: Towards a Relational Approach.' ESID Working Paper Series. Manchester: Effective States and Inclusive Development Research Centre. Accessed 10 February 2015. www.effective-states.org/wp-content/uploads/working_papers/final-pdfs/esid_wp_01_hickey.pdf.

Hossain, Akhtar. 1996a. 'The Economy: Towards Stabilisation.' pp. 50–83. In Habib Zafarullah (ed.) The Zia Episode in Bangladesh Politics. Dhaka: University Press Limited.

Hossain, Akhtar. 1996b. 'Macroeconomic Policies and Problems in Bangladesh During the Mujib Regime (1972–1975).' Canadian Journal of Development Studies/ Revue Canadienne D'études Du Développement 17 (1): 119–36. doi:10.1080/ 02255189.1996.9669642.

Hossain, Akhtar. 1999. 'Professor Amartya Sen and the 1974 Bangladesh Famine.' Journal of Bangladesh Studies 1 (1): 39–62.

Hossain, Mustak. 2006. 'Arsenic-Poisoning Lawsuit Rejected by Britain'. Mail & Guardian. 10 July. Accessed 9 February 2015. http://mg.co.za/article/2006-07-10-arsenicpoisoning-lawsuit-rejected-by-britain.

Hossain, N. 2005. Elite Perceptions of Poverty in Bangladesh. Dhaka: University Press Limited.

Hossain, Naomi. 2004. 'APPENDIX ONE The Real-Life Relationship between Donors and Recipients in Bangladesh: Exploratory Research into the Sociology of Aid Relations.' Brighton: Institute of Development Studies. http://r4d.dfid.gov.uk/PDF/ Outputs/Mis_SPC/R8248appendix1.pdf.

Hossain, Naomi. 2006. 'Inheriting Extreme Poverty: Household Aspirations, Community Poverty and Childhood in Northern Bangladesh.' Dhaka: Save the Children Fund UK.

Hossain, Naomi. 2007a. The Politics of What Works: The Case of the Vulnerable Group Development Programme in Bangladesh. CPRC working paper 92. Manchester: Chronic Poverty Research Centre.

Hossain, Naomi. 2007b. 'Expanding Access to Education in Bangladesh.' pp. 304–25. In D. Narayan and E. Glinskaya (eds) Ending Poverty in South Asia: Ideas That Work in South Asia. Washington DC: World Bank.

Hossain, Naomi. 2010a. 'School Exclusion as Social Exclusion: The Practices and Effects of a Conditional Cash Transfer Programme for the Poor in Bangladesh.' The Journal of Development Studies 46 (7): 1264–82. doi:10.1080/00220388.2010. 487096.

Hossain, Naomi. 2010b. 'Rude Accountability: Informal Pressures on Frontline Bureaucrats in Bangladesh.' Development and Change 41 (5): 907–28. doi:10.1111/j.1467-7660.2010.01663.x.

Hossain, Naomi. 2012. 'Women's Empowerment Revisited: From Individual to Collective Power among the Export Sector Workers of Bangladesh.' IDS Working Papers 389. Brighton: Institute of Development Studies. doi:10.1111/j.2040-0209.2012.00389.x.

Hossain, Naomi. 2014. 'Are We Middle Income Yet?' Dhaka Tribune, 2 December. Accessed 8 October 2015. www.dhakatribune.com/long-form/2014/dec/02/are-we-middle-income-yet.

Hossain, Naomi, and Samiha Huda. 1995. 'Problems of the Women Headed Households.' BRAC-ICDDR, B Joint Research Project working paper. Dhaka: BRAC/International Centre for Diarrhoeal Disease Research, Bangladesh.

Hossain, Naomi, and Ferdous Jahan. 2014. 'The Food Riots That Never Were: The Moral and Political Economy of Food Security in Bangladesh.' Food Riots and Food Rights: The Moral and Political Economy of Accountability for Hunger Project Reports. Brighton: Institute of Development Studies.

Hossain, Naomi, and Devangana Kalita. 2014. 'Moral Economy in a Global Era: The Politics of Provisions during Contemporary Food Price Spikes.' Journal of Peasant Studies 41 (5): 815–31. doi:10.1080/03066150.2014.895328.

Hossain, Naomi, Ramya Subrahmanian, and Naila Kabeer. 2002. 'The Politics of Educational Expansion in Bangladesh.' IDS Working Paper 167. Brighton: Institute of Development Studies.

Hossain, Naomi, Patta Scott-Villers, Nick Chisholm, and Alexandra Wanjiku Kelbert. 2016. 'Resilience, Precarity or Both? Life after the Global Food Crisis.' Life in a Time of Food Price Volatility. Brighton: Institute of Development Studies/Oxfam GB.

Hossain, Naomi, and Heidi Tavakoli. 2008. 'School Choice in Bangladesh.' Report to DFID Bangladesh. Oxford: Oxford Policy Management Limited.

Hossain, Syed Altaf. 2013. 'The World's Celebrated Business Tycoon Prince Moosa.' Business News 24, 5 November. Accessed 6 October 2015. http://businessnews24bd.com/the-worlds-celebrated-business-tycoon-prince-moosa/.

Humphrey, C. 1990. Privatization in Bangladesh: Economic Transition in a Poor Country, Boulder: Westview Press.

Huq, Lopita. 2015. 'Unpaid Care Work in Bangladesh: Policies, Practice and Evidence.' IDS Working Paper 452. Brighton: Institute of Development Studies.

Huq, Mujibul, ed. 1991. Near Miracle in Bangladesh. Dhaka: University Press Limited.

Huq, Samia. 2010. 'Negotiating Islam: Conservatism, Splintered Authority and Empowerment in Urban Bangladesh.' IDS Bulletin 41 (2): 97–105.

Husain, S. A. 1966. 'Tropical Cyclones of the Bay of Bengal affecting Pakistan'. Paper presented to the Working Group of Experts on Cyclones, Dacca (Dhaka), December 1966.

Hussain, A. M. Zakir, M. Q. K. Talukder, and Tahmeed Ahmed. 2015. 'Nutrition Background Paper to Inform the Preparation of the 7th Five Year Plan.' Dhaka: General Economics Division, Planning Commission, Government of the People's Republic of Bangladesh. www.plancomm.gov.bd/wp-content/uploads/2015/02/23_-Nutrition-Background-Paper-for-7th-FYP.pdf.

IGS. 2006. The State of Governance in Bangladesh, 2006: Knowledge, Perceptions, Reality. State of Governance in Bangladesh Report. Dhaka: Centre for Governance Studies, BRAC University.

ILO, ed. 2014a. Gender and Migration from Bangladesh: Mainstreaming Migration into the National Development Plans from a Gender Perspective. Dhaka: ILO Country Office for Bangladesh.

ILO, ed. 2014b. 'Third Supplementary Report: Situation of Trade Union Rights in Bangladesh.' Geneva, Switzerland: International Labour Organization. Accessed 21 March 2016. www.ilo.org/gb/GBSessions/GB320/ins/WCMS_235773/lang–en/index.htm.

Imran, Shahed. 2015. 'MDGs: Bangladesh Is a Role Model Now'. *The Daily Star*, 5 July 2015.

Indra, Doreen Marie, and Norman Buchignani. 1997. 'Rural Landlessness, Extended Entitlements and Inter-household Relations in South Asia: A Bangladesh Case.' Journal of Peasant Studies 24 (3): 25–64. doi:10.1080/03066159708438642.

Institute of Governance Studies. 2010. The State of Governance in Bangladesh 2009: Entitlement, Responsiveness, Sustainability. Dhaka: Institute of Governance Studies, BRAC University.

International Business Times. 2015. 'Saudi Arabia To Lift Ban On Labor Migration From Bangladesh.' 4 February. Accessed 4 April 2016. www.ibtimes.com/saudi-arabia-lift-ban-labor-migration-bangladesh-1805350.

Iqbal, Iftekhar. 2010. The Bengal Delta: Ecology, State and Social Change, 1840–1943. Basingstoke: Palgrave Macmillan.

Islam, M. Aminul. 1971. 'Human Adjustment to Cyclone Hazards: A Case Study of Char Jabbar,' Natural Hazards Working Paper Series, 18, University of Toronto. Accessed 17 April 2015. http://hermes.cde.state.co.us/drupal/islandora/object/co%3A14171.

Islam, Mohammad Mozahidul. 2012. 'The Politics of Food Security in Bangladesh.' PhD thesis. University of New South Wales. http://unsworks.unsw.edu.au/fapi/datastream/unsworks:11039/SOURCE01.

Islam, Nurul. 1972. 'Foreign Assistance and Economic Development: The Case of Pakistan'. The Economic Journal 82 (325): 502–30.

Islam, Nurul. 2003. Making of a Nation, Bangladesh: An Economist's Tale. Dhaka: University Press Limited.

Islam, Syed Serajul. 1984. 'The State in Bangladesh under Zia (1975–81).' Asian Survey 24 (5): 556–73. doi:10.2307/2644413.

Islam, Syed Serajul. 1986–7. 'Relative State Autonomy and Development Strategy in Bangladesh, 1975–81.' Pacific Affairs 59 (4): 563–76.

Jahan, Rounaq. 1973. 'Bangladesh in 1972: Nation Building in a New State.' Asian Survey 13 (2): 199–210. doi:10.2307/2642736.

Jahan, Rounaq. 1980. Bangladesh Politics: Problems and Issues. Dacca University Press Limited.

Jahan, Rounaq. 2005. Bangladesh Politics: Problems and Issues. Dhaka: University Press Limited.

Jahan, Rounaq. 2015. 'The Parliament of Bangladesh: Representation and Accountability.' The Journal of Legislative Studies 21 (2): 250–69. doi:10.1080/13572334.2014.975470.

Jahan, Rounaq, and Inge Amundsen. 2012. 'The Parliament of Bangladesh: Representation and Accountability.' CPD/CMI Working Paper no. 2. Dhaka: Centre for Policy Dialogue & Chr. Michelsen Institute.

Jahangir, B. K. 1976. 'Differentiation, Polarisation and Confrontation in Rural Bangladesh.' PhD thesis. Durham University: Durham. http://etheses.dur.ac.uk/7456/.

Jahangir, B. K. 1978. 'Peasant Mobilisation Process: The Bangladesh Case.' Journal of Social Studies 1: 25–42.

Jahangir, B. K. 1995. 'Famine and Politics.' Journal of Social Studies 68: 91–101.

Jain, Pankaj, and Mick Moore. 2003. 'What Makes Microcredit Programmes Effective? Fashionable Fallacies and Workable Realities.' IDS Working Paper 177. Brighton: Institute of Development Studies.

Jannuzi, F. Tomasson, and James T. Peach. 1979. 'Note on Land Reform in Bangladesh: The Efficacy of Ceilings.' Journal of Peasant Studies 6 (3): 342–7.

Jannuzi, F. Tomasson, and James T. Peach. 1980. The Agrarian Structure of Bangladesh: An Impediment to Development. Boulder: Westview Press.

Jansen, Erik G. 1986. Rural Bangladesh: Competition for Scarce Resources. Oslo: Norwegian University Press.

Jisheng, Yang. 2012. Tombstone: The Great Chinese Famine, 1958–1962. New York: Farrar, Straus and Giroux.

Kabeer, Naila. 1988. 'Subordination and Struggle: Women in Bangladesh.' New Left Review 168: 95–121.

Kabeer, Naila. 1999. 'Resources, Agency, Achievements: Reflections on the Measurement of Women's Empowerment.' Development and Change 30 (3): 435–64. doi:10.1111/1467-7660.00125.

Kabeer, Naila. 2000. 'Inter-Generational Contracts, Demographic Transitions and the "quantity–quality" Tradeoff: Parents, Children and Investing in the Future.' Journal of International Development 12 (4): 463–82. doi:10.1002/1099-1328(200005) 12:4<463::AID-JID684>3.0.CO;2-S.

Kabeer, Naila. 2001a. 'Conflicts Over Credit: Re-Evaluating the Empowerment Potential of Loans to Women in Rural Bangladesh.' World Development 29 (1): 63–84. doi:10.1016/S0305-750X(00)00081-4.

Kabeer, Naila. 2001b. 'Ideas, Economics and "the Sociology of Supply": Explanations for Fertility Decline in Bangladesh.' The Journal of Development Studies 38 (1): 29–70. doi:10.1080/00220380412331322181.

Kabeer, Naila. 2002. The Power to Choose: Bangladeshi Garment Workers in London and Dhaka. London: Verso.

Kabeer, Naila. 2011. 'Citizenship Narratives in the Face of Bad Governance: The Voices of the Working Poor in Bangladesh.' Journal of Peasant Studies 38 (2): 325–53. doi:10.1080/03066150.2011.559011.

Kabeer, Naila, and Naomi Hossain. 2004. 'Achieving Universal Education and Eliminating Gender Disparity in Bangladesh.' Economic and Political Weekly 39 (36) 4093–100.

Kabeer, Naila, Lopita Huq, and Simeen Mahmud. 2013. 'Diverging Stories of "Missing Women" in South Asia: Is Son Preference Weakening in Bangladesh?' Feminist Economics, November, 1–26. doi:10.1080/13545701.2013.857423.

Kabeer, Naila, and Simeen Mahmud. 2004. 'Globalization, Gender and Poverty: Bangladeshi Women Workers in Export and Local Markets.' Journal of International Development 16 (1): 93–109. doi:10.1002/jid.1065.

Kabeer, Naila, Simeen Mahmud, and Jairo G. Isaza Castro. 2012. 'NGOs and the Political Empowerment of Poor People in Rural Bangladesh: Cultivating the Habits of Democracy?' World Development 40 (10): 2044–62. doi:10.1016/j.worlddev.2012.05.011.

Kabeer, Naila, Simeen Mahmud, and Sakiba Tasneem. 2011. Does Paid Work Provide a Pathway to Women's Empowerment? Empirical Findings from Bangladesh. IDS Working Paper 375. Brighton: Institute of Development Studies. www.ids.ac.uk/files/dmfile/Wp375.pdf.

Kabeer, Naila, and Munshi Sulaiman. 2015. 'Assessing the Impact of Social Mobilization: Nijera Kori and the Construction of Collective Capabilities in Rural Bangladesh.' Journal of Human Development and Capabilities 16 (1): 47–68. doi:10.1080/19452829.2014.956707.

Kandiyoti, Deniz. 1988. 'Bargaining with Patriarchy.' Gender & Society 2 (3): 274–90.

Karim, Lamia. 2011. Microfinance and Its Discontents: Women in Debt in Bangladesh. Minneapolis, MN: University of Minnesota Press.

Karim, Lamia. 2014. 'Disposable Bodies.' Anthropology Now 6 (1): 52–63.

Karim, M., and N. Mimura. 2008. 'Impacts of Climate Change and Sea-Level Rise on Cyclonic Storm Surge Floods in Bangladesh.' Global Environmental Change 18 (3): 490–500.

Karim, S. A. 2005. Sheikh Mujib: Triumph and Tragedy. 2nd edition. Dhaka: University Press Limited.

Kasarda, John D., and Greg Lindsay. 2011. Aerotropolis: The Way We'll Live Next. London: Macmillan.

Kathuria, Sanjay, and Mariem Mezghenni Malouche. 2015. Toward New Sources of Competitiveness in Bangladesh: Key Insights of the Diagnostic Trade Integration Study. Washington DC: The World Bank. http://elibrary.worldbank.org/doi/book/10.1596/978-1-4648-0647-6.

Khan, A. Q. 2013. Bittersweet Victory: A Freedom Fighter's Tale. Dhaka: University Press Limited.

Khan, Mushtaq H. 1995. 'Class, Clientelism and Communal Politics in Contemporary Bangladesh.' In The Making of History: Essays Presented to Irfan Habib, 572–606. http://core.ac.uk/download/pdf/2785777.pdf.

Khan, Mushtaq H. 2002. 'Corruption and Governance in Early Capitalism: World Bank Strategies and Their Limitations.' In J. Pincus and J. Winters (eds) Reinventing the World Bank. Ithaca, NY: Cornell University Press. http://eprints.soas.ac.uk/2432/1/Corruption_in_Pincus.pdf.

Khan, Mushtaq H. 2008. 'Vulnerabilities in Market-Led Growth Strategies and Challenges for Governance.' Mimeo. London: School of Oriental and African Studies.

Khan, Mushtaq H. 2010. 'Political Settlements and the Governance of Growth-Enhancing Institutions.' Monograph. London: School of Oriental and Asian Studies. Accessed 11 March 2013. http://eprints.soas.ac.uk/9968/.

Khan, Mushtaq H. 2011. 'The Political Settlement and Its Evolution in Bangladesh.' Mimeo. London: School of Oriental and African Studies. http://eprints.soas.ac.uk/12845/1/The_Political_Settlement_and_its_Evolution_in_Bangladesh.pdf.

Khan, Mushtaq H. 2012. 'Growth, Institutional Challenges and the Political Settlement in Bangladesh.' Mimeo. London. http://core.ac.uk/download/pdf/2794514.pdf.

Khan, Mushtaq H. 2013. 'Bangladesh: Economic Growth in a Vulnerable Limited Access Order.' pp. 24–69. In Douglass North, John Wallis, Steven Webb, and Barry Weingast (eds) In the Shadow of Violence: Politics, Economics and the Problems of Development. Cambridge: Cambridge University Press. http://eprints.soas.ac.uk/11680/.

Khan, Mushtaq H. 2014. 'Aid and Governance in Vulnerable States: Bangladesh and Pakistan since 1971.' The Annals of the American Academy of Political and Social Science 656 (1): 59–78. doi:10.1177/0002716214543900.

Khan, Zillur R. 1996. The Third World Charismat: Sheikh Mujib and the Struggle for Freedom. Dhaka: University Press Limited.

Khandker, Shahidur R., and Hussain A. Samad. 2014. 'Dynamic Effects of Microcredit in Bangladesh.' World Bank Policy Research Working Paper no. 6821. Washington DC: World Bank. http://papers.ssrn.com/abstract=2417519.

Khanna, Pragya. 2011. 'Making Labour Voices Heard During an Industrial Crisis: Workers' Struggles in the Bangladesh Garment Industry'. Labour, Capital and Society 44 (2): 106–29.

Khatun, Fahmida, M. Rahman, D. Bhattacharya, K. G. Moazzem, and A. Shahrin. 2007. 'Gender and Trade Liberalization in Bangladesh: The Case of the Ready-Made Garments (Greater Access to Trade Expansion (GATE) project report).' Dhaka: United States Agency for International Development.

Khondker, Habibul Haque. 1985. 'Governmental Response to Famine: A Case Study of the 1974 Famine in Bangladesh.' PhD thesis, University of Pittsburgh.

Khondker, Habibul Haque. 1992. 'The Political Imperatives of 1988 Flood in Bangladesh.' Section in Five Views of the Flood Action Plan for Bangladesh. Natural Hazards Working Paper Series no. 77. Boulder, Co. USA: University of Colorado. Accessed 10 September 2015.

Khondker, Habibul Haque. 1995. 'Politics, Disasters and Refugees: The Bangladesh Case.' pp. 173–84. In Jin Hui Ong, Kwok Bun Chan, and Soon Beng Chew (eds) Crossing Borders: Transmigration in Asia Pacific. Singapore: Prentice Hall.

Khondker, Habibul Haque. 2010. 'The Curious Case of Secularism in Bangladesh: What Is the Relevance For The Muslim Majority Democracies?' Totalitarian Movements and Political Religions 11 (2): 185–201. doi:10.1080/14690764.2010.512743.

Kibria, Ashiq Mahmud Bin Gholam, Sabrina Matin, Md. Motahar Hossain, and Dilara Irin. 2014. 'Suspension of GSP: Image Crisis for Bangladesh.' European Journal of Business and Management 6 (19): 222–7.

Kibria, Nazli. 1995. 'Culture, Social Class, and Income Control in the Lives of Women Garment Workers in Bangladesh.' Gender & Society 9 (3): 289–309. doi:10.1177/089124395009003003.

Kibria, Nazli. 1998. Becoming a Garments Worker: The Mobilization of Women into the Garments Factories of Bangladesh. UNRISD paper. Geneva: United Nations Research Initiative on Social Development. http://www.unrisd.org/unrisd/website/document.nsf/ab82a6805797760f80256b4f005da1ab/523115d41019b9d980256b67005b6ef8/$FILE/opb9.pdf.

Kibria, Nazli. 2008. 'Muslim Encounters in the Global Economy: Identity Developments of Labor Migrants from Bangladesh to the Middle East.' Ethnicities 8 (4): 518–35. doi:10.1177/1468796808097077.

Kinealy, Christine. 1994. This Great Calamity: The Irish Famine 1845–52. Dublin: Gill & Macmillan.

Kinealy, Christine. 2002. The Great Irish Famine. Basingstoke: Palgrave.

Klein, Naomi. 2007. The Shock Doctrine: The Rise of Disaster Capitalism. London: Macmillan.

Kochanek, Stanley A. 1994. Patron-Client Politics and Business in Bangladesh. New Delhi/Thousand Oaks, CA. USA: SAGE Publications.

Koehlmoos, Tracy Perez, Ziaul Islam, Shahela Anwar, Shaikh A. Shahed Hossain, Rukhsana Gazi, Peter Kim Streatfield, and Abbas Bhuiya. 2011. 'Health Transcends Poverty: The Bangladesh Experience.' pp. 47–82. In Dina Balabanova, Martin McKee, and Anne Mills (eds) 'Good Health at Low Cost' 25 Years On: What Makes a Successful Health System? London: London School of Hygiene and Tropical Medicine.

Korten, David C. 1980. 'Community Organization and Rural Development: A Learning Process Approach.' Public Administration Review 40 (5): 480. doi:10.2307/3110204.

Kothari, Rajni. 1984. 'The Non-Party Political Process.' Economic and Political Weekly 19 (5): 216–24.

Kramsjo, B., and G. D. Wood. 1992. Breaking the Chains: Collective Action for Social Justice among the Rural Poor in Bangladesh. Rugby: Intermediate Technology Publications.

Kreft, Sönke, and David Eckstein. 2013. Global Climate Risk Index 2014. Who Suffers Most from Extreme Weather Events? Weather-Related Loss Events in 2012 and 1993 to 2012. Bonn: Germanwatch Nord-Süd Initiative e.V.

Kynch, Jocelyn. 1997. 'Tightening the Constraints: Famine, Relief and Gender Relations.' Gender, Technology and Development 1 (1): 47–74.

Kynch, Jocelyn. 1998. 'Famine and Transformations in Gender Relations.' pp. 108–34. In Cecile Jackson and Ruth Pearson (eds) Feminist Visions of Development. London and New York: Routledge.

Laws, Edward. 2012. 'Political Settlements, Elite Pacts, and Governments of National Unity: A Conceptual Study.' Development Leadership Programme Background Paper 10. Birmingham: Development Leadership Program.

Leslie, Jacques. 1975. 'Mujib's Man-Made Disaster Area.' The Guardian, 18 February.

Levy, Brian. 2014. Working with the Grain: Integrating Governance and Growth in Development Strategies. New York: OUP USA.

Lewis, David. 1993. 'Going It Alone: Female-Headed Households, Rights and Resources in Rural Bangladesh.' The European Journal of Development Research 5 (2): 23–42. doi:10.1080/09578819308426586.

Lewis, David. 2011. Bangladesh: Politics, Economy and Civil Society. Cambridge: Cambridge University Press.

Lewis, David. 2013. The paradoxes of Bangladesh's Shahbag protests. Blogpost. Accessed 9 February 2016. lse.ac.uk/southasia/2013/03/21/the-paradoxes-of-bangladeshs-shahbag-protests/.

Li, Tania Murray. 2007. The Will to Improve: Governmentality, Development, and the Practice of Politics. Durham: Duke University Press.

Lifschultz, Lawrence, and Kai Bird. 1979. Bangladesh: The Unfinished Revolution. London: Zed Books.

Lifschultz, Lawrence, and Martin Woollacott. 1975. 'Bangladesh: A New Disunity.' The Guardian, 23 August.

Lipset, Seymour Martin. 1959. 'Some Social Requisites of Democracy: Economic Development and Political Legitimacy.' The American Political Science Review 53 (1): 69–105. doi:10.2307/1951731.

Ludden, David. 2011. 'The Politics of Independence in Bangladesh.' Economic and Political Weekly, Readings on the Economy, Polity, and Society XLVI (35): 79–85.

Mader, Philip. 2013. 'Rise and Fall of Microfinance in India: The Andhra Pradesh Crisis in Perspective.' Strategic Change 22 (1–2): 47–66. doi:10.1002/jsc.1921.

Mahmud, Faisal. 2013. 'Land Prices Put Dhaka on Par with NY or London.' 3 May. Dhaka Tribune. Accessed 6 October 2015. www.dhakatribune.com/bangladesh/2013/may/03/land-prices-put-dhaka-par-ny-or-london.

Mahmud, Simeen, and Naila Kabeer. 2003. 'Compliance versus Accountability: Struggles for Dignity and Daily Bread in the Bangladesh Garment Industry.' The Bangladesh Development Studies 29 (3/4): 21–46.

Mahmud, S., and Tasneem, S. 2011. 'The Under Reporting of Women's Economic Activity in Bangladesh: An Examination of Official Statistics.' BDI Working Paper No. 1. Dhaka: BRAC Development Institute, BRAC University.

Mahmud, Wahiduddin, Sadiq Ahmed, and Sandeep Mahajan. 2008. 'Economic Reforms, Growth, and Governance: The Political Economy Aspects of Bangladesh's Development Surprise.' Working paper 22. Commission on Growth and Development. Washington DC: World Bank.

Maniruzzaman, Talukder. 1975a. 'Bangladesh: An Unfinished Revolution?' The Journal of Asian Studies 34 (4): 891–911. doi:10.2307/2054506.

Maniruzzaman, Talukder. 1975b. 'Bangladesh in 1974: Economic Crisis and Political Polarization.' Asian Survey 15 (2): 117–28.

Maniruzzaman, Talukder. 1976. 'Bangladesh in 1975: The Fall of the Mujib Regime and Its Aftermath.' Asian Survey 16 (2): 119–29. doi:10.2307/2643140.

Maniruzzaman, Talukder. 1988. The Bangladesh Revolution and Its Aftermath. 2nd edition. Dacca (Dhaka): University Press Limited.

Maniruzzaman, T. 1992. 'The Fall of the Military Dictator: 1991 Elections and the Prospect of Civilian Rule in Bangladesh'. Pacific Affairs 65 (2): 203–24.

Mascarenhas, Anthony. 1986. Bangladesh: A Legacy of Blood. Sevenoaks: Hodder and Stoughton.

Matin, Imran, and David Hulme. 2003. 'Programs for the Poorest: Learning from the IGVGD Program in Bangladesh.' World Development 31 (3): 647–65.

Mauss, Marcel. 2002. The Gift: The Form and Reason for Exchange in Archaic Societies. London: Routledge.

May, Maria, Joseph Rhatigan, and Richard Cash. 2011. 'BRAC's Tuberculosis Program: Pioneering DOTS Treatment for TB in Rural Bangladesh.' Cases in Global Health Delivery. Cambridge, MA, USA: Harvard Medical School & Brigham and Women's Hospital. http://isites.harvard.edu/fs/docs/icb.topic985058.files/Case%20Studies/BRAC%20TB%20Rural%20Bangladesh.pdf.

McGeehan, Nicholas. 2015. Migrant Workers' Rights on Saadiyat Island in the United Arab Emirates: 2015 Progress Report. New York: Human Rights Watch.

McGregor, J Allister. 1989. 'Towards a Better Understanding of Credit in Rural Development. The Case of Bangladesh: The Patron State.' Journal of International Development 1 (4): 467–86.

McHenry, Donald F., and Kai Bird. 1977. 'Food Bungle in Bangladesh.' Foreign Policy 27: 72–88.

Microcredit Summit Campaign. 2015. 'Mapping Pathways out of Poverty: The State of the Microcredit Summit Campaign Report 2015.' Online. Microcredit Summit Campaign.

Mills, C. Wright. 1956. The Power Elite. Oxford: Oxford University Press.

Moazzem, Khondaker Golam, and Saifa Raz. 2014. 'Minimum Wage in the RMG Sector of Bangladesh: Definition, Determination Method and Levels.' CPD Working Paper. Dhaka: Centre for Policy Dialogue. http://cpd.org.bd/wp-content/uploads/2014/03/WP-106.pdf.

MoF. 2015a. 'Bangladesh Economic Review 2014.' Dhaka: Economic Adviser's Wing, Ministry of Finance of the Government of the People's Republic of Bangladesh. www.mof.gov.bd.

MoF. 2015b. 'Bangladesh Economic Review 2015.' Dhaka: Ministry of Finance of the Government of the People's Republic of Bangladesh.

Mohaiemen, Naeem. 2011. 'Flying Blind.' Economic and Political Weekly XLVI (36): 40–52.

Mohaiemen, Naeem. 2016. 'Muktijuddho: Polyphony of the Ocean.' The Daily Star, 9 April. Accessed 14 June 2016. www.thedailystar.net/in-focus/muktijuddho-polyphony-the-ocean-1206313.

Mohapatra, Sanket, and Dilip Ratha. 2010. 'The Impact of the Global Financial Crisis on Migration and Remittances.' pp. 297–320. In Otaviano Canuto and Marcelo Giugale (eds) The Day After Tomorrow: A Handbook on the Future of Economic Policy in the Developing World. Washington DC: World Bank.

Mookherjee, Nayanika. 2007. 'Available Motherhood: Legal Technologies, "State of Exception" and the Dekinning of "War-babies" in Bangladesh.' Childhood 14 (3): 339–54. doi:10.1177/0907568207079213.

Mookherjee, Nayanika. 2008. 'Gendered Embodiments: Mapping the Body-Politic of the Raped Woman and the Nation in Bangladesh.' Feminist Review 88 (January): 36–53.

Mookherjee, Nayanika. 2011. '"Never Again": Aesthetics of "Genocidal" Cosmopolitanism and the Bangladesh Liberation War Museum.' Journal of the Royal Anthropological Institute 17 (s1): S71–91.

Mookherjee, Nayanika. 2012. 'The Absent Piece of Skin: Gendered, Racialized and Territorial Inscriptions of Sexual Violence during the Bangladesh War.' Modern Asian Studies 46 (06): 1572–601. doi:10.1017/S0026749X11000783.

Mookherjee, Nayanika. 2015. The Spectral Wound: Sexual Violence, Public Memories, and the Bangladesh War of 1971. Durham: Duke University Press.

Moore, Mick. 2004. 'Revenues, State Formation, and the Quality of Governance in Developing Countries.' International Political Science Review/Revue Internationale de Science Politique 25 (3): 297–319.

Morduch, Jonathan. 1999. 'The Microfinance Promise.' Journal of Economic Literature 37 (4): 1569–614.

Muhammad, Anu. 2011. 'Wealth and Deprivation: Ready-Made Garments Industry in Bangladesh.' Economic & Political Weekly 46 (34): 23.

Mukerjee, Madhushree. 2010. Churchill's Secret War. New York: Basic Books.

Mukherjee, Janam. 2015. Hungry Bengal: War, Famine and the End of Empire. Oxford: Oxford University Press.

Muqtada, Mohammed. 1981. 'Poverty and Famines in Bangladesh.' The Bangladesh Development Studies 9 (1): 1–34.

Murphy, Michelle. 2012. Seizing the Means of Reproduction: Entanglements of Feminism, Health, and Technoscience. Durham: Duke University Press.

Murshid, Nadine S. 2013. 'The Shahbag Uprising.' Economic & Political Weekly 48 (10): 13–15.

Myers, Deaix. 1973. 'Civil War in Bangladesh: Relief Planning and Administration in an Insurgency Situation.' pp. 206–24. In L. C. Chen (ed.) Disaster in Bangladesh: Health Crises in a Developing Nation. New York and London: Oxford University Press.

Nally, David. 2008. '"That Coming Storm": The Irish Poor Law, Colonial Biopolitics, and the Great Famine.' Annals of the Association of American Geographers 98 (3): 714–41. doi:10.1080/00045600802118426.

Nally, David. 2011. 'The Biopolitics of Food Provisioning.' Transactions of the Institute of British Geographers 36 (1): 37–53. doi:10.1111/j.1475-5661.2010.00413.x.

Narain, Mona. 2009. 'Dean Mahomet's Travels, Border Crossings, and the Narrative of Alterity.' SEL Studies in English Literature 1500–1900 49 (3): 693–716. doi:10.1353/sel.0.0070.

Nargis, Nigar, and Mahabub Hossain. 2006. 'Income Dynamics and Pathways out of Rural Poverty in Bangladesh, 1988–2004.' Agricultural Economics 35 (s3): 425–35.

Naved, Ruchira Tabassum. 2013. 'Sexual Violence Towards Married Women in Bangladesh.' Archives of Sexual Behavior 42 (4): 595–602. doi:10.1007/s10508-012-0045-1.

Naved, Ruchira Tabassum, and L. A. Persson. 2010. 'Dowry and Spousal Physical Violence Against Women in Bangladesh.' Journal of Family Issues 31 (6): 830–56. doi:10.1177/0192513X09357554.

Nazneen, Sohela. 2009. 'Something Is Better than Nothing: Political Party Discourses on Women's Empowerment in Bangladesh.' South Asian Journal 24, 44–52.

Nazneen, Sohela, Naomi Hossain, and Maheen Sultan. 2011. 'National Discourses on Women's Empowerment in Bangladesh: Continuities and Change.' IDS Working Paper 368. Brighton: Institute of Development Studies. www.ids.ac.uk/files/dmfile/Wp368.pdf.

Nicholas, Ralph. W. 1973. 'Elites, Classes and Factions in Indian Politics: A Review Article'. South Asian Review 6 (2): 145–53.

NIPORT. 2013. 'Bangladesh Demographic and Health Survey 2011.' Dhaka, Bangladesh and Calverton, MD, USA: National Institute of Population Research and Training, Ministry of Health and Family Welfare, Mitra and Associates and ICF International.

Norris, Pippa. 1999. Critical Citizens: Global Support for Democratic Government. Oxford: Oxford University Press.

Ó Gráda, Cormac. 2000. Black '47 and Beyond: The Great Irish Famine in History, Economy, and Memory. Princeton: Princeton University Press.

Ó Gráda, Cormac. 2009. Famine: A Short History. Princeton and Oxford: Princeton University Press.

O'Rourke, P. J. 2007. All the Trouble in the World: The Lighter Side of Overpopulation, Famine, Ecological Disaster, Ethnic Hatred, Plague, and Poverty. New York: Grove Press.

Ortner, Sherry B. 1978. 'The Virgin and the State.' Feminist Studies 4 (3): 19–35. doi:10.2307/3177536.

Osmani, S. R. 1991. 'The Food Problems of Bangladesh.' pp. 307–46. In Jean Drèze and Amartya Sen (eds) The Political Economy of Hunger: Volume 3: Endemic Hunger. Oxford: Oxford University Press.

Osmani, S. R. 2015. 'The Impact of Microcredit on Rural Labour Market in Bangladesh.' InM Working Papers no. 37. Dhaka: Institute of Microfinance. http://inm.org.bd/wp-content/uploads/2016/01/Workingpaper37.pdf.

Osmani, S. R., and Wahiduddin Mahmud. 2015. 'How Does Microcredit Work? A Review of the Theories of Microcredit.' In Institute of Microfinance Working Papers no. 35. Dhaka: Institute of Microfinance.

Paddock, William, and Paul Paddock. 1968. Famine-1975! London: Weidenfeld and Nicolson.

Papanek, Hanna. 1973. 'Purdah: Separate Worlds and Symbolic Shelter.' Comparative Studies in Society and History 15 (03): 289–325.

Parry, Jonathan. 1986. 'The Gift, the Indian Gift and the "Indian Gift".' Man 21 (203), 453–73.

Pateman, Carole. 1980. 'Women and Consent.' Political Theory 8 (2): 149–68.

Pateman, Carole. 1988. The Sexual Contract. Stanford: Stanford University Press.

Pateman, Carole, and Charles Wade Mills. 2007. Contract and Domination. London and New York: Polity.

Paul, Bimal Kanti. 2009. 'Why Relatively Fewer People Died? The Case of Bangladesh's Cyclone Sidr.' Natural Hazards 50 (2): 289–304. doi:10.1007/s11069-008-9340-5.

Paul, B. K., and S. Dutt. 2010. 'Hazard Warnings and Responses to Evacuation Orders: The Case of Bangladesh's Cyclone Sidr.' Geographical Review 100 (3): 336–55.

Paul, B. K., H. Rashid, M. S. Islam, and L. M. Hunt. 2010. 'Cyclone Evacuation in Bangladesh: Tropical Cyclones Gorky (1991) vs. Sidr (2007).' Environmental Hazards 9 (1): 89–101.

Phillips, N. 2011. 'Informality, Global Production Networks and the Dynamics of "Adverse Incorporation".' Global Networks 11 (3): 380–97.

Phillips, Nicola. 2016. 'Labour in Global Production: Reflections on Coxian Insights in a World of Global Value Chains.' Globalizations, February, 1–14. doi:10.1080/14747731.2016.1138608.

Pilger, John. 1975. An Unfashionable Tragedy. Documentary broadcast in January 1975. Accessed 17 April 2016. Archived at http://johnpilger.com/videos/an-unfashionable-tragedy.

Pitt, Mark M., and Shahidur R. Khandker. 1996. 'Household and Intrahousehold Impact of the Grameen Bank and Similar Targeted Credit Programs in Bangladesh.' WDP320. Washington, DC: The World Bank.

Pitt, Mark M., and Shahidur R. Khandker. 1998. 'The Impact of Group-Based Credit Programs on Poor Households in Bangladesh: Does the Gender of Participants Matter?' Journal of Political Economy 106 (5): 958–96. doi:10.1086/250037.

Plümper, Thomas, and Eric Neumayer. 2009. 'Famine Mortality, Rational Political Inactivity, and International Food Aid.' World Development 37 (1): 50–61. doi:10.1016/j.worlddev.2008.05.005.

Prasad, Ravi. 2014. 'Bangladesh Focuses on Bay of Bengal.' Exploration and Production. 19 November. Accessed 4 May 2015. www.epmag.com/bangladesh-focuses-bay-bengal-762006.

Quadir, Fahimul. 2000. 'The Political Economy of Pro-market Reforms in Bangladesh: Regime Consolidation through Economic Liberalization?' Contemporary South Asia 9 (2) 197–212.

Quddus, M., and C. M. Becker. 2000. 'Speculative Price Bubbles in the Rice Market and the 1974 Bangladesh Famine.' Journal of Economic Development 25 (2): 155–75.

Quibria, M. G., ed. 1997. The Bangladesh Economy in Transition. Delhi: Asian Development Bank/Oxford University Press.

Quibria, M. G., and Shafi Ahmad. 2007. 'Aid Effectiveness in Bangladesh.' Munich Personal RePEc Archive paper. Accessed 19 January 2015. http://mpra.ub.uni-muenchen.de/10299/.

Rabinow, Paul, and Nikolas Rose. 2006. 'Biopower Today.' BioSocieties 1 (2): 195–217.

Raghavan, Srinath. 2013. 1971: A Global History of the Creation of Bangladesh. Cambridge: Harvard University Press.

Rahman, A., 1987. 'Impact of Grameen Bank Intervention on the Rural Power Structure'. BIDS Research Report 61, Dhaka: Bangladesh Institute of Development Studies.

Rahman, Anis. 2011. 'A Political Economy of the Emerging Television News Industry in Bangladesh.' Revista de Economía Política de las Tecnologías de la Información y Comunicación 11 (2). http://seer.ufs.br/index.php/eptic/article/view/134.

Rahman, Hossain Zillur. 1995. 'The Political Economy of Poverty-Alleviation.' pp. 274–9. In Hossain Zillur Rahman and Mahabub Hossain (eds) Rethinking Rural Poverty: Bangladesh as a Case Study. New Delhi and Thousand Oaks: SAGE Publications.

Rahman, Mustafizur, and Syed Saifuddin Hossain. 2012. 'Migrant Workers Outflow and Remittance Inflow: Current Trends, Challenges and Future Options for Bangladesh (Ch 5).' In State of the Bangladesh Economy in FY2010-11. Dhaka: Centre for Policy Dialogue. http://cpd.org.bd/wp-content/uploads/2014/09/FY2012_-Migrant-Workers-Outflow-and-Remittance-Inflow-Current-Trends-Challenges-and-Future-Options-for-Bangladesh.pdf.

Rahman, Mustafizur, Khondaker Golam Moazzem, and Syed Saifuddin Hossain. 2009. Impact of the Global Economic Crisis on the Employment and Labour Market of Bangladesh: A Preliminary Assessment. Dhaka: Centre for Policy Dialogue.

Rahman, M. S. 1991. Administrative Elite in Bangladesh. New Delhi: Manak Publishing.

Raihan, Selim. 2013. The Political Economy of Food Price Policy: The Case of Bangladesh. Helsinki: UNU/WIDER.

Raihan, Selim, S. R. Osmani, and M. A. Baqui Khalily. 2015. 'Contribution of Microfinance to the Gross Domestic Product (GDP) of Bangladesh.' In Institute of Microfinance

Working Paper 44. Dhaka: Institute of Microfinance. http://inm.org.bd/wp-content/uploads/2016/01/Workingpaper44.pdf.

Rangan, Kasturi. 1974. 'Subcontinent's Leaders Face The Enemies Within; In Pakistan, India and Bangladesh: Resistance to Government Policies, Corruption and the Threat of Starvation.' The New York Times, 27 October.

Rashiduzzaman, M. 1977. 'Changing Political Patterns in Bangladesh: Internal Constraints and External Fears.' Asian Survey 17 (9): 793–808.

Ravallion, Martin. 1985. 'The Performance of Rice Markets in Bangladesh during the 1974 Famine.' The Economic Journal 95 (377): 15–29.

Ravallion, Martin. 1997. 'Famines and Economics.' Journal of Economic Literature 35 (3): 1205–42.

Rawls, John. 1993. 'The Law of Peoples.' Critical Inquiry 20 (1), 36–68.

Razzaque, Abdur. 1989. 'Sociodemographic Differentials in Mortality during the 1974–75 Famine in a Rural Area of Bangladesh.' Journal of Biosocial Science 21 (1): 13–22. doi:10.1017/S0021932000017697.

Reille, X., and Sarah Forster. 2008. 'Foreign Capital Investment in Microfinance.' CGAP Focus Note 44. Washington, DC: Consultative Group to Assist the Poorest. Accessed 4 July 2015. www.cgap.org/publications/foreign-capital-investment-microfinance-0.

Reilly, Benjamin. 2009. Disaster and Human History: Case Studies in Nature, Society and Catastrophe. Jefferson: McFarland.

Roe, Emery M. 1991. 'Development Narratives, or Making the Best of Blueprint Development.' World Development 19 (4): 287–300. doi:10.1016/0305-750X(91)90177-J.

Rosling, Hans. 2007. 'Bangladesh Miracle.' Gapminder. Accessed 13 January 2016. www.gapminder.org/videos/gapmindervideos/gapcast-5-bangladesh-miracle/.

Ross, Eric B. 1998. The Malthus Factor: Poverty, Politics and Population in Capitalist Development. London: Zed Books.

Rosselli, John. 1980. 'The Self-Image of Effeteness: Physical Education and Nationalism in Nineteenth-Century Bengal.' Past and Present 86: 121–48.

Rothschild, Emma. 1976. 'Food Politics.' Foreign Affairs 54 (2): 285–307. doi:10.2307/20039573.

Rozario, Santi. 2006. 'The New Burqa in Bangladesh: Empowerment or Violation of Women's Rights?' Women's Studies International Forum, Islam, Gender and Human Rights, 29 (4): 368–80. doi:10.1016/j.wsif.2006.05.006.

Rubin, Olivier. 2009. 'The Merits of Democracy in Famine Protection—Fact or Fallacy?' European Journal of Development Research 21 (5): 699–717. doi:10.1057/ejdr.2009.37.

Rutherford, Stuart. 1995. ASA: The Biography of an NGO. Dhaka: Association for Social Advancement.

Rutherford, Stuart. 2009. The Pledge: ASA, Peasants Politics, and Microfinance in the Development of Bangladesh. Oxford: Oxford University Press.

Ruttan, Vernon W., and Yujiro Hayami. 1984. 'Toward a Theory of Induced Institutional Innovation.' Journal of Development Studies 20 (4): 203–23. doi:10.1080/00220388408421914.

Ruud, Arild Engelsen. 2012. 'Democracy in Bangladesh: A Village View.' pp. 45–70. In Stig Toft Madsen, Kenneth Bo Nielsen, and Uwe Skoda (eds) Trysts with Democracy: Political Practice in South Asia. London: Anthem Press.

Sachs, Jeffrey. 2005. The End of Poverty: Economic Possibilities for Our Time. New York: Penguin Press.

Saikia, Yasmin. 2011. Women, War, and the Making of Bangladesh: Remembering 1971. Durham: Duke University Press.

Sattar, Maher. 2016. 'Bangladesh Editor Faces 79 Court Cases After an Unusual Confession—The New York Times.' The New York Times, 27 March. www.nytimes.com/2016/03/28/world/asia/bangladesh-editor-faces-79-court-cases-after-saying-he-regrets-articles.html?_r=0.

Sattar, Zaidi, and Sadiq Ahmed. 2012. 'Reducing Vulnerability in Export Performance: The Export Diversification Challenge in Bangladesh.' IGC Working Paper. London: International Growth Centre. www.theigc.org/wp-content/uploads/2014/05/Sattar-Ahmed-2012-Working-Paper.pdf.

Saxena, Sanchita Banerjee, and Véronique Salze-Lozac'h. 2010. 'Competitiveness in the Garment and Textiles Industry: Creating a Supportive Environment.' A Case Study of Bangladesh. The Asia Foundation Occasional Paper 1. The Asia Foundation. www.asiafoundation.org/resources/pdfs/1OccasionalPaperNo.1BGGARMENTwithCover.pdf.

Schanberg, Sydney, H. 1970. 'After Pakistani Storm: Grief, Indifference; After the Pakistani Storm: Grief, Terror, Indifference.' The New York Times, 30 December, pp. 1–2.

Schuler, Sidney Ruth, Syed M. Hashemi, and Shamsul Huda Badal. 1998. 'Men's Violence against Women in Rural Bangladesh: Undermined or Exacerbated by Microcredit Programmes?' Development in Practice 8 (2): 148–57. doi:10.1080/09614529853774.

Schuler, Sidney Ruth, Rachel Lenzi, Sohela Nazneen, and Lisa M. Bates. 2013. 'Perceived Decline in Intimate Partner Violence Against Women in Bangladesh: Qualitative Evidence.' Studies in Family Planning 44 (3): 243–57. doi:10.1111/j.1728-4465.2013.00356.x.

Schwartz, Walter. 1974. 'Disaster Is Real in the Land that Cried Wolf.' The Guardian, 17 August, p. 1.

Schwarz, Walter. 1974a. 'Kissinger's War on Famine.' The Observer, 3 November, p. 9.

Schwarz, Walter. 1974b. 'Losing Battle against Hunger.' The Guardian, 4 November, p. 1.

Scott, James C. 1987. Weapons of the Weak: Everyday Forms of Peasant Resistance. New Haven: Yale University Press.

Sen, Amartya. 1981. Poverty and Famines: An Essay on Entitlement and Deprivation. Oxford: Oxford University Press.

Sen, Amartya. 2013. 'What's Happening in Bangladesh?' The Lancet 382 (9909): 1966–8.

Sen, Binayak, and Zulfiqar Ali. 2015. 'Ending Extreme Poverty in Bangladesh During the Seventh Five Year Plan: Trends, Drivers and Policies.' Background Paper for the Seventh Five Year Plan. Dhaka: General Economics Division, Planning Commission. www.bangladeshgateway.com/doc/7th5th/25_Ending-Extreme-Poverty-in-Bangladesh.pdf.

Sen, Binayak, and David Hulme. 2004. 'Chronic Poverty in Bangladesh: Tales of Ascent, Descent, Marginality and Persistence.' Dhaka: Bangladesh Institute of Development Studies (in Process). Accessed 17 September 2015. www.prcpb-bids.org/chronic_poverty_bangladesh/chronic_poverty_in_bangladesh.pdf.

Sen, Binayak, Mustafa K. Mujeri, and Quazi Shahabuddin. 2007. 'Explaining Pro-poor Growth in Bangladesh: Puzzles, Evidence, and Implications.' pp. 79–118. In Timothy J. Besley, and Louise Cord (eds) Delivering on the Promise of Pro-Poor Growth. Washington DC and Basingstoke: World Bank/Palgrave Macmillan.

Sen, Rangalal. 1986. Political Elites in Bangladesh. Dhaka: University Press Limited.

Sharlach, Lisa. 2000. 'Rape as Genocide: Bangladesh, the Former Yugoslavia, and Rwanda.' New Political Science 22 (1) 89–102. doi:10.1080/713687893.

Shehabuddin, Elora. 2008. Reshaping the Holy: Democracy, Development, and Muslim Women in Bangladesh. New York: Columbia University Press.

Shepherd, Jack. 1975. The Politics of Starvation. New York: Carnegie Endowment for International Peace.

Shibli, Abdullah. 2014. 'Will Rising Minimum Wage Affect the RMG Sector?' The Daily Star, 1 October. Accessed 8 October 2015. www.thedailystar.net/will-rising-minimum-wage-affect-the-rmg-sector-44091.

Shirras, G. Findlay. 1931. 'Indian Migration.' In International Migrations, Volume II: Interpretations, pp. 591–616. NBER. www.nber.org/chapters/c5120.pdf.

Siddiqi, Dina M. 2000. 'Miracle Worker or Womanmachine? Tracking (Trans)national Realities in Bangladeshi Factories.' Economic and Political Weekly 35 (21/22): L11–17.

Siddiqi, Dina M. 2009. 'Do Bangladeshi Factory Workers Need Saving? Sisterhood in the Post-Sweatshop Era.' Feminist Review 91: 154–74.

Siddiqui, Kamal, Sayeda Rowshan Qadir, Sitara Alamgir, and Sayeedul Huq. 1990. Social Formation in Dhaka City: A Study in Third World Urban Sociology. Dhaka: University Press Limited.

Siddiqui, Tasneem. 2003. Migration as a Livelihood Strategy of the Poor: The Bangladesh Case. Monograph. Dhaka: Refugee and Migratory Movements Research Unit, Dhaka University. http://r4d.dfid.gov.uk/pdf/outputs/migrationglobpov/wp-c1.pdf.

Siddiqui, Tasneem. 2005. 'International Labour Migration from Bangladesh: A Decent Work Perspective.' ILO Policy Integration Department Working Paper 66. www.uni-kassel.de/einrichtungen/fileadmin/datas/einrichtungen/icdd/dateien/Webportal_Publications/Strategies_of_Empowerment_for_Decent_Work/International_Labour_Migration_from_BangladeshA_Decent_Work_Perspective.pdf.

Siegle, Lucy, and Jason Burke. 2014. We Are What We Wear: Unravelling Fast Fashion and the Collapse of Rana Plaza. Guardian Shorts Book 13. London: The Guardian.

Singer, Peter. 1972. 'Famine, Affluence, and Morality.' Philosophy & Public Affairs 1 (3): 229–43.

Sisson, Richard, and Leo Rose, E. 1990. War and Secession: Pakistan, India, and the Creation of Bangladesh. Berkeley: University of California Press.

Smillie, Ian. 2009. Freedom from Want: The Remarkable Success Story of BRAC, the Global Grassroots Organization that's Winning the Fight against Poverty. Harford: Kumarian Press.

Smith, Allan H., Elena O. Lingas, and Mahfuzar Rahman. 2000. 'Contamination of Drinking-Water by Arsenic in Bangladesh: A Public Health Emergency.' Bulletin of the World Health Organization 78 (9): 1093–103. doi:10.1590/S0042-96862000000900005.

Sobhan, Rehman. 1969. 'East Pakistan's Revolt against Ayub: Old Resentments and New Needs.' The Round Table 59 (235): 302–7. doi:10.1080/00358536908452822.

Sobhan, Rehman. 1979. 'Politics of Food and Famine in Bangladesh.' Economic and Political Weekly 14 (48) 1973–80.

Sobhan, Rehman. 1982. The Crisis of External Dependence: The Political Economy of Foreign Aid to Bangladesh. (Dacca) Dhaka: University Press Limited.

Sobhan, Rehman. 1991. 'The Politics of Hunger and Entitlement.' pp. 79–113. In Jean Drèze and Amartya Sen (eds) The Political Economy of Hunger. Oxford: Oxford University Press.

Sobhan, Rehman. 2000. 'The State of Governance in Bangladesh.' pp. 77–114. In R. Sobhan (ed.) Changes and Challenges: A Review of Bangladesh's Development 2000. Independent Review of Bangladesh's Development. Dhaka: Centre for Policy Dialogue.

Sobhan, Rehman, and Muzaffer Ahmad. 1980. Public Enterprise in an Intermediate Regime: A Study in the Political Economy of Bangladesh. Dhaka: Bangladesh Institute of Development Studies.

Sobhan, Rehman, and Binayak Sen. 1988. 'The Social Background of Entrepreneurship in Bangladesh.' BIDS Research Report 71. Dhaka: Bangladesh Institute of Development Studies.

Sommer, Alfred, Nilton Arnt, and Stanley Foster. 1973. 'Post-Civil War in Bangladesh: The Smallpox Epidemic.' pp. 225–40. In Lincoln C. Chen (ed.) Disaster in Bangladesh: Health Crises in a Developing Nation. New York and London: Oxford University Press.

Sommer, Alfred, and Wiley H. Mosley. 1972. 'East Bengal Cyclone of November, 1970: Epidemiological Approach to Disaster Assessment.' The Lancet, Originally published as Volume 1, Issue 7759, 299 (7759): 1030–6. doi:10.1016/S0140-6736(72)91218-4.

Sorokin, Pitirim A. 1975. Hunger as a Factor in Human Affairs. 1st edition. Gainesville: University Press of Florida.

Stasavage, David. 2005. 'Democracy and Education Spending in Africa.' American Journal of Political Science 49 (2): 343–58. doi:10.1111/j.0092-5853.2005.00127.x.

Stirrat, R. L., and Heiko Henkel. 1997. 'The Development Gift: The Problem of Reciprocity in the NGO World.' Annals of the American Academy of Political and Social Science 554 (November): 66–80.

Streatfield, Peter Kim, Nahid Kamal, Karar Zunaid Ahsan, and Quamrun Nahar. 2015. 'Early Marriage in Bangladesh.' Asian Population Studies 11 (1): 94–110. doi:10.1080/17441730.2015.1012785.

Sultana, Umme Busra Fateha. 2015. 'Gender, Sexuality and Contraceptive Advertisements in Bangladesh: Representation and Lived Experience across Social Classes and Generations.' DPhil thesis. University of Sussex. http://sro.sussex.ac.uk/55285/.

Sutter, Camille. 2011. 'State Legitimacy and Famines in Sub-Saharan Africa.' Mimeo. http://mpra.ub.uni-muenchen.de/37621/.

Swaan, Abram De, James Manor, Else Øyen, and Elisa P. Reis. 2000. 'Elite Perceptions of the Poor: Reflections for a Comparative Research Project.' Current Sociology 48 (1): 43–54. doi:10.1177/0011392100048001006.

Tariquzzaman, Sheikh, and Naomi Hossain. 2009. 'The Boys Left Behind: Where Public Policy Has Failed to Prevent Child Labour in Bangladesh.' IDS Bulletin 40 (1): 31–7.

Taslim, M. A., and M. S. Haque. 2011. 'Export Performance of Bangladesh: Global Recession and after.' IGC Working Paper. Dhaka/London: Bangladesh Foreign Trade Institute/The International Growth Centre.

Taylor, Marcus. 2011. '"Freedom from Poverty Is Not for Free": Rural Development and the Microfinance Crisis in Andhra Pradesh, India.' Journal of Agrarian Change 11 (4): 484–504.

The Economist. 2013. 'Revenge of the Migrants' Employer?' The Economist, 26 March. Accessed 4 April 2016. www.economist.com/blogs/banyan/2013/03/bangladesh-and-saudi-arabia.

The Guardian. 2014. 'Bangladesh Court Convicts British Journalist for Doubting War Death Toll.' 2 December. Accessed 13 March 2015. www.theguardian.com/world/2014/dec/02/bangladesh-convicts-british-journalist-david-bergman.

The New York Times. 1972. 'Basket Case.' Editorial. 8 October. p. 267.

Thompson, E. P. 1971. 'The Moral Economy of the English Crowd in the Eighteenth Century.' Past & Present 50: 76–136.

Thompson, E. P. 1991. 'The Moral Economy Reviewed.' pp. 59–351. In E. P. Thompson, Customs in Common. London: Penguin.

Thorp, J. P. 1978. Power among the Farmers of Daripalla: A Bangladesh Village Study. Dacca: Caritas Bangladesh.

Timmins, Nicholas. 1994. 'Labour Rejects Pounds 5m Offer "on Principle."' The Independent, 29 August. Accessed 5 October 2015. www.independent.co.uk/news/uk/labour-rejects-pounds-5m-offer-on-principle-1379387.html.

Torry, William I. 1984. 'Social Science Research on Famine: A Critical Evaluation.' Human Ecology 12 (3): 227–52. doi:10.1007/BF01540590.

Toufique, Kazi Ali, and Cate Turton, eds. 2002. Hands Not Land. Dhaka and London: Bangladesh Institute of Development Studies/Department for International Development. www.theidlgroup.com/documents/handsnotlandbook.pdf

Tripathi, Salil. 2014. The Colonel Who Would Not Repent: The Bangladesh War and Its Unquiet Legacy. Daryaganj: Aleph.

Turner, Billie L., and A. M. Shajaat Ali. 1996. 'Induced Intensification: Agricultural Change in Bangladesh with Implications for Malthus and Boserup.' Proceedings of the National Academy of Sciences 93 (25): 14984–91.

Tweeten, Luther. 2001. 'Review.' American Journal of Agricultural Economics 83 (4): 1098–100.

U.S. Department of State Office of the Historian. 1976. 'Document 46—Foreign Relations of the United States, 1969–1976, Volume E–8, Documents on South Asia, 1973–1976—Historical Documents—Office of the Historian.' Historical Documents—Office of the Historian. Foreign Relations of the United States, 1969–1976, Volume E–8, Documents on South Asia, 1973–1976. Washington DC: United States Department of State. https://history.state.gov/historicaldocuments/frus1969-76ve08/d46.

Unb, Rangpur. 2008. 'Moeen Seeks to Dispel Fear of Silent Famine.' 17 March. The Daily Star. Accessed 1 December 2015. http://archive.thedailystar.net/newDesign/story.php?nid=28094.

United States Department of State. 1971. Minutes of Washington Special Actions Group Meeting. Document 235—Foreign Relations of the United States, 1969–1976, Volume

XI, South Asia Crisis, 1971—Historical Documents—Office of the Historian. Accessed 31 March 2015. https://history.state.gov/historicaldocuments/frus1969-76v11/d235.

United States Department of State. 1974. Document 37—Foreign Relations of the United States, 1969–1976, Volume E–8, Documents on South Asia, 1973–1976—Historical Documents—Office of the Historian. Accessed 31 March 2015. https://history.state.gov/historicaldocuments/frus1969-76ve08/d37.

United States Department of State. 1975. Document 42—Foreign Relations of the United States, 1969–1976, Volume E–8, Documents on South Asia, 1973–1976—Historical Documents—Office of the Historian. Accessed 21 December 2015. https://history.state.gov/historicaldocuments/frus1969-76ve08/d42.

Unterhalter, Elaine, Jake Ross, and M. Alam. 2003. 'A Fragile Dialogue? Research and Primary Education Policy Formation in Bangladesh, 1971–2001.' Compare 33 (1): 85–100.

US Embassy Dacca. 1974a. 'FEAR OF FAMINE.' Official cable. 1974DACCA04337_b. Dacca: US Embassy Dacca. Accessed 19 December 2014. http://wikileaks.org/plusd/cables/1974DACCA04337_b.html.

US Embassy Dacca. 1974b. 'QUARTERLY REVIEW: WHAT AWAITS THE SECRETARY IN BANGLADESH.' Confidential Cable to US Secretary of State and others, declassified 2005 1974DACCA04634_b. Dacca (Dhaka): American Embassy Dacca. Accessed 12 December 2014. http://wikileaks.org/plusd/cables/1974DACCA04634_b.html.

USAID. 1997. 'Food Aid in Bangladesh: A Gradual Shift from Relief to Reform.' Impact Evaluation. Washington DC: USAID. http://pdf.usaid.gov/pdf_docs/pnaby242.pdf.

USAID. 2007. 'Final Report: The Office of U.S. Foreign Disaster Assistance (OFDA) of the United States Agency for International Development (USAID): A Critical Juncture Analysis, 1964–2003.' Washington, DC: Office of U.S. Foreign Disaster Assistance (OFDA) of the United States Agency for International Development (USAID). Accessed 19 May 2015. http://web.archive.org/web/20070414002649/http://www.usaid.gov/our_work/humanitarian_assistance/disaster_assistance/publications/ofda_cjanalysis_02_21-2005.pdf.

USTR. 2015. 'GSP Review of Bangladesh Recognizes Progress, Urges That More Be Done on Worker Safety and Rights.' Washington, DC: Office of the United States Trade Representative. Accessed 8 October 2015. https://ustr.gov/about-us/policy-offices/press-office/press-releases/2015/january/gsp-review-bangladesh-recognizes.

Vaessen, J., A. Rivas, M. Duvendack, R. Palmer Jones, F. L. Leeuw, G. Van Gils, R. Lukach, N. Holvoet, J. Bastiaensen, J. G. Hombrados, and H. Waddington. 2014. 'The Effects of Microcredit on Women's Control over Household Spending in Developing Countries: A Systematic Review and Meta-analysis.' Campbell Systematic Reviews 2014: 8.

Van Schendel, Willem. 2009. A History of Bangladesh. Cambridge: Cambridge University Press.

Verba, S., S. Kelman, G. R. Orren, I. Miyake, J. Watanuki, I. Kabashima, and G. D. Ferree, Jr. 1987. Elites and the Idea of Equality. Cambridge: Harvard University Press.

Wade, Robert. 2013. 'Our Misleading Measure of Income and Wealth Inequality: The Standard Gini Coefficient.' Blogpost on Triple Crisis. Accessed 28 September 2015.

http://triplecrisis.com/our-misleading-measure-of-income-and-wealth-inequality-the-standard-gini-coefficient/#more-8133.

Wazed, Sheikh Hasina. 2010. High Level Plenary Meeting-Millennium Development Goals (MDGs) Statement by Her Excellency Sheikh Hasina, Prime Minister Government of the People's Republic of Bangladesh. New York. Presented at the High Level Plenary on the Millennium Development Goals. New York, 20–22 September.

Weinraub, Bernard. 1974. 'Bangladesh, at Age 3, Is Still a Disaster Area; A Worrisome Portent Key Enterprises Taken Over Premier's Nephew Accused Sluggish Bureaucracy U. S. Leads the Donors.' The New York Times, 13 December. p. 14.

Wemheuer, Felix. 2014. Famine Politics in Maoist China and the Soviet Union. New Haven: Yale University Press.

Werbner, Pnina. 1999. 'Political Motherhood and the Feminisation of Citizenship: Women's Activisms and the Transformation of the Public Sphere.' pp. 221–45. In Pnina Werbner and Nira Yuval Davis (eds) Women, Citizenship and Difference. London: Zed Books.

White, Sarah C. 1992. Arguing With the Crocodile: Gender and Class in Bangladesh. London: Zed Books.

White, Sarah C. 1999. 'NGOs, Civil Society, and the State in Bangladesh: The Politics of Representing the Poor.' Development and Change 30 (2): 307–26. doi:10.1111/1467-7660.00119.

White, Sarah C. 2002. 'Thinking Race, Thinking Development.' Third World Quarterly 23 (3): 407–19. doi:10.1080/01436590220138358.

Wood, G. D. 1994. Bangladesh: Whose Ideas, Whose Interests? Dhaka: University Press Limited.

Wood, G. D. 2000. 'Prisoners and Escapees: Improving the Institutional Responsibility Square in Bangladesh.' Public Administration and Development 20 (3): 221–37.

World Bank. 1970. 'Appraisal of a Reconstruction Project for the Cyclone Damaged Coastal Areas of East Pakistan Pakistan.' Report. Washington DC: World Bank.

World Bank. 1972. 'Reconstructing the Economy of Bangladesh.' Vol. 1. Report no. SA-35a. Washington DC: World Bank. Accessed 14 April 2014. www-wds.worldbank.org/external/default/WDSContentServer/WDSP/IB/2002/11/11/000178830_98101903374031/Rendered/PDF/multi0page.pdf.

World Bank. 1977. 'Bangladesh Food Policy Review.' Washington DC: World Bank.

World Bank. 1981. 'Labour Migration from Bangladesh to the Middle East.' World Bank Staff Working Paper 454. Washington DC: World Bank.

World Bank. 1994a. Bangladesh: From Stabilization to Growth. Washington DC: World Bank.

World Bank. 1994b. Bangladesh: Privatization and Adjustment. Washington DC: World Bank.

World Bank. 2003. 'Bangladesh: Development Policy Review: Impressive Achievements but Continuing Challenges.' Development Policy Review 26154-BD. Washington DC: World Bank.

World Bank. 2006. 'The World Bank Annual Report 2006.' Washington DC: The World Bank.

World Bank. 2007. 'Whispers to Voices: Gender and Social Transformation in Bangladesh.' Dhaka: World Bank/AusAid.

World Bank. 2008. 'Poverty Assessment for Bangladesh: Creating Opportunities and Bridging the East–West Divide.' Bangladesh Development Series no. 26. Dhaka: World Bank.

World Bank. 2010. 'Bangladesh—Country Assistance Strategy for the Period FY11-14.' Document no. 54615. Dhaka/Washington DC: World Bank. Accessed 17 September 2015. http://documents.worldbank.org/curated/en/2010/07/12649110/bangladesh-country-assistance-strategy-period-fy11-14.

World Bank. 2010. Food Price Increases in South Asia: National Responses and Regional Dimensions. Washington DC: World Bank.

World Bank. 2013. 'Bangladesh Poverty Assessment: Assessing a Decade of Progress in Reducing Poverty, 2000–2010.' Bangladesh Development Series Paper 31. Dhaka: Bangladesh World Bank Country Office.

World Bank. 2016. 'Migration and Remittances Factbook 2016.' Washington, DC: Global Knowledge Partnership on Migration and Development (KNOMAD).

Yang, Dali, L. 1996. Calamity and Reform in China: State, Rural Society and Institutional Change Since the Great Leap Famine. Stanford: Stanford University Press.

Yanguas, Pablo. 2016. 'The Role and Responsibility of Foreign Aid in Recipient Political Settlements'. ESID working paper no. 56. Manchester: Effective States and Inclusive Development Research Centre.

Yunus, Muhammad. 2008. Creating a World Without Poverty: Social Business and the Future of Capitalism. Dhaka: Subarna Press.

Yunus, Muhammad. 2009. 7th Nelson Mandela Annual Lecture. Video Recording. Nelson Mandela Foundation. Accessed 4 December 2014. www.youtube.com/watch?v=oK6IdPERTRw&feature=youtube_gdata_player.

Yunus, Muhammad, and Alan Jolis. 1999. Banker To The Poor: The Autobiography of Muhammad Yunus, Founder of the Grameen Bank. London: Aurum Press.

Zafarullah, H. M. 1987. 'Public Administration in the First Decade of Bangladesh: Some Observations on Developments and Trends.' Asian Survey 27 (4): 459–76.

Zafarullah, Habib, ed. 1996. The Zia Episode in Bangladesh Politics. Dhaka: University Press Limited.

Zaman, Hassan. 2004. 'The Scaling-up of Microfinance in Bangladesh: Determinants, Impact, and Lessons.' World Bank Policy Research Working Paper 3398. Washington DC: World Bank.

Zeitlin, Arnold. 2013. 'Bewildered by Bangladesh.' South Asia Journal 8. Accessed 7 October 2015. http://southasiajournal.net/bewildered-by-bangladesh/.

Zeitlyn, Benjamin. 2014. 'Watching the International Crimes Tribunal from London.' South Asia Multidisciplinary Academic Journal 9 (July). Accessed 7 October 2015. http://samaj.revues.org/3711.

Zhang, Xiabo, Shahidur Rashid, Kaikaus Ahmad, Valerie Mueller, Hak Lim Lee, Solomon Lemma, Saika Belal, and Akhter Ahmed. 2013. 'Rising Wages in Bangladesh.' IFPRI Discussion Paper 01249. Washington DC: International Food Policy Research Institute.

Index

The manufacturer's authorised representative in the EU for product safety is Oxford University Press España S.A. of El Parque Empresarial San Fernando de Henares, Avenida de Castilla, 2 – 28830 Madrid (www.oup.es/en or product.safety@oup.com). OUP España S.A. also acts as importer into Spain of products made by the manufacturer.

Printed in the USA/Agawam, MA
August 11, 2025

891792.003